Belarus
at the Crossroads

Edited by Sherman W. Garnett
and Robert Legvold

Carnegie Endowment for International Peace
Washington, D.C.

BOE 8247 - 4/2

© 1999 Carnegie Endowment for International Peace
1779 Massachusetts Avenue, N.W.
Washington, D.C. 20036
Tel. 202-483-7600
Fax. 202-483-1840
www.ceip.org

Belarus at the Crossroads
ISBN 0-87003-172-4 (paper) $12.95

To order, contact Carnegie's distributor:
The Brookings Institution Press
Department 029, Washington, D.C. 20042-0029, USA
Tel: 1-800-275-1447 or 202-797-6258
Fax: 202-797-6004, E-mail: bibooks@brook.edu

Library of Congress Cataloging-in-Publication Data
Belarus at the crossroads / Sherman W. Garnett and Robert Legvold, editors.
    p.   cm.
    Includes bibliographical references.
    ISBN 0-87003-172-4 (pbk.)
    1.   Belarus—Foreign relations—1991-   I.   Garnett, Sherman W., 1955- .
II.   Legvold, Robert, 1940- .
DK507.8175.B45 1999
327.478—dc21   99-38034
                                                                              CIP

Cover design: Laurie Rosenthal
Printing: Automated Graphic Systems, Inc.

Contents

Foreword

On December 8, 1991, the leaders of Russia, Ukraine, and Belarus met in Minsk to drive the final nail into the coffin of the Soviet Union. Belarus, it seemed then, offered promise as a state anxious to move into a brighter, post-Soviet era.

Since those heady days, however, the picture has dimmed, as Belarus has struggled to establish its own, independent identity. Political and economic reform has lagged badly behind other states in the region. The desire among Belarusians to reconstitute a union with other post-Soviet states has increased. And under the autocratic presidency of Aleksandr Lukashenko, Belarus has been written off by many Western analysts and governments as a hopeless backwater reminiscent, on a much smaller scale, of the Soviet Union.

Yet Belarus's geographic location and the ambitions of its president make it an important factor in the region and in Europe as a whole. Consigning Belarus to the geopolitical margins is short-sighted and could prove to be costly.

This study focuses on Belarus's place in the evolving European security environment. What makes it unique are the diverse chapters by specialists from Belarus, Russia, Poland, Ukraine, Lithuania, and the United States. At stake, the authors agree, is whether Belarus, a frontline state bordering an enlarged NATO, will become a bridge or a barrier to the West. Two key factors that will determine Belarus's future are Lukashenko and Russia. This book originated from a conference the two editors, Sherman Garnett and Robert Legvold, along with Carnegie Moscow Center deputy director Dmitri Trenin, sponsored with the Development and Security Research Institute in Minsk in November 1997 with support from the Smith Richardson Foundation.

JESSICA T. MATHEWS
President
Carnegie Endowment for
International Peace

Acknowledgments

As editors we were fortunate to take part in a genuinely collaborative effort, beginning with the unique partnership between the Carnegie Endowment for International Peace and the Committee on International Security Studies (CISS) of the American Academy of Arts and Sciences. The Carnegie Endowment, founded in 1910, is a private, nonprofit organization dedicated to advancing cooperation between nations and promoting active international engagement by the United States. It supports one of the premier research programs on Russian and Eurasian affairs as well as the Carnegie Moscow Center, the first wholly independent public policy research center in the former Soviet Union.

The Academy's CISS, founded in 1982, oversees a diverse research program that emphasizes emerging challenges to global security. Current and recent projects have included Light Weapons and Internal Conflict; The International Criminal Court and U.S. National Security; Environmental Scarcities, State Capacity, and Civil Violence; and Emerging Norms of Justified Intervention. CISS also oversees the activities of the U.S. Pugwash Committee, part of the international Pugwash Conferences on Science and World Affairs, recipient of the 1995 Nobel Peace Prize.

We were fortunate to have a strong collaborative base of funding. We gratefully acknowledge support that was provided to the Academy and CISS by the Bechtel Foundation and the John D. and Catherine T. MacArthur Foundation, and to the Carnegie Endowment by the Smith Richardson Foundation.

We are grateful for the support of talented people in both institutions who looked on our work with the same enthusiasm for our understudied but important topic. We appreciate the encouragement given to us by Carl Kaysen, the chairman of the CISS and by Endowment officers, President Jessica Matthews and Vice President Paul Balaran as well as the former vice president for Russian and Eurasian affairs Arnold Horelick. We are grateful for the excellent work done by Dmitri Trenin, the deputy director of the Carnegie Moscow Center and editor of the Russian language edition of this book; the excellent organizational backup of Jeffrey Boutwell, senior program director of the CISS; and, as always, David Kramer, the associate director of the Endowment's Russian and Eurasian Program. Madelyn Ross did an outstanding job of copy editing, and Tom Skladony and Sherry Pettie provided important comments on the manuscript and the technical follow-through that turned it into a book.

We also were fortunate to have the able assistance and sound judgment of Elizabeth Reisch, Rachel Lebenson and, during the final organizational and editing stage, Marcus Fellman and Vanda Felbabova, four of the Endowment's talented junior fellows. At various stages of the project, each performed a wide variety of research, organizational and editing assignments with great professionalism. There would be no book without them.

Last, but certainly not least, we are grateful for those who contributed in this book, either as authors or as participants in our October 1997 seminar in Minsk. In addition to the authors in this volume, Oleksy Haran (Ukraine), Marik Karp (Poland), Andrey Sannikov, and Ural Latypov (both from Belarus) took part in the seminar. Alexander Yegorov, director of the Minsk-based Development and Security Research Institute, was the local organizer of the event. He and his staff made sure we had great facilities and the warmest hospitality possible. They made the seminar one of the best organized and most productive with which we have been involved in recent years.

The book's many authors represent a variety of often conflicting views. No topic this important and complex could generate unanimity. But these essays also reflect the spirit of free inquiry, mutual respect, and seriousness that marked the seminar in Minsk. Indeed, if this spirit could be replicated in the wider Belarusian political context, it would have a transforming effect on the debate. Neither of us, as outsiders, wish to complicate an already complex political situation in Belarus with our personal views. Both of us came away from this project with a sure sense that Belarus is more interesting, important and complex than currently imagined in the West. Wherever we went, we found willing interlocutors on both sides and can only hope these interlocutors are allowed to find each other. Finding some common ground is the way to the freer and more prosperous future in Europe that the Belarusian people deserve.

SHERMAN W. GARNETT AND
ROBERT LEGVOLD

List of Acronyms

BPF	Belarusian Popular Front
BSSR	Belarusian Soviet Socialist Republic
CEFTA	Central European Agreement on Free Trade
CFE	Treaty on Conventional Armed Forces in Europe
CEI	Central European Initiative
CIS	Commonwealth of Independent States
CPB	Communist Party of Belarus
CSCE	Commission on Security and Cooperation in Europe (later the OSCE)
EAPC	Euro-Atlantic Partnership Council
EU	European Union
ICBM	Intercontinental ballistic missile
IMF	International Monetary Fund
NACC	North Atlantic Cooperation Council
NATO	North Atlantic Treaty Organization
NIS	Newly independent states
NPT	Nuclear Non-Proliferation Treaty
OPIC	Overseas Private Investment Corporation
ORT	Russian state television station
OSCE	Organization for Security and Cooperation in Europe
PFP	Partnership for Peace
RFE/RL	Radio Free Europe/Radio Liberty
START	Strategic Arms Reduction Treaty
USSR	Union of Soviet Socialist Republics
VAT	Value-added tax
WTO	World Trade Organization

1

Introduction: Assessing the Challenge of Belarus

Sherman W. Garnett
and Robert Legvold

Belarus is the wild card in Central Europe's political and economic game of poker. It sits astride the axes linking Russia to Europe and the Baltic states to the south, forming a vital strategic arena not only for them but also for Ukraine and Poland. Despite its location, Belarus falls through the cracks. Neither governments nor analysts have given much thought to the country's larger significance and its potential impact on the stability of Europe. Thus, this book.

This neglect on the part of the United States or even Western Europe may be understandable, albeit no less ill advised. Belarus is a disappointment. Its march toward democracy has not merely been unsteady, but is in apparent full retreat. Economic reform has not merely run into obstacles, as in many neighboring states; it has been consciously sidetracked by an increasingly repressive and hidebound leadership. In a Europe invigorated by the triumph of modern democracy over communist failure, a Europe that so many of the ex-socialist states are clamoring to enter, the major powers do not have much time for retrograde nations.

The lack of attention and analysis on the part of Belarus's immediate neighbors is harder to explain. They cannot afford simply to avoid Belarus because of its distasteful policies, for whatever happens there will directly affect their own fortunes. Leaders in Ukraine, Poland, Lithuania, and Latvia know this, and when they meet, they often worry together over what is to be done and how to do it. Still, their periodic anxiety does not add up to a systematic evaluation of the strategic challenge raised by Belarus or how Belarus figures in the larger trends shaping their region. Nor have they been much helped by the analytical communities within their countries who, for whatever reasons, rarely take up the subject.

Among Russians, Belarus *is* a prominent topic. Politicians often compete with one another to demonstrate their support of Russian-Belarusian integration, although the August 1998 financial crisis had a sobering effect on many, making them increasingly aware of the costs of the potential union. Still, significant enthusiasm persists for the Russia-Belarus union. The media and public also recognize the country as an important part of their political landscape, although in these discussions the real Belarus and its role in the emerging and complicated security environment often get lost. Russians take it for granted that Belarus will remain close and that the two countries may even become one again. Belarus is often in the Russian news, either because political leaders are debating the latest move to bind the societies closer together or, less auspiciously, because the Belarusian regime has done something to offend Russian sensibilities. Thinking regularly of Belarus, however, is not the same as thinking deeply about Belarus. The tendency of Russians—analysts as well as policy makers—to concentrate on Belarus in a narrow Russian domestic context impedes their readiness and ability to consider Belarus in a larger European context.

As we who have collaborated on this volume can attest, Belarus is not an easy subject. From the start it has defied normal expectations. While the neighboring Soviet republics of Estonia, Latvia, Lithuania, Ukraine, and Moldova rushed toward independence when the chance came, Belarus only drifted into it. Had the conservative party bureaucrats who dominated the Belarusian political scene at the time had their way, the putschists in Moscow would have prevailed in August 1991. When the conspiracy in Moscow collapsed, however, Belarusian party bureaucrats embraced independence largely for the same reasons that they had declared Belarusian sovereignty the year before: to preserve their power and their conservative, largely Soviet ways against the liberal influences initially of Mikhail Gorbachev's perestroika and then—worse—Boris Yeltsin's Russia.

Unsurprisingly, therefore, Belarus's not-so-new leaders did not rush to throw over the old order and launch wide-ranging economic and political reform after independence. On the contrary, Belarus stood out not only as one of the least venturesome of the new states, but also as an active defender of comfortable and familiar ways, including the old economic arrangements among the former Soviet republics. When a more liberal and nationally minded element had emerged during the last years of the Soviet Union, bolstered by public outrage over the Chernobyl disaster (the effects of which were particularly harsh in Belarus), it failed to rally significant popular support. The Belarusian Popular Front (BPF), the core of the democratic opposition, eventually captured a small share of seats in the parliament. But unlike the popular fronts in the Baltic states and Ukraine, it remained too feeble to seize the initiative or to edge the national agenda in more progressive directions. When the Popular Front and its allies pushed for pre-term elections in 1992 in hopes of refurbishing the political establishment, the push failed.

The fact that Belarus cooperated with Russia and Ukraine in undoing the Soviet Union and launching a dozen states on a path of independence was, therefore, out of character. Belarus's role stemmed from the actions of Stanislau Shushkevich, the lone-wolf parliamentary chairman, whose capacity to imagine a Belarus on its own rather exceeded that of most other Belarusian politicians. As the effective head of state, he claimed the authority to join the other two Slavic republics in annulling the original 1924 treaty by which they had established the Soviet Union. Shushkevich, however, needed more than formal authority to make something of his new country's independence, and that he lacked. He spent his two years in power fighting pitched battles with Viacheslau Kebich, who was then prime minister, over less-than-clear issues. In the process sporadic thoughts of economic reform flickered and died. Thoughts of a government and legislature renewed and legitimized through elections were held off as long as possible.

Belarus was the last of the new post-Soviet states to hold elections. It finally scheduled presidential elections in 1994—as provided for in a new constitution—and parliamentary elections in 1995. The electorate, on balance as conservative and enamored of the past as the political establishment, selected Aleksandr Lukashenko as the country's first president. Lukashenko, a collective farm chairman from the northeastern part of the country, had built popular support as a member of parliament by charging much of the existing national leadership with corruption. Among the general public, his reputation apparently was also enhanced by the myth that in 1991 he was the deputy who cast the sole vote in the Belarusian parliament against the agreement dismantling the USSR.

Since June 1994, Belarus's emergence as a problem state has been swift and steady. The concern derives primarily from developments within the country—and not, until recently, from its behavior abroad. Three dimensions, in particular, form the basis of outside criticism and displeasure: human rights abuses, the movement away from constitutional government toward authoritarianism, and Belarus's staunch criticism of the expansion of the North Atlantic Treaty Organization (NATO) and of the policies of the United States.

In the first instance, Belarus's European neighbors, together with the United States and Canada, have made an increasing issue of human rights abuses by official agencies. Belarus's record on this score was hardly unblemished in the period before Lukashenko's election, but the range and scale of incidents since have galvanized a far sharper reaction in the outside world. Within six months of Lukashenko's election, the independent press, always in a parlous position because of the state's control over newsprint, found itself shut down for lack of printing facilities. Freedom of expression, an elemental test for the West of a regime's democratic intentions, seemed to be choked off from many different directions. Television media, still a state monopoly, once again became the regime's tame mouthpiece; adventurous reporters were turned into targets of intimidation; and would-be political opponents had fewer and fewer means of making a case. Early in the Lukashenko era, in April 1995, these trends came to a dramatic head when parliamentary deputies from the BPF "sat in" on the Supreme Council to protest a presidential action—and the leadership turned loose its special police force in a club-swinging rejoinder.

The West's more critical view of Belarus, however, stemmed not just from the country's increasingly marred human rights record, but also from its substitution of authoritarian for constitutional government. From the start Lukashenko and his people seemed to place a low value on constitutional constraints and the need to build power within law-governed institutions. Soon after his election, Lukashenko sought parliamentary approval to appoint governors for Belarus's six regions.[1] Not long after, he dropped the pretense of respecting parliamentary authority and set about eroding parliamentary power. A referendum held in May 1995 strengthened the executive's hand at the expense of the legislature. Even more telling were the president's openly disdainful gestures during the accompanying parliamentary elections. The following year he set aside the 1994 constitution, crafted one to his own liking, and submitted it to a referendum. Both the process and the result persuaded Europeans and Americans that Belarus under Lukashenko, rather than struggling with the problems of building democracy, was to a remarkable extent recreating its Soviet past. Lukashenko's internal policies also dismayed many in Russia, with Viktor Chernomyrdin, who was then prime minister, attempting unsuccessfully to mediate a compromise on the eve of the 1996 referendum. Finally, Lukashensko's foreign policy toward the West has not added a positive spirit to Belarus-West relations. His vocally hostile stance toward NATO expansion, as well as his criticism of other Western policies, as might be expected, have failed to improve Belarus's image in the West.

Western governments are accustomed to setbacks and imperfections along the path to democracy. They have seen a fair number of each in Spain, Portugal, Greece, and Turkey and again in the new Eastern Europe. What they find untenable in modern Europe is leadership that appears to be consciously and purposefully pursuing an undemocratic path. Even more than Belarus's failure to remodel its economy and open the way to market-oriented behavior, its seeming political defection preoccupies Western policy makers.

By the accident of geography, however, Belarus's role in Europe cannot be reduced to the bad example it sets among states making the post-Soviet transition. Its location makes its role broader and more basic. Belarus is where the post-Soviet space meets an expanding Europe. Together with Ukraine, parts of the Caucasus, Central Asia, and the Russian Far East—other meeting places between the former USSR and the outside world—Belarus will determine whether change in what was once the Soviet Union contributes to stability and cooperation or instability and conflict in the world at large. At stake is whether Belarus, a frontline state bordering an enlarged NATO, will become a bridge or a barrier.

A wide range of states have a stake in the path down which Belarus proceeds: Ukraine, Poland, Lithuania, Latvia, and Russia, because they are immediate neighbors; Scandinavia and Germany, because they are neighbors-once-removed; the rest of Western Europe, because its stability is prey to instability in Central Europe; and the United States, because it has good, selfish reasons to care about stability in Europe. The precise stake in Belarus, however, varies from state to state. Not only does the Polish stake obviously differ from the Russian, but so, too, does the West European from the Ukrainian, and the U.S. from the Central European.

By assembling authors from these different countries, we have sought to give the reader a sense of Belarus's great but varied significance beyond its borders. Belarus matters in complex and not always self-evident ways, as the multi-perspective analysis of the book reveals. Presented with many facets and contrasts, the reader must assess their meaning. How much do distinct, at times competing, views of the challenges posed by Belarus complicate the task of designing effective responses? How should these varying assessments be factored into U.S., European Union, Ukrainian, Polish, Lithuanian, or Russian national policy?

Ahead of this task, the challenge itself must be assessed. In this book, authors from six different countries explore Belarus's importance to European security. Five of the six authors examine trends in Belarusian politics and foreign policy from their country's perspective, and then review their country's response. The sixth author, Anatoly Rozanov from Belarus, reconstructs the way the world looks from a Belarusian vantage point and offers his own critique of current Belarusian policy.

The six authors unite around some key themes while diverging on others. Where they come together and where they draw apart reveals much of the underlying challenge posed by Belarus. The six are unified in stressing the significance of Belarus to the region and far beyond. They formulate its geostrategic role in strikingly similar terms. They agree in linking developments within Belarus to the character of its relations with the outside world. They all emphasize the impact of one figure, Aleksandr Lukashenko, on the country's development. Finally, they emphasize the importance of the Russian-Belarusian relationship and identify Russia as the single most important external factor in Belarus's evolution.

But differences among the authors in this volume start precisely where their convergence ends, with the meaning of the Belarusian-Russian relationship. They have different views of the prospects, and still more emphatically, the reasons for cooperation or even integration between the two countries. Behind this contrast stands a still more basic difference in their reading of Russian foreign policy and the way it adds to or subtracts from the Belarusian issue. They also think differently about the potential threat Belarus represents to the outside world. For the non-Belarusian authors, this difference in thinking in turn entails equally distinctive notions of how Belarus impinges on the interests of their particular country. Given these differences, not surprisingly they advocate often dissimilar policies in promoting a healthy role for Belarus among its neighbors and a constructive contribution to European security.

All the authors agree that Belarus is, in a geopolitical sense, a crossroads state. In chapter 5, Ukrainian author Hrihoriy Perepelitsa describes Belarus as at the junction of four dynamically developing European subdivisions. To its west are the countries of Central Europe (Poland, the Czech Republic, and Hungary) moving rapidly toward and into Europe's vibrant western half. To the north is the Baltic region, whose countries are integrating among themselves and with the five Nordic countries. To the south are the states of the Black Sea region (Ukraine, Moldova, and countries to the south), countries struggling to make something of their new subregion. To the east, of course, is Russia. Belarus, Perepelitsa suggests, links all these "subdivisions" along two axes. Along the east-west axis, Belarus is Russia's vital corridor for economic relations with Central Europe. Along the north-south axis, Belarus could be a bridge between the Black Sea region and the Baltic area. More grimly, because of its pivotal location, Belarus could also serve as a rampart of Russian military power, allowing Moscow to intimidate states to the north, west, and south.

Antoni Kaminski, viewing the problem from Warsaw, sees Belarus's geopolitical significance a bit differently (chapter 3). Poland and Belarus, he writes, once belonged to the space between Germany and Russia but now form the area "between a united Europe and Russia." With Poland in NATO and prospectively in the European Union, this intermediate area shrinks to Belarus alone. If Belarus unifies with Russia, the space disappears entirely, and the border of Poland with Belarus becomes the border between the Commonwealth of Independent States (CIS) and a united Europe.

As Vyacheslav Nikonov makes plain in his essay on the perspective of Russian foreign policy (chapter 6), for Russia, Belarus is indeed Russia's "window on Europe," permitting or impeding the flow of Russian goods, ideas, and influence into the central and western reaches of the continent. Belarus is also the primary obstacle to the emergence of a "so-called Baltic–Black Sea zone isolating Russia." But it is also the piece that contains the possibility of turning the CIS into more than an empty and shattered entity opposite an expanded and integrated Western Europe, should the union between Belarus and Russia gather momentum.

Belarus's geostrategic location is, however, only a backdrop. The country's real impact derives from the way its neighbors interpret trends within the physical setting and the way they reconstruct Belarus's part in the flow of events along the north-south and east-west axes. Seen from a Ukrainian perspective, the critical flow originates in the east. Russia, Perepelitsa stresses, sets the terms by which Belarus comes to affect other states. In Perepelitsa's view, since Russia is bent on restoring its sway over much of what was once the Soviet Union, then Belarus matters principally as a target of Moscow's efforts to reincorporate large parts of the former Soviet Union. To the extent that Russia means to turn the collective security arrangements within the CIS into a "mechanism for the political-military domination" of the region, Belarus has a cardinal role to play. According to Perepelitsa, deep military collaboration between Belarus and Russia creates an anchor for the otherwise uncertain process of melding the scattered portions of the post-Soviet space into a functioning defense alliance, one that would remain over-whelmingly an instrument of Russian foreign policy. In much the same fashion, an economic union between Belarus and Russia under-pins Russian efforts to gather the new states again into a Russian-dominated sphere of trade and investment.

Thus, for Perepelitsa, Belarus's role only takes on significance as an echo of Russian policy. So long as Russia refuses to reconcile itself to the loss of control over developments within and among neighboring states, Belarus's alignment with Russia inevitably renders Belarus a beachhead of Russian military power. Ukraine, he contends, faces dangers, not enemies, and historically the gravest of these dangers has been Ukraine's vulnerability to aggressors approaching from the north—that is, through Belarus. The threat, even if only hypothetical, forces Ukraine to orient its own defenses accordingly. In much the same way, according to Perepelitsa, Bela-rus's incorporation in the Russian economic sphere raises a dual challenge to Ukraine. On the one hand, it feeds the Russian appetite for supranational institutions and threatens the independence of members of the CIS. On the other hand, by harmonizing Belarusian and Russian trade policy, Russia's discriminatory measures against Ukraine are imitated by Belarus.

For Kaminski, too, the Russian dimension is important, but it works its effect differently. According to him, the worrying dynamic starts with domestic developments on the Belarusian side and within the country. By turning its back on reform and settling for authoritarian solutions, Belarus, he argues, constricts its foreign policy options. Reformers turn naturally to the West, while anti-reformers have nowhere to go but toward Russia. Moreover, lacking other sources of legitimacy, the anti-reformers seize on nationalist themes and the "myth of external threat to national survival" to justify their undemocratic ways. In the process, "the search for external enemies" turns the country into a "regional troublemaker." When Russia then chooses to embrace a state like Belarus—in part because it sees partnership in its own interest and in part because of resentment toward the regimes of Eastern and Central Europe—the threat is simply that much greater. To complete the circle, Russia preserves Belarus's anti-reform option by providing political and financial support to Lukashenko and his people—perhaps because they are more amenable to Russian aspirations within the CIS than the Belarusian opposition.

From this perspective, Belarus is not only a cat's-paw of Russian ambition but also the source of trouble—not necessarily as an aggressor, but as an exporter of instability. Kaminski fears that if conditions deteriorate within the country, desperate Belarusians may begin flowing in large numbers across the Polish border. Or perhaps even sooner, the sizable Polish minority in Belarus might be made the scapegoats of an angry and frustrated population. Kaminski acknowledges the possibility that, if constructively fashioned, a Russian-Belarusian union could promote stability within Belarus and the region. However, his analysis of current trends in the country and the Russian readiness to oblige Lukashenko make him treat such an option as a largely theoretical possibility.

Alghirdas Gricius of Lithuania stresses in chapter 4 the importance of the Russian link, but sees its role more positively. At least he starts with the assumption that the "East," primarily Russia, better understands the Lukashenko regime and how to influence it than does the West. Without Russian assistance, he argues, the West, including "an economically powerful European Union," has slim possibility of influencing internal policies in Belarus.

For Gricius, as for Perepelitsa and Kaminski, the question of what type of union might emerge between Belarus and Russia looms large. As with his Ukrainian and Polish coauthors, Gricius does not question the right of these two countries to draw together, on the condition that the drawing together does not threaten the security of other states. The wrong kind of integration, he maintains, is military, and the wrong kind of action is, for example, the Belarusian threat to bring Russian nuclear weapons back to Belarus, as Lukashenko suggested in the heat of the NATO debate.

Lithuania shares with Poland a peculiar concern. A small piece of Russia (historic Koenigsburg, later renamed Kaliningrad by the Soviets) sits tucked between Poland and Lithuania, cut off from the rest of Russia. Belarus in turn separates Russia from Poland and Lithuania. The combination of a sizable Russian military force in the Kaliningrad region and considerable Russian nervousness over its long-term grip on the enclave seems to the Poles and Lithuanians a ready-made basis for trouble. And Belarus, depending on the way it chooses to play its hand, will be central to Russian choices.

Belarus, as Gricius notes, poses challenges to Lithuanian foreign policy quite apart from the shadow cast by Russia. For one, it is a major corridor of illegal Asian and Central Asian refugee traffic into Lithuania, and when it adopts a hard-line unresponsive approach to the problem, Lithuania's headaches mount. For another, when Belarus tries to use its choice of shipping port on the Baltic as a form of leverage on Vilnius, the pressure is felt. Or, were Belarus to disrupt Lithuania's transportation links to Russia, nearly all of which pass through Belarusian territory, it could "create substantial difficulties" for a vital portion of Lithuanian foreign trade.

Viewed from Moscow, the picture, not surprisingly, looks rather different. Vyacheslav Nikonov makes the point in chapter 6 that Belarus poses a challenge for Russia as well, but a positive rather than negative one. More than any other country Belarus stands as a natural ally of Russia. The cultures of the two countries are very close, their sense of identity with one another is great, and their common interests are extensive. As a result, ties with Belarus are a crucial factor in Russia's foreign policy under any leadership. These ties bring Russia a long list of advantages: direct access to Central Europe; an obstacle to a Baltic–Black Sea zone intended to isolate Russia; added means of influencing Ukraine; a useful resource in the dialogue with Poland and the Baltic states; a positive example facilitating integration among the states of the CIS; an enhanced strategic position vis-à-vis the West; aid in sustaining the Russian position in the Kaliningrad region; and more space for maneuver within the boundaries covered by the Organization for Security and Cooperation in Europe (OSCE). All of these benefits are before tallying the potential economic benefits of the relationship.

For most Russian analysts, therefore, the issue is not whether integration of the two countries is desirable, but whether it is feasible. Even more than for Belarus's other neighbors, issues surrounding the Belarusian-Russian union dominate Russian thinking about Belarus and its place in the world. Unlike the cases of Ukraine, Poland, or Lithuania, these issues arise for Russia less as dangers than as trade-offs. When Nikonov carefully compiles the list of potential costs of a more thoroughgoing Russian-Belarusian integration, he presents them more as negatives for Russia than as threats to stability in East-Central Europe. These negatives include the possibility that Poland and Ukraine, and Poland and Lithuania, as well as the Baltic states, will draw closer together, thereby reducing Russia's room for maneuver; or leading Ukraine to strain harder to pull away from Russia and toward the West; or adding to the tensions between Russia and the West; or jeopardizing Russia's access to the resources of international financial institutions.

Even more fundamentally, and unlike his coauthors, Nikonov's criteria for judging the Russian-Belarusian union do not particularly involve the nature of the union, that is, whether a union will strengthen or weaken security in the region. Instead his eye is on its economic viability and whether the growing disparities between the character of the two economies can be spanned; on the risk that more Belarusian actions, such as the arrest and trial of Russian journalists in the summer of 1997, would poison the popular Russian mood and destroy support for integration; and on the quarrels that the idea of union with Lukashenko's Belarus sparks among Russian political elites.

Because Nikonov frames the question in this fashion, he finds less reason to make a fuss over Lukashenko's antidemocratic detour.

Rather than accent the link between the deterioration of political conditions within the country and the dangers that it raises for the outside world, Nikonov tends to stress the parallel with many other post-Soviet states. Seen in this light, internal political developments within Belarus do not differ greatly from those elsewhere in Russia's immediate neighborhood. For the most part Russia chooses to live with these regimes, a tolerance that makes the West's consternation seem both misplaced and counterproductive.

Among the six authors, Nikonov and Perepelitsa appear farthest apart in their views, save for one important convergence. Only these two authors emphasize the significance Belarus has for politics within their own countries. In Ukraine, Perepelitsa reports, the specter of Belarusian-Russian integration has a divisive effect. By energizing those forces on the left traditionally eager to preserve close ties with Russia, a talk of union between Russia and Belarus leads to a polarization of Ukrainian politics. Those who favor Ukraine's "eastern option" not only press for some form of union with Russia along the same lines, but they also attack cooperation with NATO. Those on the other side of the issue, that is, those who resent the weight of Russian power and want Ukraine to turn its face westward, pull still more insistently in the opposite direction. As a result, national institutions like the Rada, Ukraine's parliament, descend into paralyzed acrimony over the entire thrust of Ukrainian foreign policy.

Nikonov, too, emphasizes the broad reverberations in Russian politics of the disagreements over union with Belarus. Not only do Russia's liberal economic reformers question the desirability of merging the two economies, fearing that Belarus's unreconstructed economy will distort and hamstring Russia's own reform efforts, but they also worry that "encouraging authoritarianism" in Belarus will damage Russia's own democratic transition—not to mention cast a bad light on the idea of Russian-Belarusian integration. Others, determined to bring the two together no matter what, resent the opposition of the economic reformers and what they see as their undermining of the 1997 Union Treaty between Russia and Belarus from their various governmental posts. Matters grow still more complicated because, on the one hand, Belarus's moderate reformers— those politicians who should be more attractive to the Yeltsin regime and its supporters—tend to be the least supportive of integration with Russia and the most prone to embrace Western options. On the other hand, many Russian intellectuals also fear that Lukashenko, who seems to be an ally of integration, hopes to build a political base for himself within an enlarged Russian-Belarusian community by appealing to the more reactionary elements of Russian society. The last adds another area where the analyses of Perepelitsa and Nikonov overlap and, in this instance, their misgivings overlap as well.

In chapter 2, Anatoly Rozanov attacks the problem from yet another direction, a Belarusian perspective. For him the central issue is to preserve Belarusian independence, which for his country, as he acknowledges in subtle but unmistakable terms, means a delicate balancing act. Belarus, no one should doubt, has every reason to harmonize its policy with Russia and to foster close relations and, perhaps, even some level of integration. At the same time, Belarus has a no less urgent a need to help shape its general security environment by participating in the design of the European security regime. Belarus has, or at least should have, its own independent vision of an architecture that promotes its security. As a Belarusian, Rozanov lays out his version of what this vision should be. Provided the Western powers are open to a broadly based European system and do not insist on subordinating the management of European security to an unreconstructed NATO, Belarus has nothing to fear from a constructive relationship with NATO. A constructive relationship with an auspiciously restructured NATO, and an active role in building European institutions that strengthen Belarusian security by enhancing mutual security, can and ought to be primary objectives of Belarusian foreign policy.

Where, then, is the problem? Oddly it is the risk that Belarus will deny itself such an option. Although Rozanov's language is muted, he still suggests that the further the Belarusian leadership proceeds down its present domestic path, the more it constricts its foreign policy choices. By disregarding the West's increasingly hostile reaction—even deluding itself into believing that the West must come to terms with realities it cannot change—the government weakens its voice in European politics. Much as it may wish to pursue a balanced policy, creating optimal conditions for Belarus in West and East alike, the leadership doubly disadvantages itself by acting unwisely at home. First, it cuts in half its field of maneuver and leaves itself dependent on Russia as its only ally, a self-created isolation. Second, it sacrifices a flexibility that Russian leaders would not think of giving up themselves. Russia, for example, objected as vehemently to NATO enlargement as Belarus did, but when the time came, Russia's leaders protected their interests by reaching an agreement with NATO. Belarus's leadership, at least for the moment, has cheated itself out of the chance.

There is in Rozanov's argument an echo of Kaminski's point: anti-reform regimes among the former socialist states often have nowhere to turn but to Russia. His conclusion, however, differs fundamentally from Kaminski's. Where Kaminski worries that such regimes risk becoming local troublemakers, Rozanov fears that stunted relations with the West will deprive Belarus of control over its own international fate. The worst outcome, he warns, would be for Belarus to lose the opportunity to build a "belt of good-neighborly relations" along all its borders and thereby find itself reduced to some kind of "gray zone" between Russia and a NATO whose shape it has no prospect of influencing.

From across the Atlantic Ocean or even from London and Brussels, Belarus seems a good deal more distant. It has none of the imminence that it does for those next door. There is nothing comparable to its palpable presence in the internal politics of Ukraine and Russia, nothing comparable to the immediacy Poland or Lithuania feel over the likely effects of instability within Belarus or trouble over Kaliningrad. As a result, leaders in the major Western powers, including the United States, are not naturally inclined to conceive of Belarus in a security context. Instead, they react first to its political evolution, to its sharp deviation from their hopes for democracy and market reform in the former Soviet Union. As Robert Legvold argues in chapter 7, this slant is not entirely unconnected with their conception of European security. Their determination to hold European states to a standard of democracy relates to a half-articulated assumption that the modern (West) European international order, and by extension a future European order, rests on the democratic character of the states comprising it.

The association, however, obscures rather than highlights the more tangible and particular impact of Belarus on European security. The United States and its allies, Legvold contends, would do well to give greater attention to this other dimension, not the least because they, more than Belarus's neighbors, should have less trouble putting it in perspective. Looked at from afar, Belarus's significance for European security has multiple angles. The root of the problem is the sum of the concerns expressed in the essays in this volume. That each of Belarus's neighbors has fears involving Belarus—often contrasting and sometimes totally opposed fears—creates an unhappy point of departure. Trends within Belarus and its foreign policy do not encourage consensus and unity among the states of the region. They have the opposite effect. Worse, these trends are taken as criteria by which to judge the (supposedly malicious) intentions of third parties. They are used to derive insight into Russian purposes for Ukrainians, Poles, and Lithuanians, as well as into Ukrainian, Polish, and Lithuanian (and Western) purposes for Russians.

Second, Belarus risks figuring in a variety of destabilizing configurations. A Russian-Ukrainian-Belarusian triangle would produce unsettling effects in Central Europe. A like-minded Belarus allied with a Russia alienated from the West would considerably enhance the range of hostile Russian response. A Belarus alienated from the West and willing to abet strong-armed Russian policies would gravely complicate life for any state in the neighborhood that had raised Russian ire. And a Belarus adrift and casting about for alignments would generate considerable nervousness, especially among the Russians.

Third, Belarus is a critical piece of the Central European mosaic. Belarus could tie together a variety of states and international enterprises or obstruct any such possibility; it could serve as a stable hinge between the post-Soviet space and the rest of Europe or as a dangerous void between the two Europes; and it could solidify the peace among the new states of the former Soviet Union or leave it under a perpetual cloud.

Fourth, a stable and prospering Belarus will export into surrounding areas one set of effects, an unstable and decaying Belarus, another set. U.S. leaders can plausibly argue that the prospects for a stable and prospering Belarus depend on its advancing toward democracy and a modern market-based economy, but nothing guarantees that getting there will be incombustible or accident-free. Hence, part of the task of thinking through the implications of Belarus for European security, when it comes to the internal dimension, involves not only the direction of change, but also the stability of the process.

Nothing in this more highly wrought notion of Belarus's relevance to European security calls into question the centrality of the Russian-Belarusian relationship. Legvold shares with the other authors the view that what becomes of the union between the two will, more than any other factor, determine Belarus's influence on the rest of Europe. But two further things are relevant on this score. First, and from this none of the authors dissents, it is far from a forgone conclusion that the union between Russia and Belarus will ultimately materialize, let alone take on pathological qualities. Second, and on this point only Rozanov offers an echo, Legvold suggests that influence flows west to east, not merely east to west: that is, the United States and Western Europe can, depending on the strategy they adopt, have much to say about the shape the union assumes.

Belarus, as most of the authors stress, is both subject and object in this book. Not only what happens to Belarus, but also what it *chooses* to do, will determine the outcome. Thus, how Belarusian officials and elites perceive their basic strategic choices is an important element in the analysis. Rozanov identifies three basic options. In the early post-independence days, parties such as the BPF and other forces on the left advocated what they termed "a return to Europe." By this they meant both an effort to integrate Belarus into European institutions and a conscious distancing of the country from Russia and its various imperial enterprises. Because, as Rozanov indicates, few within the general population shared the desire to separate from Russia, the idea was doomed from the start.

A second approach favored by many in the foreign policy establishment in Belarus—foreign ministry officials and specialists in international relations—leaned toward neutrality. This posture would not be in any way anti-Russian. On the contrary, Belarus would remain sensitive to the "geostrategic considerations of Moscow," taking them into account and responding to them intelligently. But the emphasis would be on the European context of Belarus's foreign policy interests, and Belarus would pursue them by avoiding entanglement in any political-military alliance, existing or future, east or west. Rozanov describes it as a distinctive form of "Finlandization."

While this approach may still be viewed sympathetically in some quarters, as an articulated approach it belongs largely to the early years of independent Belarus. Since the mid-1990s, Rozanov writes, the dominant view—at least the official view—has stressed a tilt toward alignment, indeed, integration, with Russia. More recently, the emphasis has shifted from integration to preserving Belarusian statehood and sovereignty. But events within Belarus still prevent the country from following a genuinely balanced policy between East and West and leave it, half by intent and half by default, with only a Russian option. Moreover, it is an option whose purpose and content grow more ambiguous and shapeless.

Rozanov's summary leads to several propositions that seem essential in any analysis seeking to stay close to reality. First, Belarus will be odd-country-out among the post-Soviet states in the European part of the former Soviet Union. Gradually it may come to be as jealous of its sovereignty as any of the others are. But unlike all the others, Belarusian sovereignty is not likely to be defined in juxtaposition to Russia. For economic, cultural, and historical reasons Belarusian governments, whatever their character, will genuinely care about keeping their foreign policy in harmony with Russia's. Even were the West to give Belarus the choice, Belarus would be unlikely to choose the West over Russia—again, not a claim to be made about any other post-Soviet state. Hence, whether the union of the two gathers momentum or, to the contrary, collapses, there is likely to remain a basic, underlying consonance in their foreign policies.

Second, within that constraint there still exists room for Belarus to pursue an active, independent policy toward its neighbors and in the broader European setting. Although the United States and the major powers of Western Europe—and at times even Belarus's immediate neighbors—have trouble seeing the precise ways that Belarus matters to their larger interests, their vague appreciation of Belarus's importance creates opportunities for Belarusian policy. If Belarus's leadership wishes to play a role in shaping Europe's security arrangements, it can. Even less than Russia can it exercise a veto over developments that it dislikes. But there is scope for initiative between veto and impotence if Belarus can overcome self-imposed obstacles to engagement.

There follows directly a third point: much as President Lukashenko and those around him may resent Belarus's ostracism by the West and attribute it to ill-considered motives or worse, the situation is not likely to change until trends within Belarus change as well. Even were the United States, the European Union, and the majority of Belarus's neighbors, or some portion of them, to abandon the sharper and more explicit penalties imposed on Belarus for human rights abuses, they would not welcome Belarus back into the community of European nations. Belarus's position would still be compromised and its influence limited.

At the same time, it seems shortsighted for the United States and the other Western powers to write Belarus off, to assume that, so long as Lukashenko remains in power, little can be done to integrate Belarus into European processes or, still more despairingly, that Lukashenko will remain in place indefinitely. It is equally shortsighted to sink into the habit, so clearly regretted by Rozanov, of treating Belarus as nothing more than an extension of Russia. If the United States and its principal European allies start from a carefully constructed calculation of their stakes in the evolution of Belarus and its role in Europe, few will think they can afford to slight the country.

Once the stakes are understood, the challenge of dealing with Belarus grows commensurately. None of the authors in this book underestimates the difficulty of integrating Belarus into the work of designing Europe's security architecture, while at the same time attempting to divert its leadership from the authoritarian temptation back to the path of democracy and economic reform. To the degree that different countries disagree over which of these objectives should have priority, each will be less effective in achieving its objectives. To the extent that Russia denies or ignores the challenge altogether, it makes the challenge facing others formidable indeed. It also almost certainly complicates the challenge that Belarus will present to Russian policy down the road.

NOTES

[1] Kathleen J. Mihalisko, "Belarus: Retreat to Authoritarianism," in Karen Dawisha and Bruce Parrott, eds., *Democratic Changes and Authoritarian Reactions in Russia, Ukraine, Belarus, and Moldova* (Cambridge, U.K.: Cambridge University Press, 1997), p. 254. Mihalisko's essay is a good survey of these developments and their broader background.

2

Belarus: Foreign Policy Priorities

Anatoly Rozanov

The history, cultural tradition, and economic and intellectual potential of Belarus form a favorable context for its advancement along the lines of its European neighbors. It should be participating fully in European affairs, including the creation of a new security structure for Europe. Regrettably, Belarus has yet to find a way to fulfill its European promise. Instead, it remains largely at the periphery of European developments.

Even as disputes with the West have grown, top government officials have repeatedly stressed their desire for a "multidirectional" foreign policy, one that continues to form strong ties with Russia while developing closer relations with Europe. The reality, however, is that such a foreign policy remains largely on paper. In practice Belarus's foreign policy agenda revolves around the East, particularly Russia.

If Belarus itself focuses primarily on Russia, it is not surprising that the international community tends to see Belarus through the Russian prism. Western analysts have doubts about whether Belarus has or should have an independent role in the world, or even on the European scene. They often refer to Belarus as if it were a mere extension of Russia. Belarus has been described as "a highly autonomous, but not truly independent state."[1] Until recently such views have rarely, if at all, been called into question in the West.

In addition, a mature multi-directional foreign policy is constrained by the emerging mechanisms of foreign policy formulation and implementation in Belarus. Foreign policy assumptions and key objectives were laid down in the Declaration of State Sovereignty adopted by the Belarusian Supreme Soviet on July 27, 1990, and recorded in the Constitution of the Republic of Belarus adopted by the Supreme Soviet on March 15, 1994. The basic objectives remain the same today: Belarus aims to become a nuclear-free neutral state.

A debate on the parameters of Belarusian neutrality took place in the first half of the 1990s, culminating in the National Security Concept of the Republic of Belarus approved by the Security Council of the Republic of Belarus on March 27, 1995. The National Security Concept is the only functioning document containing an official description of the neutrality policy that Belarus intends to pursue. The document states that Belarus will "not be involved in current or possible future international armed conflicts." It will not "supply to any belligerent, either directly or indirectly, weaponry, ammunition, or goods declared to be military contraband." Belarus territory is not to be used for the recruitment or creation of "armies or armed formations of parties to military conflicts." The text also places restrictions on the movement of troops or weapons of mass destruction through Belarusian territory.[2]

The deepening of Belarusian-Russian military integration, which opened up prospects for a military alliance, as well as continuing disagreements with the West, raised serious questions about what a policy of neutrality meant. Official foreign policy statements hardly mention neutrality in describing the country's foreign policy.

Since the publication of the National Security Concept the Belarusian government has been working on a broader foreign policy concept. It has yet to be submitted for public discussion, although the Ministry of Foreign Affairs prepared a version in 1997 and submitted the document to the president for approval. This document, in part, discusses the unity of domestic and foreign policy. When applied to Belarus, the thesis of mutual interdependence and interconnection between internal and foreign policies becomes evident.

TROUBLES IN THE WEST

In fact, Belarus's moves in the international arena are frequently the result, directly or indirectly, of domestic developments. The domestic policy favored by the current leaders of Belarus has an impact on the nation's foreign policy, making the country stand out on the current European scene. The peculiar attitude displayed by Belarus to the West and, in particular, to the United States corresponds to the Belarusian government's negative views on market reform and private enterprise, democracy, and human rights. These basic differences have been widened by a long dispute over ambassadorial residences, NATO enlargement, and recent events in Kosovo.

Despite the great gap that now exists between Minsk and Western capitals, the West has a strategic stake in Belarus. Western politicians should prefer an independent, democratic Belarus, given its location on the eastern border of NATO.

At the close of the twentieth century, Belarus is going through a dramatic period in its relationship with the major Western nations. It might even be thought that recent events have fundamentally undermined these relations: Russian-Belarusian integration, diplomatic disputes, and differences over evolving security policy in Europe. Although Western politicians officially disavow any attempt to isolate Belarus, the Belarusian leadership cannot but see the West's current policy as aimed at excluding Belarus from key European institutions and processes. This course is likely to have far-reaching and negative consequences.

Belarus's current relationship with the West can be understood in different ways. Belarusian President Lukashenko put a bold face on the situation in late 1997, stating that "the West and the United States need time to once again embark on a dialogue with Belarus, while still saving face."[3] Others, including a number of independent Belarusian experts, argue that the chances of resuming a full-fledged dialogue between Belarus and the West are not good.

Given the tension between stated foreign policy objectives and the policy results, the question arises whether Belarus has a fully developed and strictly consistent foreign policy? The answer is obviously no. Outside of Russian-Belarusian integration Belarus has made little more than individual moves and improvisations on the international arena.

THE EUROPEAN SECURITY AGENDA

The dilemma of Belarusian foreign policy is best illustrated by looking at what Minsk sees as four key issues on the European security agenda. The first is Minsk's preferred security architecture, which is one that relies more on the OSCE than on NATO. The second is NATO enlargement. The third is the advancement of a nuclear-free zone in Central and Eastern Europe. The last is Belarusian-Russian integration.

Toward a Single Security Space in Europe

The end of the Cold War brought forth competing proposals on the future of Europe's security architecture. One proposal that has been popular with many in the West envisions a prevailing role for NATO and the transformation of NATO into something resembling a collective security organization. Another proposal makes NATO subordinate to a pan-European collective security organization. Still another suggests a well-planned and reasonable separation of security efforts among NATO, the OSCE, and other European institutions.

Many advocates of NATO's primacy believe that the North Atlantic alliance will evolve into a new entity and will, in addition to the function of collective defense, assume collective security obligations. Opponents argue that collective defense (the core mission of the alliance) must not be sacrificed to the wider and vaguer mission of collective security. In this view, NATO should remain NATO and keep its present identity.

Many experts in both the East and West once saw the Commission on Security and Cooperation in Europe (now known as the OSCE) as the top contender to become the functional mechanism for collective security. However, the OSCE's critics rightly criticized its amorphous nature. The crises in Bosnia and Kosovo further damaged public confidence in the OSCE's ability to carry out a meaningful role in a serious crisis. Nevertheless, for Belarus the OSCE remains a valuable and, in its own way, irreplaceable component of an emerging European security architecture.

After Belarus gained independence in 1991, it was able to participate in OSCE negotiations on the reduction of armed forces and armaments, to formulate positions on a range of European security problems, and to deliberate on confidence-building measures. This experience was valuable for developing Belarus's foreign policy cadre and for raising Belarus's appreciation of the OSCE as an institution. The OSCE also provided a forum for Belarus to put forward specific initiatives that would help it define itself in European politics, as well as outline the kind of European security environment

Minsk would like to see. In keeping with its stated foreign policy goals, Belarus tabled initiatives that would reduce the military potential of all European nations to the minimum level sufficient for their defense. Belarus also sought to underscore the importance of the environmental aspects of security, in view of the country's tragic experience with Chernobyl and its aftermath.

According to Minsk, Europe will only enter the twenty-first century in peace if its continental security system meets certain basic criteria:

- First, it must address both old and new threats such as regional conflicts, terrorism, organized crime, and other non-traditional security problems.

- Second, the new system must keep a fair balance between the interests of European nations, all of which should have equal rights when it comes to making decisions affecting the future of Europe.

- Third, it is necessary to select a security model that will bring nations together rather than threaten yet another division of Europe.[4]

Belarus concluded that only the OSCE could provide an underlying structure for a system that meets the above criteria and makes effective use of existing institutions, including NATO. The OSCE's role had to be that of a coordinator for European and Euro-Atlantic institutions in the overall effort to maintain peace and stability in Europe.

Belarus seeks to contribute to the development of just such a model of European security. It shares the fundamental OSCE principles regarding comprehensive security arrangements that are common to all. No state or group of states may enhance its security at the expense of another. There can be no spheres of influence or divisions within the common security space. The new security model should be based on a concept of cooperation and on mutual security guarantees, not on mutual deterrence.

Belarus strongly supports having the OSCE as coordinator of the new security system. On the whole, Belarus supports Russia's position that the OSCE should be a leader among the institutions involved in the creation of a new European security structure. Western nations have indicated that they are ready to accept a somewhat stronger and more influential OSCE, but they are opposed to the idea of a hierarchic security system. NATO members, in particular, want the freedom to use the alliance to address problems such as Kosovo, with or without the support and approval of other European states and institutions.

To make an OSCE-led security structure a reality, Belarus favors creating a legal environment and a system of treaties. There are many different views on the idea of adopting legally binding documents of this sort. The United States, for instance, questions whether OSCE activities require a legally binding foundation. Belarus, for its part, wants an appropriate agreement that builds on the Helsinki Final Act and other OSCE documents and gives them legal force.

Belarus follows Russia in emphasizing the need for a European security charter that has equal footing with the Helsinki Final Act. At the same time, the charter should make the strategic development of the OSCE the normative basis of this process. Belarus also favors enhancing OSCE's peacekeeping capabilities but has indicated that it understands the complexity of the problem. It is hard to give the OSCE its own peacekeeping task force when even the United Nations, in spite of its vast experience and potential, has not always succeeded in its peacekeeping missions,[5] and NATO has assumed the de facto lead.

Relationship with NATO and Regional Structures

It is important to stress that in principle the Belarusian approach to European security is not anti-NATO, although Minsk has strongly criticized both the enlargement of NATO and its intervention in Kosovo. While the OSCE may provide the optimal general framework for a pan-European political dialogue on security issues, NATO could make a sizable contribution to the military aspect of European security and stability. After all, NATO has been successfully setting up new types of political and military relations in Europe through the Partnership for Peace (PFP) and Euro-Atlantic Partnership Council (EAPC).

It would be shortsighted, however, to idealize the process of NATO transformation and its internal and external adaptation to the newly emerging realities in Europe. NATO's adjustment to an undivided Europe has been far from painless, and one should not exaggerate its impact. However, a change in the functions of NATO, increased emphasis on the political component of security, and new nuances in how the alliance functions are quite visible. It is a different matter, of course, that the NATO's internal adaptation seems to lag behind that of its enlargement.

Minsk in fact has consistently opposed NATO expansion. It thought expansion would result in new dividing lines in Europe through the expansion of military alliances. Even now, after the event, it still appears to many in the East that the decision to expand NATO was a mistake.

Russia and Belarus have valid reasons to be concerned that NATO enlargement might push them to the outskirts of European politics. Should a NATO-based security system evolve in Europe, Russia would cease to be a major player in defining the parameters of European security, the reason the OSCE is a particular focus of Russian diplomacy. Nonetheless, all serious analysts understand that the future of European security depends primarily on the Russia-NATO relationship, not on lengthy debates within the OSCE. Minsk accepts this basic reality.

In its foreign policy Belarus would do well to give proper consideration to the various motives and interests behind NATO enlargement. Belarus could have been more cautious in this area. It could have not closed the doors to bilateral cooperation while still maintaining its opposition to enlargement. Belarus should not have focused so single-mindedly on supporting Russia's stand vis-à-vis the Atlantic alliance. In fact, Minsk's policy demonstrated less flexibility than the Russian approach did. Ultimately, Russia accepted the NATO-Russian Joint Council, while Minsk failed to achieve any special bilateral arrangements with NATO. While Russian and Belarusian interests are highly compatible, they are not identical. Each country has its own geopolitical realities. Belarus should be developing its own vision of a new security architecture in Europe that complements—but is not subsumed by—Russia's proposals.

The issue of NATO enlargement directly relates to the U.S. presence in Europe and to the American role in building a new European security structure. If America's stabilizing role in Europe were to be seen as containing Germany's geopolitical push to the east, then Minsk could look on NATO enlargement more calmly. One positive long-term outcome would be a situation in which Central Europe would not become an arena for Russian-German rivalry. The prevention of the so-called renationalization of the defense policies of European nations could also be seen as a positive result of enlargement.

Given the facts, Belarus's anti-enlargement posture does not seem wholly convincing. It is possible that NATO can make a positive contribution to designing the military component for a European security system, since other relevant organizations do not have influential and capable military components, while the institutions of the CIS are barely making an impact on European developments. Of course, for such an arrangement to work NATO could not assume the unilateral role it did in Kosovo.

Considering its small size and relative isolation, Belarus should have thought through its position on NATO more thoroughly. Belarus's national interests would be best served by constructive interaction and cooperation with every multilateral structure involved in ensuring European security. It is hoped that the possibility of returning to a more constructive dialogue between Belarus and NATO has not been lost. Over time, Belarus is prepared to make a constructive contribution to avoid a confrontational relationship and new lines of division between Eastern and Western Europe. Despite recent disputes, I believe Belarus is prepared to build useful interaction with NATO and new security structures such as the EAPC.

The principles and structure of security cannot be imposed from above by some supranational forum, be it NATO or the EAPC. They should rely on solid grassroots support at the regional level, taking into account the historical overlap in interests among certain nations and regional security specifics. This approach would make such a security model a natural addition to the current geopolitical situation and take proper account of the interests of all nations and international institutions. For this reason, the regional dimension may emerge as an important avenue of the EAPC and other European security activities.

Belarus has virtually no border disputes with neighboring countries. The issues of delimitation of Belarusian borders were successfully dealt with through bilateral negotiations. As a landlocked country, however, Belarus takes a keen interest in the situation around the Baltic Sea. Undoubtedly, Belarus will be a motivated participant in all special working groups that may be formed within the EAPC framework to discuss Baltic issues.

At the regional level, Belarus's steps toward integration with Russia deserve mention. From the perspective of the Belarusian leadership, the Union Treaty of 1997 between Belarus and Russia makes a regional contribution to Euro-Atlantic security. Such diplomatic forums as tripartite and multilateral consultations may help establish neighborly relations and enhance regional and overall security. Belarus is prepared to use such proven mechanisms in cooperating with its neighbors Poland, Ukraine, Lithuania, and Latvia.

Given this complicated but not unfavorable picture, the growing gap between Belarus and NATO is a serious obstacle to overall improvement in Belarus's relations with the West. Despite a continuing dispute over enlargement—particularly if NATO expands farther to the east into the Baltic region—and harsh words over Kosovo, a new NATO-Belarusian dialogue is possible. Such a dialogue is built not on wishful thinking but on hard strategic facts. Belarus is of strategic interest to NATO, especially as NATO moves east. As Sherman Garnett has noted, "If Poland becomes a member of NATO, Belarus will increasingly become a matter of the alliance's interest as well."[6] Because of the prominent geostrategic location of Belarus and the trends in Belarus-Russia rapprochement, Minsk will remain, as Michael Dobbs wrote in the *Washington Post*, "a long-term strategic headache for Washington."[7] Does the West really want to abandon any leverage it might have over Russian-Belarusian integration and deal exclusively with Moscow?

Although its excessively anti-NATO rhetoric and rigid support of Russia have placed Belarus at a relative disadvantage in dealing with NATO, the Russian-NATO example of limited cooperation remains instructive. Both Russia and Ukraine were able to maneuver adroitly to fashion a special link with NATO. In Russia's case that link is still weak and frayed by Kosovo, but the link still exists. Belarusian diplomacy should take a lesson from history and realize its interest in sustaining a zone of good neighborliness in and around itself. NATO can help support such a zone. President Lukashenko stated clearly the strategic benefits of such a link when he commented that "Russia's and Ukraine's agreements with NATO to build up confidence measures and create obstacles in the way of advancement to the east of troops, arms, and military infrastructures objectively meet the interests of our country as well."[8] It would be good to see Belarus make a contribution of its own to the establishment of a constructive partnership with NATO.

Belarus would benefit from an even, stable, and dynamic relationship with the Atlantic alliance. Such a relationship is hard to build, however, when Belarus continues denying the Western values that essentially underlie NATO. The preamble of the North Atlantic Treaty, signed on April 4, 1949, in Washington, D.C., specifies that the member states "are determined to safeguard the freedom, common heritage, and civilization of their peoples, founded on the principles of democracy, individual liberty, and the rule of law." Few outside of Belarus or Russia accept Belarus's own interpretation of democracy and human rights. This obstacle to dialogue must be faced squarely.

Obviously, the near-term prospects for establishing special relations between Belarus and NATO (similar to those between NATO and Russia or NATO and Ukraine) are not favorable. Belarus's earlier unwillingness to explore ways of cooperating with NATO and its relatively inactive role in PFP make the current task of restoring some form of a link even harder. What Belarusian diplomacy needs right now is patience, just as Western diplomacy needs greater imagination and strategic insight. Belarus would do well to display greater flexibility and genuine pragmatism in its foreign policy, and thereby open up new options and prevent Minsk from being caught off guard.

Perhaps the best way to proceed is slowly, focusing on specific, discrete areas. It is no secret that Belarusian public opinion is prejudiced against NATO because of the decades of anti-Western and anti-NATO propaganda. The lack of objective information about NATO, and about how the alliance has changed since the end of the cold war, is a serious obstacle to cooperation. Perhaps that problem could be addressed by setting up in Minsk, as was done in Moscow and Kiev, a NATO documentation center. Such a center would help create a favorable background for further, more ambitious steps to restore NATO-Belarusian dialogue.

A Proposed Nuclear-Weapon-Free Zone in Central Europe

The proposal for "a nuclear-weapon-free space in Central and Eastern Europe," as announced by President Lukashenko on July 3, 1996, remains the country's most meaningful and large-scale foreign policy initiative to date.[9] Considerable effort is being exerted to attract the international community's attention to the idea, although with little success. Belarus saw implementation of this initiative as a way to promote the process of further disarmament, and particularly as a way to rule out the possibility of resumed nuclear confrontation in Europe. The proposal conforms to the letter and spirit of the nuclear Non-Proliferation Treaty (NPT) and the decisions of the 1995 conference for extension of the NPT.

As new arrangements on conventional forces in Europe take shape, a parallel treaty on a nuclear-free zone could be the final link in the legal regime of arms limitation in Europe. However, the United States and its closest allies in NATO have consistently opposed such a zone. The non-nuclear principle still does not fit into NATO's strategic assumptions and military planning, even with the alliance's promises not to introduce nuclear weapons into the new member states. While its profile in NATO's military-political guidelines has become lower, the nuclear aspect, as before, occupies an exceptionally important place in NATO strategy. To many in the West, the denuclearization of Europe or of its central segment would effectively call into question the military designation of NATO as the West's reliable instrument for collective defense.

The West has long tried to erode the appeal of a nuclear-free zone in Europe. It has argued that such a zone would create the risk of conventional hostilities and that nations have no need legally to record their nuclear-free status if they are already de facto nuclear-free. Finally, some feel that nuclear-free zones make no sense because it is impossible to guarantee that they will not fall prey to a nuclear attack from outside. According to that position, nuclear-free zones can be created at the stroke of a pen, but no zone can be truly safe from the use of nuclear weapons.

All the above make implementation of Belarus's nuclear-free proposal highly unlikely, although no less desirable. Given the bitter aftertaste of enlargement and NATO's unilateral intervention in Yugoslavia, renewed attention to nuclear and conventional limits is more important than ever. The momentum of demilitarization and cooperation in security matters in this region of Europe must be sustained. Perhaps the nuclear-free zone proposal cannot be made viable, especially given the Soviet-style of diplomacy that supports it, but the impulse within Belarus that gave rise to it is as relevant to the future military stability of the region as ever.

BELARUS-RUSSIA INTEGRATION: VARYING INTERPRETATIONS

The relationship between Belarus and Russia is in many ways unique and stands out against the overall bleak background of CIS integration. Russia is Belarus's top economic and trade partner. Russia supplies nearly 100 percent of Belarus's oil and gas. After the breakup of the USSR, Belarus paid more attention than any other CIS nation to Russia's position on settling disputes concerning the reduction and limitation of nuclear and conventional weapons. Belarus and Russia share almost identical approaches on many pressing European issues. Their common historical and societal-cultural traditions are also a factor in Belarus-Russia integration.

The dynamics of the two countries' rapprochement have alarmed the West, which tends to interpret Russia's efforts at restoring and strengthening ties with Belarus and other former Soviet republics as a manifestation of Russian "neo-imperialism." It should be noted, however, that, while Russian-Belarusian cooperation is real, integration appears to be more show than substance. It is quite obvious that major agreements, including the 1997 Union Treaty and the 1998 summit pledge to create a unified monetary system in 1999, are simply not being implemented. Integrationist expectations in both countries have declined as a result of the failure to implement existing plans, as well as the lack of tangible results from cooperation, particularly in the economic sphere.

A broad range of assessments on the significance and prospects of Belarus-Russia integration can be found in analytical papers and political statements not only in Belarus and Russia but also in other countries. In late April 1997, the Politika Foundation, a Russian strategic research institution, and the Council for Foreign and Defense Policies published a joint report that stands out among other Russian research papers on bilateral issues. The report analyzes the positive and negative implications of the accelerated integration of Belarus and Russia.[10] Inasmuch as the contributing authors appear to be authorities on Russian affairs, their realistic and balanced opinions are worthy of further study.

In their description of the domestic political situation in Belarus, these Russian researchers argue that, as a result of the acute political crisis in Belarus (October–December 1996) and its attendant constitutional reform through referendum, a "moderately authoritarian regime" has been established in Belarus. On the one hand, this regime may advance unification by such acts as removing opponents of Belarus-Russia rapprochement from government agencies. On the other hand, it can discredit the unification process in the eyes of Russian reformers and expose Russia to charges of "encouraging authoritarianism."

The report stresses the real benefits from eventual integration, including Russia's direct access to the borders of the Central European region, removal of the potential threat of a Baltic Sea–Black Sea "Russia isolation belt," access to additional leverage on Ukraine, and optimization of Russia's strategic situation on its western periphery, including room for maneuver in the framework of the Treaty on Limitation of Conventional Armed Forces in Europe. Russia's foreign policy and defense interests view the benefits of faster integration predominantly in a geopolitical and geostrategic context.

The authors also present some negative implications of unification: it would lead to closer relations between Poland and Ukraine and between Poland and Lithuania, and further consolidate the Baltic nations; it would encourage the West to pay greater attention to Ukraine; and it would heighten certain differences in Russia's relations with the West, primarily with the United States.

Western analysts, especially in the United States, tend to see the union of Belarus and Russia in dark colors. In fact, it is difficult to find any positive treatment of the Belarusian regime in prominent Western publications. The United States has been closely watching the progress of the Belarus-Russia relationship. Washington's official assessment of Belarus-Russia integration has been cautious; nevertheless it has been concerned about the possibility of a new union of states in the territory of the former USSR and the reemergence of an influential power center in what is Eurasia's key region. Besides, argues Sherman Garnett, "a change in the status of Belarus would shift the regional balance of power."[11]

Integration of Belarus and Russia is a complex and controversial process that requires subtle analysis and a multidimensional perspective, not hysteria. The fact that the issue has invited such varying assessments in both Russia and the United States indicates that it is perceived in different ways. More attention needs to be given to what in fact the two states can accomplish, given political and economic conditions in the two countries and the interests of immediate neighbors and important outside powers.

Frankly, the Russian economic and financial crisis at the end of 1998 cannot be separated from the situation in Belarus. The crisis has had an increasingly negative influence on the Belarusian economy, including a high level of inflation (21 percent in October 1998), a sharp drop in exports, and a series of shortages of fundamental foodstuffs. Furthermore, the crisis in Russia was used in Belarus to discredit the market economy model and to develop a proposal for the state to play an increasing regulatory role in the economy. Bad economic influences are not going to make integration more likely, unless Russia is prepared to control and fully subsidize the Belarusian economy and Belarusian leaders are prepared to give Russia such control. Neither is likely.

Observers should also note that Russian-Belarusian strategic cooperation does not mean that Russian and Belarusian interests and actions are identical. At a meeting of the first session of the Parliamentary Assembly of the Union of Belarus and Russia in June 1997, President Lukashenko stated that Belarus and Russia have achieved "considerable success" in coordinating and implementing their foreign policies. He added, however, that "it is a mistake to believe that we will automatically implement foreign policy decisions made in Moscow. . . ."[12] In practice, nevertheless, the foreign policies are virtually identical.

IN SEARCH OF AN OPTIMAL FOREIGN POLICY STRATEGY

The scope of the public debates in Belarus over foreign policy since the country won independence in 1991 has not been particularly wide or diverse. The leaders of the opposition Belarusian Popular Front and affiliated political groups have campaigned for a return to Europe. Their interpretation of a return to Europe has emphasized not so much the need for integration into European structures, which could not of itself have caused any objection, but the prospect of putting political distance between Belarus and Russia, whose imperialistic impulses have been portrayed as an attribute of Russian statehood. The anti-Russian bias of that position, even if disguised, prevented the opposition groups from winning sizable popular support. The majority of people in Belarus see their country's future as linked to that of Russia.

Another proposal that was put forth, although with no obvious anti-Russian agenda, provided for the dominance of a European vector, somewhat along the lines of a "Finlandization" of Belarus's foreign policy. Advocates of that position suggested that, while taking into account and reacting reasonably to Moscow's geostrategic considerations, Belarus should nevertheless pursue a firm policy of neutrality and keep out of military-political alliances. That position was being worked on at one time in Belarus's foreign ministry, with support from experts on international affairs.

In the mid-1990s, however, official statements turned away from both of these variants. Belarus emphasized the need for unification and closer ties with Russia. The "Russian vector" in the foreign policy of Belarus, which received a great deal of attention, represented an upsurge of integrationist sentiments. This ideological emphasis on the Russian vector proved overly optimistic, occurring at a time when integration itself was producing few results. Gradually, the government's rhetoric began to emphasize the need to maintain Belarusian statehood and sovereignty no matter how advanced the integration process became. As of the late 1990s, the key concept in official foreign policy rhetoric is a "multi-vectored approach." Advocates of this approach argue that Belarus's foreign policy efforts ought to be evenly distributed in all directions, although there is little evidence of this occurring.

The tension in Belarus's relationships with the United States, Western nations, and European institutions, as well as problems in its relations with Russia, demonstrate the questionable effectiveness of Belarus's past international activities. In principle, a balanced foreign policy agenda for Belarus might consist of efforts to build good neighborly relations with Russia and other neighbors, balanced with a stated readiness for integration into European cooperation and security mechanisms. This agenda, while justified both geopolitically and historically, is not easy to translate into reality under current conditions such as the difficult domestic conditions in Belarus.

To expand its options and respond to its national interests, Belarus needs to strengthen its reputation as an independent nation with its own national and geopolitical interests and foreign policy preferences. It is particularly important to ensure that Belarus's foreign policy follows a clear-cut "European vector," not a Eurasian one. This does not mean some kind of "Ukrainization" of Belarus's policy, which would place strong emphasis on relations with the West. Such a policy could hardly appeal to the average Belarusian. Instead, it means creating an optimal environment in which Belarus can participate in the building of new European structures and contribute fully to European developments as an independent international player, not just as a participant in the Belarus-Russia union.

It is of great importance for Belarus to find the right tone in its dealings with NATO. Disapproval of the enlargement of the NATO alliance or NATO actions in Kosovo does not need to be overdramatized or accompanied by alarmist statements about increased threats to national security. NATO enlargement is part of the transformation of the alliance since the end of the cold war. Just as Belarus and Russia vehemently opposed NATO's intervention in Kosovo, so now do both countries need to play a role in defining the post-intervention settlement.

Belarus needs to assess its chances of establishing a special relationship with NATO more realistically. Codification of the relationship can only come at the end of long and thorough efforts to expand the range of cooperation with NATO and a visible demonstration of Belarus's political will for genuine interaction. At the current stage it appears that the only option for Belarus is to become more actively involved in discrete and modest aspects of the PFP and in the work of the EAPC.

In view of the reluctance of Western nations to discuss seriously a nuclear-free zone in the center of Europe, Belarus should stop lobbying for it. The Soviet-style tradition of presenting unrealistic initiatives that are unacceptable to partners and then trying to sell them aggressively does not reflect well on Belarusian diplomacy.

As to the policy of integration with Russia, Belarus should end its superfluous declarations and instead outline the shape and reasonable limits of integration. The controversial dynamics of the integration process and its questionable efficiency, as well as neighbors' reaction to Belarus-Russia integration, all call for a comprehensive reassessment of the problems that are arising.

Belarus cannot accomplish any of these steps without greater openness within its foreign and security policy establishment. Its foreign policy strategy should be subject to top-level analysis, including by independent experts, instead of being the exclusive playground of government officials. The country's strategy must be open to various scenarios and provide for flexibility in reacting to changes in the international arena. Otherwise, Belarus will continue to languish in isolation, creating problems for itself, its neighbors and Europe as a whole.

NOTES

[1] A. M. Zaccor, "Belarus," in *Instabilities in Post-Communist Europe* (Camberley, U.K.: RMA Sandhurst, 1994).
[2] *National Security Concept of the Republic of Belarus*, Security Council of Belarus, Minsk, March 27, 1995, p. 11.
[3] *Sovetskaya Belorussia*, October 11, 1997.
[4] See remarks by Aleksandr Lukashenko, president of the Republic of Belarus, at a meeting of the heads of state and government of the OSCE member states on December 2, 1996, reprinted in *Bulletin of the Ministry of Foreign Affairs* (1997), pp. 60–61.
[5] "Principled Approaches of Belarus to the Security Model for Europe in the Twenty-first Century," *Current Archives of the Ministry of Foreign Affairs of the Republic of Belarus* (November 1996).
[6] Sherman W. Garnett, *Keystone in the Arch: Ukraine in the Emerging Security Environment of Central and Eastern Europe* (Washington, D.C.: Carnegie Endowment for International Peace, 1997), p. 106.
[7] Michael Dobbs, "Political Shift in Belarus Poses U.S. Policy Dilemma," *Washington Post*, April 4, 1997, p. A18.
[8] *Sovetskaya Belorussia*, October 11, 1997.
[9] *Sovetskaya Belorussia*, July 4, 1996.
[10] *NG-Stsenarii* (Monthly supplement to *Nezavisimaya gazeta*), April 29, 1997.
[11] Garnett, *Keystone in the Arch*, p. 106.
[12] *Sovetskaya Belorussia*, June 17, 1997.

3

Belarus as an Object of Polish Security Concerns

Antoni Kaminski

A nation's direct and indirect security concerns usually fall into one of three categories: (1) threats to its sovereign existence, (2) threats to the functioning of its political and economic institutions, and (3) the inability to achieve political and economic development. Given these categories, does Belarus pose a threat either to Poland's ability to survive as an independent state or to the functioning of its political and economic institutions? And how does Belarus matter to the security of Poland, the region, and Europe?

To answer these questions two factors must be taken into account. First, both Belarus and Poland belong to an important geopolitical area between the Baltic, the Adriatic, and the Black Sea, and between Germany and Russia. This area has long been crucial to the stability of Europe as a whole, and developments there have been a good yardstick of the ebb and flow of German and Russian power. It has also been a route for invasion, used by both Russian troops on their way to Europe, and by European armies on their way to Russia. What happens in this area and to the states that it encompasses, including Belarus, is important not only for Poland, but also for the whole of Europe.

Second, Belarus is part of the post-communist world that is often struggling with instability. The transition to democracy and a market economy has been most successful in the western part of Central Europe—Hungary, the Czech Republic, and Poland. It has also passed the point of no return in Estonia, Lithuania, and Latvia. Even Ukraine has undertaken some efforts toward reform despite its enormous economic and political problems. But Belarus has drifted in another direction, reverting to the authoritarian practices of the past. An economic and political catastrophe in Belarus would have ominous consequences for Russia and Ukraine and could affect Hungary, Poland, Romania, and Slovakia.

These basic arguments suggest why Poland has to be concerned with Belarus—with both its internal developments and its relations with its great eastern neighbor, Russia. To understand Polish interests in and concerns about Belarus fully, this chapter first places the Belarusian challenge within a broad historical context, as well as within the context of the liberal-democratic transition of the post-communist world. The analysis then looks at Poland's political and economic reorientation in the 1990s as a crucial factor in defining Polish national interests and Polish policy toward Belarus and the rest of the former Soviet Union. The final two sections address Russian-Belarusian relations, beginning with Russia as a factor in Belarusian internal developments and then turning to the prospects for Russian-Belarusian integration. These two modes for Russian-Belarusian relations have a significant impact on Poland.

THE ROLE OF HISTORY

Polish reactions to Belarus are largely shaped by the past. History also looms large in the public statements of some leading Russian and Belarusian politicians.[1] A brief historical overview shows how fluid and volatile geopolitical conditions in the region have been, how strongly these conditions have influenced each other, and how they in turn have affected global political developments. The historical review also highlights the common historical and cultural heritage that binds the people of this region together.

Two events in the thirteenth century significantly influenced the region's future for centuries: the settlement of Teutonic Knights in eastern Pomerania as vassals of the Dukes of Mazovia, and the invasion of Kievan Rus by the Mongols. Duke Konrad of Mazovia invited the Order of Teutonic Knights to protect his province against the raids of tribes that lived in the inaccessible woods of the present northeastern Poland, Kaliningrad *oblast*, Lithuania, and Latvia. The knights were also expected to "Christianize and civilize" the "pagans," while loyally serving their hosts, the Dukes of Mazovia.

As they gained power, however, the knights rejected the bonds of vassalage and became a major independent force in European politics of that period.

Meanwhile, the Mongols invaded Kievan Rus and temporarily conquered the open, unprotected land of Ukraine and Belarus. The change in the power status quo of the region provided an opportunity for Lithuania, the last non-Christian nation in Europe, to come forward as a major regional power and reconquer parts of Belarus and Ukraine. The Lithuanian warlords quickly commingled with the Ruthenian aristocracy, adopting many of its cultural patterns.

Even the Lithuanian warlords were not safe for long in this volatile region. The crusade of the Pomeranian Teutonic Knights against barbarians, that is, their eastward expansion, soon posed a deadly threat to Lithuania as well as to Poland. As war became inevitable, the strategic interests of Poland and Lithuania produced an alliance. Aided also by a personal union of the Grand Duke of Lithuania and the Queen of Poland, the Commonwealth of Poland and Lithuania emerged to survive for four hundred years despite frequent battles with the aggressive Teutonic Knights.

In the sixteenth century, as the Grand Duchy of Moscow liberated Russia, a new political center emerged in the territories of the former Kievan Rus, still under Mongol control. Following its success, Moscow looked with increasing interest to the south and the west. Russia rationalized its territorial expansion in three ways: to reunify "Old Rus" by recovering Constantinople, to reunify Orthodox Christianity, and, finally, to reunify the Slavs. This again led to a series of wars.

In this way the decline of the strategically located Polish-Lithuanian Commonwealth was accompanied by the rise of its Russian neighbor to international prominence. The partitions of the Polish-Lithuanian state in the eighteenth century served Russia well. Territory of present-day Belarus and most of Ukraine came under Moscow's rule. The remainder was divided between Prussia and the Hapsburg Empire. Although the end of World War I brought the demise of the Hapsburg Empire and provided independence for many of the states and regions discussed above, Stalin's and Hitler's expansionism in the 1930s and 1940s resulted in the region being carved up once again. The end of World War II did not fully liberate the region: the territories that were not already part of the USSR were gripped firmly in the Soviet sphere of influence until the collapse of the USSR in 1989–1991.

This brief historical review captures the crux of developments in this region: the constant challenge from the West and the East. Whether the Eastern challenge meant the Mongols, the Russians, or the Soviet Union, and the Western challenge the Teutonic Knights, the Hapsburgs, the Prussians, or Hitler, these two forces determined the destiny of the region where they clashed, that is, of Central and Eastern Europe.

This geographical space has often been called the area "between Germany and Russia." This expression connotes the region's significance and derives from its history, as well as from the fact that whoever controlled it militarily could control the continent. European integration has changed the geopolitical position of Germany to the extent that this expression has lost its past meaning. Poland and Belarus are now in an area "between a united Europe and Russia." However, with Poland becoming a member of NATO in 1999, and intending to join the EU, the area "between" will narrow to Belarus. The discussed union of Russia and Belarus would extend Russia westward, the space "between" would disappear, and the Polish-Belarusian border would become the border between the CIS (or at least the Russian-Belarusian union) and that of a united Europe. Especially with the CIS, as it is conceived now, representing Russia's "sphere of influence," this border could become tense and unstable.

What kind of international order fills the space "between"? The order created by European integration and the NATO alliance has been built around the idea of international cooperation designed to realize the interests of its participants in a peaceful way and to support political democracy and respect for international law. The economic and political structures and processes of a united Europe are the main reasons Poland sought to join NATO and seeks to join the EU. Poland views NATO as a stabilizing factor in European affairs. NATO enlargement will remove Poland's traditional security concerns, which have been a main factor in its relations with its Eastern European neighbors. Does Russia accept and follow the same strategy and the same philosophy of international cooperation? *Can* Russia follow this strategy? The answer to the first question appears at present to be negative. The second one remains open. There is no doubt, however, that weak or not, Russia is a major factor in the region.

LIBERAL DEMOCRATIC TRANSITIONS IN THE POST-COMMUNIST WORLD

The demise of the communist system was preceded by a long period of decay that involved all aspects of life: demographic, such as the decline in life expectancy since the mid-1960s, economic stagnation, and political disintegration. Efforts to reform the system proved unsuccessful: the cold war was ultimately lost on the internal front.

The liberal-democratic transition in the post-communist world has, however, proven to be difficult because it embodies a social revolution: it is a move from one type of social order to its logical contradiction. The more successful a country had been in building its communist regime, the more difficult it is for it to carry out the liberal-democratic transformation. Obviously other variables intervene: the length of time under the communist system (or number of generations socialized under the system), the status of the country within the "communist family of nations," and a past tradition of an independent statehood. Judging by these criteria, the nations that had experience with independence and that came under communism as late as 1945 were in a better position to adopt liberal-democratic institutions than those with the opposite features were. Such a theoretical framework suggests that Belarus and Ukraine would be among the difficult cases, while Poland would belong to the group of countries in which conditions for a successful transition would be more opportune.

The political decision to move a post-communist country in a liberal-democratic direction involves two important changes: the first is in the composition of the political elite and the second is in the basic geopolitical orientation. As far as the first change is concerned, the party *nomenklatura*—including members of the party apparatus, managers of heavy industry, directors of state farms, and representatives of the army and security services—needs to be replaced with new elements from the liberal intelligentsia and professional milieus.

The second change implies a westward reorientation of foreign policy, trade linkages, and cultural ties. It is natural that reforming countries look to the West for technical know-how, financial assistance, policy directions, and institutional models. For this reason a successful first round of transition is often measured by a country's ability to redirect its trade from the closed economic structures of the socialist community to the outside world. The post-communist states still depend, to varying degrees, on Russian energy, gas, and fuel supplies. Until these states become independent in terms of resources or diversify their suppliers, they will inevitably remain closely tied to Russia.

Countries that for some reason abandoned the path of transition altogether (such as Belarus and Serbia) or that implemented only partial reforms because of political constraints (such as Slovakia) are in such a situation. Their rulers legitimize the authoritarian patterns of government by using nationalist themes accompanied by the myth of an external threat to national survival. In the case of Belarus, the lack of economic reform means not only that the Belarusian economy stands no chance of becoming competitive on world markets, but also that even the Russian market will be closed to its products. The lack of political reforms creates serious problems with respect to human rights and consequent difficulties with European institutions like the OSCE or the Council of Europe. Inside or outside these countries, scapegoats must be found. The search for external enemies turns these countries into regional troublemakers. As such, they cannot count on the goodwill of either their neighbors or the international community. Yet they cannot function in total isolation—they must look for allies, and they find one in the Russian Federation.

The political reorientation that has taken place in most of East-Central and Eastern Europe has ended unilateral dependency on Russia. Russia has become just another state—surely a highly important one in every respect, but not an omnipotent empire. Russia's significance depends on the value of the cooperation it can offer or the amount of disruption it can cause. To the reforming countries Russia offers very little in positive terms—not only because Russian resources are limited, but also because Russia has demonstrated little inclination to engage constructively in regional affairs. Russia's destructive potential is, therefore, of greater concern than is its potential as a partner.

Russia has reacted bitterly to its decline in influence and to the westward orientation of governments in the region. Moreover, nations with underdeveloped national identity often tend to define their national identity in opposition to Russia. Both developments are temporary. To achieve a balanced situation in East-Central and Eastern Europe, an active Russian role is indispensable. Yet Russian politics have been oriented toward the short-term perspective, and politicians in Moscow have shown little patience with nations that they used to treat as inferiors.[']

Until now, the Russian tactic has consisted of welding close ties with states that abandoned the liberal-democratic transition. Fearing international isolation, these states have no alternative ally to Russia. As a member of the UN Security Council and still a major power, Russia can stultify or delay international sanctions against them. These potential troublemakers usually have strained relations with their neighbors, so that there is the potential for military conflict and possibly local war. As far as such matters attract international concern, Russia enjoys an opportunity to present itself as a valuable mediator and thereby gains the trust of the problem country.[2] This cycle adds to East-Central Europe's distrust of Russian intentions.

POLAND'S POLITICAL AND ECONOMIC REORIENTATION IN THE 1990S

Poland is among the most resolute of the post-communist world countries that have embarked on the path of liberal democratic reforms. The return to power of the left-wing coalition, following its 1993 parliamentary and 1995 presidential victories, has not altered these strong trends for reform. Nor has the return of a center-right government in 1997. Shock therapy, unavoidable in the Polish case, was applied to the economy at the beginning of 1990. Foreign trade was quickly and effectively reoriented away from the USSR. Economic growth picked up in 1992 and has continued ever since at a pace of between 5 percent and 7 percent of GNP annually.

Poland has sought increasing cooperation with and membership in Europe's two most important institutions, the EU and NATO. Negotiations for Poland's Association Agreement with the European Community began in 1990, and the agreement came into force on January 1, 1992. In 1998 the EU placed Poland on the list of countries with which it would hold accession talks.

In 1991 the Polish government made public its intention to apply for NATO membership. In July 1997, at the NATO summit in Madrid, Poland was invited, together with the Czech Republic and

Hungary, to start accession talks for NATO membership. Poland formally became a member in April 1999 at NATO's fiftieth anniversary summit in Washington, D.C.

Poland perceives NATO not only as a defensive alliance, but also as a deterrent to the political forces in the region that consider promoting their objectives by force of arms. As mentioned, in Poland's view NATO enlargement will move military security concerns from the realm of bilateral relations to that of multilateral negotiations. Governments will be free in their bilateral dealings to concentrate on economic, political, environmental, and cultural cooperation. From this Polish perspective, a strong NATO is the most effective instrument for improving the chances for peace in Europe.

Moreover, before actually undertaking enlargement, NATO has made a great effort to develop links with countries that will not be eligible for NATO membership in the foreseeable future. First it established the North Atlantic Cooperation Council (NACC), its initial effort at integrating non-NATO states into a forum for dialogue. In 1994, it established the Partnership for Peace (PFP), an outgrowth of the NACC, which promotes closer military collaboration, particularly for peacekeeping purposes, among states in and out of NATO. Finally, in 1997 NATO established the Permanent NATO-Russia Council and signed a treaty of cooperation with Ukraine. These have all been important steps in demonstrating the peaceful intentions of the alliance.

After some initial misunderstandings, Polish-German relations have improved without encountering serious obstacles. The enlargement of the EU and NATO to include Poland is clearly in Germany's national interest, since an unstable Poland could threaten Germany's stability. Through the enlargement of NATO, Germany has become a reliable ally in matters of greatest concern to Warsaw. Poland has also developed close ties with the United States and other Western states as evidenced by numerous treaties and declarations, but above all by close everyday cooperation.

Within Poland itself, progress on both NATO and EU enlargement has tempered the fear that more active regional cooperation would hinder Polish integration with European institutions. All the major parties in Poland agree that the country should be more concerned with regional cooperation, particularly with its eastern neighbors.

Even before the demise of the USSR, Warsaw had initiated—with Moscow's full consent—"double track" relations with the USSR. In

1990, in addition to regular diplomatic contacts with the Soviet Union, Poland established quasi-diplomatic relations with neighboring republics of the USSR: Ukraine, Lithuania, and Belarus. After the demise of the USSR, Poland signed Treaties of Friendship and Cooperation with all its neighbors. These treaties included a definition of existing borders and respect for the rights of ethnic minorities. In September 1992, a Polish-Kaliningrad Roundtable was held to promote closer economic, administrative, and cultural cooperation between the *oblast* and Poland's northern governorships. Nevertheless, Poland's eastern policy has been criticized as excessively passive and not worthy of an important regional power.[3] Polish relations with Russia are stable but still lack both breadth and depth. Poland's chief interest lies in political stability and economic growth in the region, while some aspects of Russia's policies, namely those that aim at reintegration of the former Soviet space, endanger the fulfillment of Poland's objectives.

The primary issue for Polish security policy is Russia, where reformers have experienced both ups and downs. The August 1998 financial crisis brought to power a national consensus government led by Yevgeny Primakov, who seemed bent on finding an illusive third way to reform, with the help of the Russian left. Yet Russia has also acted pragmatically, as in the run-up to NATO enlargement, when it finally, after years of delay, concluded both a Friendship Treaty and an agreement with Ukraine on the division and basing of the Black Sea fleet. Whether Russia follows a path of opposition to or reconciliation with emerging regional trends will be a key determinant of the future of the region, particularly of Belarus.

Poland understands that Russia's opposition to NATO enlargement is serious and deep-seated, but Russia's reasons ring hollow. Russia claims to perceive NATO enlargement as a threat to its security. However, far more than an actual security challenge, it seems that within Russia, NATO enlargement stands as a difficult psychological problem because it confronts Russia with the reality of its diminished position and a striking new pattern of political and economic cooperation in Europe. Russians also sometimes see Poles as potential competitors in the territory "between Russia and Poland." Yet Poland is and will remain too weak politically and economically to dominate the region either now or in the foreseeable future. Nor does Poland have any intention of doing so. Polish strategy after the demise of the communist regime has consisted, and will most likely continue to consist, of promoting constructive cooperation with all its neighbors, with its main strategic interest to gain full membership in the West's core institutions. Poland is on the way to becoming a commercial republic, whose long-term interests are connected with political stability and economic prosperity in the region. These interests have been, by and large, reflected in Poland's foreign policy during the present decade.

For these reasons, the democratic opposition in Belarus has turned to Poland for inspiration and support. They have indeed received support—although it is more moral than material—because Poland perceives that the political regime that has evolved in Belarus is not only unethical, but also one that will lead the country to catastrophe. Polish support for democracy does not directly contradict Russian interests in Belarus. The sorry state of Belarus should be a matter of regional concern and cooperation.

Last but not least, Poland's position on Belarus is not different from that of the OSCE, the EU, and the Council of Europe. Polish policies are based on the European approach to the evolving European order. This order must be based on shared values and assumptions. A new division of Europe will be created not by an enlargement of European institutions, but above all by the rejection by societies and governments of the values and norms upon which the new Europe is developing.

BELARUS'S FAILED TRANSITION AND THE "RUSSIAN FACTOR"

There are several significant features in Belarus's past. First is the long history of coexistence of several ethnic, national, and religious groups on its territory. Belarusians have lived in relative harmony with Poles, Jews, Russians, Tartars, and Lithuanians, and with Orthodox, Catholics, Muslims, Karaims, and Protestants.[4] Second is the lack of a Belarusian national consciousness, cited by many analysts when explaining the current political situation in Belarus. The reason is mainly that speakers of the Belarusian language have mostly been peasants. When they migrated to urban centers or moved up the social ladder, they learned Russian as the idiom of the educated class. The Belarusian language became the mark of the lower class, a fact that has hampered the development of an authentic Belarusian identity.

The third important feature is the Soviet legacy. As a republic of the USSR, Belarus functioned as a military base in case of a war between the Warsaw Pact and NATO. The country was militarized in every respect: it had a huge arms industry, the highest proportion of military men to total population of all the republics of the USSR, and an educational and propaganda system that emphasized the role of the "Great Patriotic War." Considering the privileged position of the military sector under communism, Belarus was also among the wealthiest republics of the USSR. Communism had been imposed on most of the country in 1918 (with the exception of western Belarus, which remained under Polish rule until 1939). Unlike in Ukraine, however, national feelings in Belarus were never strong. Whatever aspirations Belarus might have had to independent statehood, they were buried in the second half of the 1930s and in the 1940s, at the sites of the mass executions, such as the Kuropaty forest and many others.

When the communist regime disintegrated, Belarus found itself burdened with all the characteristics that make a society unfit for easy transformation. The communist elite's grip over society was stronger in Belarus than anywhere else in the former USSR. Furthermore, because of Belarus's relative economic prosperity under communism, the sudden economic crisis and dramatic decline in living standards were blamed not on communism but on weak attempts at post-communist reforms. As with many other post-communist societies, Belarus lacked a pool of strong leaders. President Lukashenko has certainly demonstrated strength, but unfortunately he uses it to lead his country along the wrong path.

Another factor explaining the lack of a decisive attempt to reform the state and the economy of Belarus was Moscow's willingness to give political and financial support to the political circles that opposed reform. Reformers are usually active individuals intent on shaping destiny and improving the lot of their compatriots. As such, they tend to identify with the interests of Belarus rather than with those of imperial reunification. Considering current Russian priorities, Moscow cannot but look at Belarusian reformers with deep suspicion.

Belarus needs significant reform if it is to move forward. Belarus is not endowed with significant natural resources. The famous swamps, rich in fish and crabs, were mostly drained and filled in under the Soviet regime. The Chernobyl disaster afflicted Belarus more than any other country in the region. With its unreformed regime Minsk is on the road to becoming an economic and political disaster. Yet it does have a well-educated and professionally gifted population. Under opportune internal conditions the country could become a success.

The early 1990s saw a wave of reforms in all the former satellite states of East Central Europe. Reforms took place in the three Baltic republics formerly under Soviet rule and were also adopted, albeit at a slower pace, by Russia and Ukraine. Belarus initially took some hesitant steps in this direction. Nevertheless, at the end of 1992 it was already clear that the leadership lacked the political will to carry on. The liberal camp, headed by Stanislau Shushkevich, former president of the Supreme Council, was weak and indecisive. The government was in the hands of Viacheslau Kebich, an ex-chief manager of one of the big companies in the arms industry. His constituency consisted of people connected with heavy industry, the military, the secret police, nationalized agriculture, and the party apparatus.

Faced with a steep economic decline, Kebich's government had to look for solutions. Since the government was made up of the old communist privileged stratum, it had no incentive to initiate reforms. Some liberalization followed the disintegration of the USSR, but the support for it was too weak to elevate liberal intelligentsia and professionals to positions of power. Instead, Kebich found the solution to Belarus's problems in renewed cooperative ties with Russia. Belarus also desperately needed new production orders. Its energy-intensive arms industry was in need of cheap energy and fuel. Under communism it had been part of a complex network of cooperation extending throughout the Soviet Union. After the imperial demise and disintegration of the regime, both the continued supply of fuel and energy at special prices and the acquisition of new production orders depended on Russia's benevolence.

To remain in power and maintain a functioning economy while opposing any serious reforms, the Kebich government decided to trade political independence for Russian subsidies. In 1993, for example, Belarus agreed to join the military alliance established by the 1992 Tashkent Treaty in exchange for material support. Shushkevich, president of the Supreme Soviet, opposed this move on grounds that it violated the principle of strict neutrality adopted in the Constitution of Belarus. As could have been predicted, Shushkevich lost this showdown, despite some support from the democratic milieu in Russia. The conservative orientation prevailed.

On July 10, 1994, Lukashenko was elected president of Belarus. He had previously been a political officer in the army and director of a *kolkhoz*, or collective farm. He had served as a chairman of the anti-corruption committee of the Supreme Soviet. His victory over his competitors was easy—Kebich, although supported by Moscow, was compromised by corruption scandals, and Shushkevich's constituency was restricted chiefly to the urban intelligentsia. Lukashenko's program of political and, above all, economic "sanitation" called for close integration of Belarus with Russia. Thus, at least in appearance, he promised to continue the policies of Kebich.

Russia's initial reaction to Minsk's focus on integration was hesitant. Liberal reformers led by Yegor Gaidar, a former acting prime minister and later deputy prime minister, realized that support for antireformist forces in Belarus and subsidies for its outdated and uncompetitive industry were inconsistent with the task of reforming Russia.[5] From the point of view of the Russian reformers, support for neo-communist forces in the "near abroad" would strengthen similar forces in Moscow. Subsidies for Belarusian industry would also place a further drag on the Russian economy. Thus, Kebich's calls for integration were not welcome. Unfortunately, that was not the only Russian point of view. Russia's number one priority was reintegration under Moscow's control of the states that had emerged after the demise of the USSR.

In December 1994, Gaidar resigned as a deputy prime minister, citing among other reasons the decision to go ahead with Russian-Belarusian integration. During the next two years, former apparatchiks were the dominant force in Russian politics. Although they accepted the inevitability of change, they wanted to minimize it. The coalition, led by Viktor Chernomyrdin, had no doubts about the advantage of regaining Belarus for Russia: to get hold of Belarus implied control over the territories through which the Yamal natural gas pipeline was to pass. For some at least, beginning with Chernomyrdin, the interest of the state energy company Gazprom was equated with that of Russia. Moreover, support for reintegration of the two states boosted their ties with the nationalist and nationalist-communist opposition, with which integration was popular. Once Russian reformers regained influence after the 1996 presidential elections, the problem of the proposed union between Russia and Belarus once again became a subject of controversy. Leaders of the reform camp, especially Anatoly Chubais and Boris Nemtsov, strongly opposed efforts to formalize a union of the two states in early 1997. Their opposition clearly led to major changes in the draft agreement. Although the project of creating a bilateral union received a lift with the appointment of Yevgeny Primakov as prime minister in September 1998, the same financial crisis that brought him in and out of office has robbed the bilateral union of needed resources and momentum.

Parallel to developments within Russia, Lukashenko in 1996 introduced radical changes to the organization of Belarus. He dissolved the local soviets and created the so-called verticals—hierarchies assuring direct subjugation of the local and provincial administrations to the president's chancellery. These steps centralized the system of government and concentrated all power in the president's hands, producing an overgrown and extralegal presidential administration that is the true ruler of the country. The administration immediately began to appropriate for itself whatever wealth was left. Using the right to issue decrees bequested upon him by the parliament, Lukashenko made his chancellery the biggest proprietor in the country, accountable to no one but him.

Moreover, Lukashenko has replaced the chief editors of all major newspapers and put both radio and television under his control. He changes existing laws at will by presidential decree and ignores those adjudications of the Constitutional Court that do not fit his purposes. According to the law, his decrees can be abolished only when the parliament can muster a two-thirds majority against them. Such a majority is virtually impossible because Lukashenko has packed the parliament with his supporters. In 1996, Lukashenko abolished the Supreme Soviet in all but name. He also dissolved the National Election Committee when it questioned his conduct of the November 1996 referendum, and he filled the Constitutional Tribunal with individuals subservient to him. The government of Belarus possesses no real authority; the president's chancellery makes all important decisions. All these developments have estranged Lukashenko from important elements among the urban population and professional intelligentsia, although he continues to have support in the countryside and among the army and security services.

WHITHER THE RUSSIAN-BELARUSIAN UNION?

Although Belarus and Russia alone will decide on their union, their neighbors will feel its side effects. A union that stimulates positive changes in both countries would contribute to regional stability and development, while a union that hinders such trends would be viewed with anxiety. The interest of neighboring countries in developments in Belarus and in the specific relationship that develops between Moscow and Minsk should surprise no one. These countries in particular must question whether the direction of integration will stimulate positive or negative trends. Is it a "virtuous" or a "vicious" union? This question touches directly on the role Russia wishes to play in the region.

The first decisive formal steps toward integration were undertaken at the beginning of 1995. In January of that year, Aleksey Bolshakov, Russia's deputy prime minister, and Mikhail Chigyr, Belarusian prime minister, signed an agreement specifying the conditions under which Russia could use military facilities in Belarus for the next twenty-five years. The two countries also established a customs union. In February 1995, Boris Yeltsin paid a visit to Minsk, signing other documents on military collaboration between Russia and Belarus. From then on, the Russian army took over the task of guarding Belarus's borders with Lithuania, Poland, and Ukraine. The latest steps toward the integration of Belarus and Russia have been the 1997 Union Treaty and the late-1998 bilateral agreement to pursue a currency union in 1999. Although the two states remain separate under these agreements, they are seeking greater interconnectedness in political, military, and economic institutions. On the surface, the Russian attitude toward events in Belarus is simple. As two Polish observers put it, "The commentators (both from Belarus and Russia) emphasize that, for Russia, the identity of the individual who rules Belarus is irrelevant as long as he supports the process of integration between the two states."[6] In this role, Lukashenko has no serious contenders. Nearly all political factions in Belarus favor close cooperation with Russia. Some of them base their stand on emotional ties, others simply see no other way. Thus, it appears, whatever happens in the country will not directly affect Russian interests. And yet, the problem of Belarus is more complex from the Russian perspective than this superficial description suggests.

The essence of the Russian dilemma lies in Russia's economic weakness. Strong and efficient democratic and market reforms, as well as international assistance, are needed to revive the economy. To establish a well-functioning internal regime, firm political will is needed. All these elements are missing or weak in Belarus. The basic historical traditions of Russia are imperial. How can Russia rebuild an empire on the basis of an economy in deep crisis and a society in which male life expectancy is now only fifty-eight years? An autocracy, communist or not, is not a solution; the present sorry state of Russia is a direct outcome of just such a political philosophy. Liberal-democratic reforms are a must. In the grip of a contradiction between the basic traditions rooted in the political culture of the nation and the historically conditioned contingencies, Russia constantly vacillates between policies imposed by one or another constraint.[7] To change these basic instincts, a consistent reform strategy that would help form a strong civil society is needed, but this strategy requires time and favorable conditions.

Nowhere is the dilemma more evident than in the case of Russian policies toward Belarus, which can be characterized by a set of axioms: (1) among Russians, the idea of integration with Belarus is widely popular; (2) the particular type of integration worked out by Presidents Yeltsin and Lukashenko in 1996–1997 is supported by the nationalists and communists in the opposition, by much of the foreign policy elite, and by the opponents of reforms and their mild supporters; and (3) reformers realize that integration may have a negative impact on the fate of reforms in Russia, and they will therefore try to prevent it.[8] The final result of the dilemma is that Russia tries to muddle its way through: it does not want to bear the cost of integrating Belarus, but neither does it want to relinquish its plans for integration. Meanwhile, Belarus has enough autonomy to make problems for Russia, but not enough to solve its own problems.[9]

Hence, it is natural that, from the point of view of Belarus's neighbors, the union itself is less important than the circumstances under which it is being established. The problem, also widely discussed by the Russian liberal press, is whether integration may hamper the consolidation of democracy and the rule of law in Russia, as well as delay or even prevent Russia's economic revival. By adopting a course of reforms at home while supporting anti-reform forces in neighboring states, the argument runs, Russia is playing with fire and risks undermining the party of reform.

The priority given to short-term military interests in the process of integration, which preceded the Western decision to enlarge NATO, as well as provocative moves by Lukashenko both internationally and inside Belarus, suggest that Belarus can eventually become an instrument of regional instability. Moreover, Lukashenko may discover with time that he has a stake in amplifying international tension to justify antidemocratic measures and the brutal repression of the opposition. For the time being, he is trying to convince neighboring countries that he has not yet decided on integration, and that in fact he does not favor it. He makes it seem that he will be compelled to go ahead only if pressed against the wall. Hence, until now Lukashenko has portrayed Belarus as responding to Russian pressures. But it seems that Russia could well become a hostage to Lukashenko's policies and the weaknesses of Belarus.

Thus, while it is possible to assume that Moscow has inspired the threats Lukashenko has made with respect to NATO enlargement, they serve his own purposes as well. Moreover, the continuation of this hard-line approach to security issues will continue to shape the debate in Russia. It is important to remember that Lukashenko's constituency is not in Belarus alone—many Russians see him as a political hero, too.

Until 1996 Poland did not have a well-defined policy toward Belarus. Ukraine played—and continues to play—a more prominent role in Poland's considerations. Moreover, Minsk reciprocated Warsaw's relative lack of interest. In January 1995, when the Belarusian government decided to expand its cooperation with Russian border troops and extend the presence of the Russian army on Belarusian soil for the next twenty-five years,[10] there was no reaction from Warsaw, although the move changed Poland's strategic position in an important way.

It was only during the events in Belarus of late 1996—which amounted to a coup d'état—that the president of Poland, together with the presidents of Lithuania and Ukraine, expressed anxiety over developments in Belarus. From that moment on the Polish government has made clear its disapproval of the human rights violations in Belarus on a number of occasions. Moreover, events in Belarus have become a focus of greater public and media attention in Poland.

Another interesting problem in the relations between Poland, on the one hand, and Russia and Belarus, on the other, has been Russia's desire to establish a corridor between Russia and Kaliningrad through Belarus and Poland. Different spokesmen from Russia and Belarus offer different versions of the idea. According to some extreme proposals the corridor would consist of a highway, a railway, and an oil pipeline. It would also be extraterritorial. There is no chance that Poland will accept such a proposal. Poland has never posed any obstacles to the right of normal, international transit between Belarus and Kaliningrad. Thus the talk of an extraterritorial corridor has all the appearances of a pipe dream or a provocation.

LOOKING AHEAD

Geography, history, and mainly current political trends make Belarus a preoccupation of Polish foreign policy. The future of Polish-Belarusian relations is likely to turn on three key issues:

- The first is a set of difficult ethnic and border issues. There is still a half-million strong Polish minority in Belarus that could become the scapegoat of impoverished Belarusians who redirect their frustrations against "foreign agents." To date Poland has no serious complaints against Belarus, but should such problems occur, they would raise a domestic storm within Poland that would deeply affect Polish foreign policy. The deteriorating economic situation in Belarus and continued economic improvement in Poland could lead to large-scale Belarusian migration to Poland. To make Polish borders with Belarus less permeable would require considerable investment, and even if the investment were made, serious population pressures on such installations would make them inoperable.

  Poland's goal of joining the EU has led Brussels to pressure Poland to introduce stricter border controls. Poland's adherence to the EU border regime is inevitable and will likely bring considerable disruption to the movement of people and goods between Poland and its eastern neighbors. It will take considerable efforts to balance the desire for continued trade and cultural interchange with its eastern neighbors, on the one hand, and Poland's obligation to its European partners to regulate the EU's external boundary, on the other.

- The second issue relates to Belarus's political evolution. Poles are concerned that, under an autocratic government, Belarus would become an instrument in the hands of die-hard communists and nationalists at home and abroad, exacerbating political tensions in Central Europe. A stable, democratic, and prospering Belarus would be an important contributor to regional stability and a guarantor of good Polish-Russian relations. Belarus's failure to fit into the broader European pattern of economic and political freedom will become a continuous source of problems and potential conflict. It has been argued that NATO enlargement has created a military divide at the Polish-Belarusian border. From Poland's perspective, a much more important factor in producing the new division is the emergence of an autocracy in Belarus. However, if Minsk can be persuaded to do so, liberal-democratic reforms in Belarus might foster cooperation in Central and Eastern Europe and function as a buckle that ties the continent together.

- The third and final issue is the shape of Russian-Belarusian relations. Poland has no quarrel with close relations between Minsk and Moscow. The historic ties between the Russian and Belarusian peoples quite easily lead to strong ties between the two states. Poland cannot, however, remain aloof from a Moscow-Minsk relationship that is based on opposition to the trends in Europe. Poland would rather be a bridge than a bulwark, but it has made a historic choice to be part of broader European developments. Should Minsk and Moscow choose otherwise, the results will be felt along the Polish-Belarusian border first of all. This fact explains the interest Poland and its Western partners and allies have in encouraging Russian-Belarusian ties that are in harmony with Europe as a whole.

The Belarusian quagmire holds no easy solution. The answer to the problem lies partly in Belarus and partly in Moscow, since the latter can be very instrumental in securing the continuation of the present situation or in blocking all efforts to change it. Moscow's willingness to support Lukashenko's regime politically and to underwrite it financially has given Lukashenko's style of government a serious boost. Without this support the political edifice would have crumbled a long time ago. This policy is quite likely to continue. Integration of the former Soviet space continues to appeal to the

Russian political class, and a change of policy toward Belarus would be perceived as a threat to this political priority.

Hence, Belarus has become part of the broader problem of the Russian transition and must be considered in this context. Perhaps a good starting point for European institutions is to take a tough stand on the issue of human rights violations by the Lukashenko government and its complete disregard for European political and ethical standards. Severe sanctions should be considered to force Lukashenko and his supporters to return to democracy and the rule of law. In taking this course, Russia's cooperation should be sought— without it, no measures will be effective. Russia should be made aware that its refusal to cooperate would be treated as a breach of the principles underlying European cooperation. These steps may not help the Belarusian people immediately, but at least they may help preclude a new division of Europe. Belarus is a continental problem—not just a regional one.

NOTES

[1] On the occasion of the 850th anniversary of Moscow in 1997, for instance, Mayor Yuri Luzhkov assured his listeners that all territories conquered by Peter I and Catherine II would be returned to Russia. This ambition may be unrealistic, blown-up rhetoric, but it does reflect the frame of mind of an important part of the Russian ruling class. See the report on Luzhkov's remarks in *Rzeczpospolita*, September 6–7, 1997. While some analysts argue that Luzhkov's statements are not important for Russian foreign policy, the twentieth century offers too many examples of political statements of grave consequences that were judged as irrelevant at first. Moreover, the mere fact that one of the most powerful and popular Russian politicians chooses to express such views is significant.

[2] This pattern is exemplified in F. Stephen Larrabee's analysis of Russian policy toward Serbia, "Russia and the Balkans: Old Themes and New Challenges," in Vladimir Baranovsky, ed., *Russia and Europe: The Emerging Security Agenda* (Oxford: Oxford University Press, 1997), pp. 389–402.

[3] See, for instance, Sherman W. Garnett, "Poland: Bulwark or Bridge?" *Foreign Policy*, no. 102 (Spring 1996), pp. 66–82. For a different view, see Stephen R. Burant, "Poland's Eastern Policy,

1990–95: The Limits of the Possible," *Problems of Post-Communism* (March/April 1996), pp. 48–55.

4   One perceptive analyst remarked that Belarus is multi-denominational not only because many religions coexist on its territory, but also because the main feature of the cultural substratum of the nation is its spiritual diversity. Fr. Wolynczak, "Polityka Wewnetrzna. Metryka dyktatury," *Biuletyn Bialoruski*, no. 8 (January 1997) p. 4.

5   It was Yegor Gaidar, though, together with Viacheslau Kebich, who signed the twenty-one agreements on economic, political, military, and cultural cooperation on July 20, 1992. They involved, among others, the proposal for a common currency and the coordination of budget, tax, credit, and price policies. Kebich stated on the occasion that the agreements were a small step toward confederation between the two countries, noting that, "Belarus will follow its own way avoiding the tragic experience of Poland resulting from the shock therapy." *Bialorus w przededniu wyborów prezydenckich* (Warsaw: Ośrodek Studiów Wschodnich), May 1994, p. 5.

6   Elzbieta Beziuk and Anna Naumczuk, "Bialorus po referendum konstytucyjnym," *Biuletyn Bialoruski*, no. 8 (January 1997), p. 14.

7   Garnett makes a similar point: "The dilemma is whether the current ambitions of Russia's leaders to restore Russian power will stretch existing capabilities still further, perhaps to the breaking point, or whether these ambitions can be moderated to reflect and grow with existing capabilities." See Sherman W. Garnett, "Russian Foreign Policy," paper delivered at the U.S. Relations with Russia, Ukraine, and Eastern Europe Conference, Aspen Institute (Washington, D.C., 1995), and published in *U.S. Relations with Russia, Ukraine, and Eastern Europe*, Congressional Program Series, vol. 10, no. 4 (Washington, D.C.: Aspen Institute, 1995), pp. 25–30. For a similar view, see Antoni Kaminski, "East-Central Europe between the East and the West," *European Security*, vol. 3, no. 2 (Summer 1994), pp. 301–17.

8   The union between Russia and Belarus had been preceded by a lively debate in the Russian press about its advantages and disadvantages. The threats the union poses to Russian reforms have been widely realized by many journalists of the liberal-democratic orientation.

[9] A suitable illustration of the conflict between democratic reform and integration is the 1997 dispute over the arrest of a Russian television crew by Belarus security services. Lukashenko controls all the media with the exception of Russian television, which the majority of Belarusians watch because it gives more objective information about their country. The relative freedom of Russian media undermines the position of Lukashenko, who remains Moscow's closest ally. Can Lukashenko force censorship of news emitted by Russian television stations to Belarus without the imposition of censorship on Russian television in general? His demands threaten the freedom of information in Russia generally. Lukashenko is evidently aware of the dilemma, for he has consistently supported antidemocratic forces in Russia. It is alleged, for instance, that he contributed an important sum of money to the 1996 presidential campaign of Gennady Zyuganov, the Communist Party candidate who ran second to Yeltsin.

[10] The agreement did not lead to Russian troops guarding Belarus's borders; Russia pays for some equipment and maintains a military presence in Minsk.

4

The Belarus Factor: The Impact on Lithuania's Foreign Policy and on Stability in the Baltic Region

Alghirdas Gricius

Although Belarus receives relatively little coverage in the international media, except when its president, Aleksandr Lukashenko, takes the spotlight, Belarus cannot and should not be forgotten, especially by its neighbors. Nuclear weapons left behind on Belarusian territory after the breakup of the USSR attracted international attention for a while, overshadowing national political and economic trends in the country. However, with the removal of the nuclear force from Belarus to Russia in late 1996, many outside observers turned their attention elsewhere.

At about the same time that the nuclear warheads left Belarus, the human rights situation in the country deteriorated sharply. Press freedom was restricted, and in November 1996 Lukashenko engineered the approval of a new and undemocratic constitution that transferred additional powers to the president and rid the parliament of opposition. These steps forced the West to adopt a tougher stand against Minsk. The United States, major European countries, the European Union, and the Council of Europe quickly cut back on political and economic contacts with Belarus.

Belarus is too important to be ignored and left in isolation. Its geopolitical and geostrategic location makes it a considerable factor in the stability of Eastern and Central Europe as well as in the Baltic region. Neighboring countries, including Lithuania, are forced to take Belarus into account when formulating their external policies, especially on issues of security. This chapter looks at the role Belarus has played and will continue to play in Baltic—and especially Lithuanian—calculations.

FROM LITHUANIAN PRINCIPALITY TO INDEPENDENT NATION

Given the complexities of this region of Europe, the brief historical retrospective provided below helps elucidate the analysis of the current situation. From the thirteenth through the fifteenth centuries, the history of Belarus was closely interwoven with the history of the Grand Principality of Lithuania. The vast, albeit scarcely populated, tracts of land east of Vilnius enjoyed broad autonomy within the Grand Principality until the 1569 Lublin Union between Poland and Lithuania. Even so, larger political forces,the Catholic Church, and the nobility retarded the creation of a national identity, especially for Belarusians.

The partitions of Poland in the late eighteenth century once again dramatically altered the situation for both Lithuanians and Belarusians—although not in a way that aided them in developing national identities, as a period of intense Polonization gave way to forced Russification. The nineteenth century saw the emergence of new nation-states in most of Europe, but not in the area of modern Lithuania or Belarus, since both nations remained part of the Russian Empire. Because the Belarusians are Slavs, the task of Russification was easier and faster there than in Lithuania or eastern Poland, despite a fierce crackdown against the latter by the czarist government following the revolts in 1831 and 1863.[1]

The 1905 revolution in Russia brought some relief with the lifting of bans on publications in the Belarusian language. The weekly *Nasha Niva* became the ideological center for the renaissance of the Belarusian people. Against the background of World War I and yet another revolution, the Belarusian Democratic Republic was proclaimed in March 1918. The republic was short-lived, ceasing to exist in January 1919. During its brief life it was unable to translate the idea of Belarusian statehood into reality. In fact, the republic's authorities had no control over national territory, which was occupied by German troops. Yet even this brief period of statehood helped mold national identity.

The 1921 Riga Treaty divided the territory populated by Belarusians between Poland and Soviet Russia. When the Soviet Union was formed in December 1922, it incorporated the eastern part of Belarus as the Belarusian Soviet Socialist Republic, or BSSR. During the 1920s, Lenin's policies created an environment in Soviet Belarus favorable to the renaissance of Belarusian nationality, language, and culture. This environment came to an abrupt end in 1929 when Stalin declared war on Belarusian nationalism. Western Belarus was also unlucky, suffering from a policy of Polonization—accelerated after 1926—until the beginning of World War II. Even World War II, however, was no match for Stalin's cruelties.[2]

Hit harder by Nazi aggression than any other Soviet republic, Belarus also received more postwar economic assistance from the federal center of the USSR than any other republic did. This assistance brought economic recovery to the region and spurred migration to the cities. But at least until the death of Stalin, this economic development was implemented while a struggle against nationalism was being carried out that drastically slowed the emergence of national self-awareness. Indeed, the overwhelming majority of Belarusians, with the exception of a small group of intellectuals, took on a Soviet identity in that period. Given this legacy, one author argues that the difficulties with establishing democracy in Belarus are not simply the result of the personality of the current Belarusian president, but also come from the fact that the Belarusians have yet to form a modern society or nation in the full sense of the word.[3]

Belarus took the first step toward modern statehood on May 27, 1990, when the Supreme Soviet of the BSSR followed the example of the parliaments of Russia and Ukraine and declared sovereignty. Very few Belarusians at that time, however, were concerned with real independence. After the coup d'état in Moscow in August 1991 failed, on August 25 Belarus officially declared its independence for the second time in this century. In December 1991, with the Soviet Union finally dissolved, Belarus became a fully sovereign country. With mutual recognition, Minsk and Vilnius set about establishing genuine interstate relations.

THE IMPACT OF THE FAILURE OF REFORM IN BELARUS

As Poland, the Baltic states, and Russia embarked on economic reforms, laid down the foundations of democratic institutions, and encouraged the development of an independent media, Belarus was busy sorting out other complex internal political problems. Even during Mikhail Gorbachev's policy of perestroika, the Communist Party of Belarus (CPB) proved itself a highly conservative force opposed to any changes. The 100,000-strong Belarusian Popular Front (BPF), an opposition party, could not even muster enough influence to arrange conference facilities for its founding assembly in Minsk and had to convene in Vilnius instead. The 1990 elections to the Supreme Soviet of the BSSR showed that, even though many high-ranking party bureaucrats lost their races, the CPB survived as the principal political force in the national legislature. It was, however, a weakened force. The new communist majority in the Supreme Soviet was no longer the rock solid monolith it had once been, as some of the communists campaigned for reform. Nikolai Dementei, first secretary of the CPB, was not elected chairman of the Supreme Soviet until the second round of voting, and the post of his first deputy went to Stanislau Shushkevich, a BPF delegate and the deputy chancellor of the Belarusian State University.[4]

After the August 1991 coup in Moscow failed, the chairman of the Supreme Soviet in Belarus was forced to resign, since the CPB and Dementei had almost openly supported the coup. In September 1991, Shushkevich was elected his successor. During the next eighteen months, Shushkevich and Viacheslau Kebich, chairman of the Council of Ministers, working together, were able to lay down the foundations of new Belarusian statehood and launch moderate economic reforms. By late 1993 it was clear that even these modest reform steps, including liberalization of the market, were unlikely to succeed without economic assistance from Russia.

By then the democratic faction in the Belarusian Supreme Soviet had tried and failed to get the communist majority to agree to early elections. If these elections had been held, they might have broadened the political base of the reform. But such a broadening never occurred. In fact, at the initiative of the conservatives in the parliament and the government, restrictions began to be imposed on the independent media. As early as 1993, after a brief period of operation, independent television stations were shut down. Independent periodicals found themselves in dire financial straits. Finally, in January 1994, the communist majority in the parliament forced Shushkevich to resign. Although Prime Minister Kebich remained in office, Belarus's modest democratic reforms were derailed.

There are many reasons for the failure of the liberal-democratic reforms in Belarus in 1991–1994. A major factor was the strong opposition, mounted by the military-industrial complex and the collective farm managers in the Supreme Soviet of Belarus and the government. The few representatives of the BPF and other democratic forces who held seats on the Supreme Soviet also failed to rise to the occasion. They overlooked the consequences of the economic difficulties resulting from the breakup of the Soviet Union and the implications of the lack of national self-awareness among ordinary citizens. The democrats' emphasis on national values and on the historical past failed to win the population over, in striking contrast to what occurred in the Baltics.

The victory in the 1994 presidential elections of Lukashenko, a former collective farm manager and a true populist, brought the command economy back to Belarus. With the presidential elections over, the legislative and executive branches went to war. The president launched an offensive and his powers were enhanced at the expense of the Supreme Soviet. More restrictions were imposed on the independent media, and human rights violations became routine. In 1995 the Belarusian police began to crack down on street rallies and on members of parliament who disagreed with the president's policies. A group of eight members of Lithuania's parliament appealed to Lukashenko, protesting the beatings of Belarusian deputies, but with little results.[5] Unfortunately, the developments in Belarus passed unnoticed by many foreign parliaments. Perhaps this lack of reaction to the violations of human rights and freedoms convinced the Belarusian executive branch that increasingly strong-arm measures could be used to suppress dissent. As many as two hundred street marchers were arrested in March and April 1996. More than thirty concerned Lithuanian parliamentarians sent a statement to Semyon Sharetsky, chairman of the Supreme Soviet of Belarus, to the effect that "political violence points to the absence of a dialogue between the executive branch and society."[6] The statement again appeared to have little impact on the policies of the Belarusian executive.

In August 1996, Lukashenko canceled a round of parliamentary elections scheduled by the Central Election Commission for November 24, 1996. He claimed that his country had no need for the 300 deputies specified in the constitution and that the 199 active deputies were sufficient.[7] As of September 1, 1996, the Ministry of Communications shut down one of the country's few remaining independent radio stations, Radio 101.2, under the pretext that the station's transmitter interfered with two government wireless communications stations.[8]

Tension between the Supreme Soviet and the president grew daily in the fall of 1996. Sharetsky strongly criticized the draft of a new constitution that President Lukashenko submitted for a nationwide referendum. The speaker's address to the nation (distributed by nongovernment media) commented, "such a document could only be submitted to a nation for approval by a man who is driven by a maniacal lust for unlimited power."[9] The address also claimed that houses were being searched in Belarus without warrants, that people were being detained without any grounds, and that acts of provocation, threats, and blackmail were being used against the disobedient. Further attempts were made to convince Lukashenko that adoption of a constitution lacking a balance of power among the branches of government would harm the republic and damage its international reputation. The Constitutional Court, for example, proclaimed that the effective constitution "create[d] all opportunities for all branches of power to function properly," and that the national crisis had been caused not by constitutional imperfections but by "ignoring its key provisions and by direct violations of provisions of the constitution and laws."[10] In early September 1996 the Supreme Soviet suggested that the two competing constitutional drafts, that of the president and that of the parliament, be withdrawn, but the president disregarded any such suggestions.

Finally, on the eve of the referendum, the international community took an interest in the issue. In mid-October the ambassadors of Great Britain, Germany, Italy, and France conveyed to the Belarusian foreign ministry a statement on behalf of the European Union. The EU expressed deep concern over the aggravation of the political situation in the country and stated that "any constitution should conform to international standards (a principle of separation of powers and a system of checks and balances), maintain the prerogatives of the Constitutional Court and parliament, and guarantee the freedoms of speech and the press."[11] The Political Committee of the Council of Europe also discussed the situation in Belarus with representatives of both Lukashenko's administration and the Supreme

Soviet. The Political Committee to a plenary session of the Parliamentary Assembly of the Council of Europe suggested a roundtable discussion among the parties to the conflict to solve the constitutional crisis in the country.[12] The European Commission for Democracy through Law at the Council of Europe (Venetian Commission) concluded that neither the president's nor the Supreme Soviet's amendments to the Belarusian Constitution of 1994 were consistent with the minimal democratic standards set by European constitutional law. The commission suggested that the parties honor the decision of the Constitutional Court of Belarus, which was in agreement with European standards, and come up with a compromise that would dramatically differ from the amendments of both the president and the Supreme Soviet.[13]

In late November the European Parliament passed a resolution on the situation in Belarus that underscored the serious nature of the constitutional crisis in Belarus. It blamed the crisis on the actions of President Lukashenko, who had phased in an authoritarian form of government by interfering with elections to the parliament, placing restrictions on the freedom of the press, banning trade unions, and undertaking other undemocratic acts.

Neither these appeals nor statements by the U.S. State Department affected Lukashenko's decision to hold the referendum on his own terms.[14] Ten days before the referendum, he fired Viktor Gonchar, chairman of the Central Commission for Elections and Referendums, a decision that was supposed to be the prerogative of the Supreme Soviet.[15] The referendum took place, and, as expected, the overwhelming majority of the citizens (70.5 percent of those who cast their votes) supported the president's draft of a new constitution.[16] The president's political opponents contested the results of the referendum. Chairman of the Supreme Soviet Sharetsky, for example, referred to the referendum as a farce, noting that the ballots were printed by the president's administration.[17] Sergei Kalyakin, leader of the CPB, claimed that the results were rigged in different parts of the republic on a scale of 20 percent to 50 percent. He suggested that a mere 40 percent of the voters had supported the president's draft of the constitution, a figure that was consistent with earlier opinion polls.[18] Lukashenko was not deterred. Next on his agenda was the elimination of the Constitutional Court, which had long opposed him on constitutional issues. Not surprisingly, the Constitutional Court was disbanded in December 1996.

The Council of Europe reacted to the referendum and the new constitution by temporarily suspending Belarus's special invitation to participate in its work.[19] The presidents of Lithuania, Poland, and Ukraine issued a joint statement on November 20, 1996, expressing deep concern over developments in Belarus. The three leaders called on Belarusian leaders to solve the conflict using constitutional procedures in compliance with universally recognized standards, democratic principles, human rights, and civil liberties.[20]

In the first six months of 1997, the executive branch in Belarus, relying on the new constitution, imposed even more restrictions on the civil rights of the republic's citizens. These steps triggered a series of harsh statements by Western European nations and the United States, as well as decisions to limit political contacts and economic ties with Belarus. Belarus's relationship with the OSCE also deteriorated significantly.

In short, since 1995 Lukashenko's administration has dramatically narrowed democratic freedoms, terminated economic reform, and isolated the country internationally. Lukashenko, elected by democratic procedures in 1994, has been able to establish close to a one-man rule in his country. With a new constitution in effect, he has become essentially the sole decision maker on both domestic and foreign issues.

The most stunning development, however, is that in spite of Belarus's serious economic difficulties and suppressed democratic freedoms, Lukashenko remains popular domestically.[21] His popularity can be attributed to two factors. The first has been the ability of Belarusian authorities, through administrative action and assistance from Russia, to stop the economic decline and maintain a low, yet tolerable standard of living. The limited popularity of the opposition, that is the former deputies of the Supreme Soviet, is the other factor. According to Professor Manayev, director of the Independent Institute for Socioeconomic and Political Research, the Belarusian public has split into two antagonistic social segments. People belonging to the first group have a highly conservative, anti-democratic, anti-market, and anti-reform mentality. The group relies completely on the government and lacks initiative. People in the other group, in contrast, value democratic and market principles, seek reform, and are typically active in the nongovernment economic sector and in nongovernmental organizations. The first group consists primarily of older, uneducated, poor people in rural communities; the second group contains younger people in higher income brackets, residing in the capital and other large cities.[22] Whatever the balance between the two groups, the popularity of opposition leaders Shushkevich, Zenon Poznyak, Sharetsky, and others lags far behind that of President Lukashenko.[23]

In November 1996, the opposition made yet another attempt to resist the president's methods of governing. It began to collect signatures nationwide in support of the formation of a broad public movement, Charter-97.[24] The charter was signed by 100 prominent Belarusians, including three former speakers of the Supreme Soviet (Stanislau Shushkevich, Yelena Grib, and Semyon Sharetsky), former prime minister Mikhail Chigyr, and popular author Vasil Bykov. The charter asserted that the Belarusian Constitution had been trampled underfoot and that the Belarusian people had been denied the right to elect representatives to bodies of government, the right to freedom of speech, and the right to be informed about the actual situation in the country. In addition, national culture and the educational system had been destroyed, and the Belarusian language had been discriminated against. Despite Charter-97's hopeful beginning, little has happened since to suggest that it has succeeded in mobilizing the public to restore democracy in the republic or to change Lukashenko's mind.

THE EASTERN BIAS OF BELARUS'S "MULTI-DIRECTIONAL" FOREIGN POLICY

Over the past few years, Belarusian authorities have often referred to their multidirectional and balanced foreign policy. Actually, Minsk's relationship with Western European nations and institutions such as the EU, the Council of Europe, and the IMF has deteriorated noticeably since the emergence of one-man rule in Belarus in late 1996. Recent domestic political developments in Belarus and the negative response of the outside world make it hard to agree with the assertion of the Belarusian government that Belarus is pursuing a balanced, multidirectional foreign policy.

In its early years of independence, Belarus did indeed conduct a balanced, even if not very active, foreign policy. It agreed to the withdrawal of Soviet nuclear weapons, acceded to the NPT, and became actively involved in conventional arms reduction in Europe. Belarusian leaders repeatedly mentioned the possibility of Belarus becoming a nuclear-free state and proposed a nuclear-free zone in Central Europe. Belarus participated in a number of international institutions and was granted the status of "specially invited nation" at the Council of Europe in 1992. It seemed that Belarus's economic relations with neighboring nations, other parts of Europe, and the rest of the world got off to a good start.

Although Russia played a key role in Belarusian foreign policy from the very beginning, 1994 was a major turning point when Russian influence on Belarus's foreign policy increased. To some extent this shift can be attributed to Belarus's difficult economic situation and heavy dependence on Russian energy, as well as on the nostalgic feelings of ordinary Belarusians about the recent past and their desire for closer ties with Russia. In May 1995, the customs barriers between Belarus and Russia gave way to representative offices of the Russian Customs Service in Belarus on the Lithuanian, Latvian, Polish, and Ukrainian borders.[25] President Lukashenko began frequently to remind Russian leaders of the opportunities for closer cooperation in defense and for strengthening mutual defense capabilities. Many Russian politicians and international affairs analysts encouraged this turn in Belarus's foreign policy.[26] Hard evidence of the eastward shift in Belarus's foreign policy was provided by the Agreement on Creation of a Commonwealth of the Sovereign States of Belarus and Russia, signed in Moscow by the two presidents on April 2, 1996. Most of the recent official trips made by Belarusian dignitaries overseas, including by the president, have been to Asian, rather than Western European, countries—another sign that Minsk places the bulk of its emphasis on relations with the East.

As a part of this Eastern orientation, President Lukashenko has waged the loudest campaign for the integration of Belarus and Russia. His major motivations probably include Belarus's economic dependence on Russia and the ideal of Slavic brotherhood. Nor should the personal ambitions of Lukashenko himself be ignored. The current orientation of the Belarusian economy exclusively to Russia may, however, have grave consequences in the future, by isolating Belarus from the Western European and U.S. economies. Although pro-integration enthusiasm reached fairly high levels in 1996, it started subsiding by the time of the signing of a subsequent

Union Treaty in May 1997. The financial crisis of August 1998 also cooled the exuberance of many pro-integration Russians. As time goes by, integration will inevitably be slowed by the lack of synchronization in the two countries' economic reforms and by their different approaches to democracy and government. A landmark case in point was the 1997 conviction by a Belarusian court of Pavel Sheremet, a reporter for Russia's ORT television channel, for illegally crossing the Belarusian border.[27]

Minsk's emphasis on the East and its planned union with Russia constitute the sovereign right of Belarus. These actions by themselves are not a legitimate cause for objection by other countries, including Belarus's neighbors, as long as Belarus's actions do not threaten their security. Given the developments in Belarus, however, other countries, and especially Belarus's neighbors, cannot rest assured that their security will not be compromised. Such apprehension has understandably grown since the pronouncements by Belarusian officials about the possibility of a return of nuclear weapons to Belarus[28] and the strengthening of Belarus's military alliance with Russia.[29] Nor are all Russian analysts happy about the prospect of the Russian-Belarusian union. Some have pointed out the negative implications of unification with Belarus, such as the recent intensified rapprochement between Poland and Ukraine and between Poland and Lithuania, as well as further consolidation of the Baltic states and their pro-Western orientation.[30]

The current regime in Belarus has reduced the country's relations with European democracies and international financial institutions such as the IMF and the World Bank to a minimum. To improve relations with these groups Minsk needs to be willing to reach compromise solutions on key questions of internal and foreign policy and to undertake democratic and market reforms. Lukashenko's personality renders these steps unlikely. If anyone were able to persuade Lukashenko to soften his regime, it would be someone from the East, not the West. Even the economically powerful EU is unlikely to make an impact on Belarus other than through Moscow.

FUNDAMENTALS OF LITHUANIAN FOREIGN POLICY

In contrast to the foreign policy of Belarus, the key elements of Lithuania's foreign policy strategy include its complete integration into European and North Atlantic political, economic, and security structures; maintenance of good constructive relationships with its neighbors; positive and mutually beneficial cooperation with all democratic and friendly nations; and the encouragement of multifaceted regional cooperation. Lithuania sees good relations with its neighbors as key to enhancing security both within the immediate region and in all of Europe. Because Lithuania is interested in having positive neighborly relations with Belarus, it naturally takes an interest in internal developments in that country.

Lithuania is often considered part of several regions at the same time: the Baltic states and the wider Baltic Sea region, as well as Central Europe. In its regional policies Lithuania gives priority to security and economic relations and to cooperation with the nations of the north and west, especially Poland. Current Lithuanian-Polish relations have reached an unprecedented level of cooperation.

Lithuania also wants to structure its relations with Russia on the principles mentioned above, that is on the principles of good neighborliness, mutual understanding, equality, and mutual benefit. The Kaliningrad region occupies a special place in Lithuania's foreign policy. Lithuania would like to see this region become a priority zone of economic cooperation and intends to encourage in every way possible its political, economic, and cultural integration into the community of the Baltic Sea nations.

Analysis of the top priorities in Lithuanian foreign policy indicate that Vilnius has achieved very good results in several areas, especially in its relations with both Warsaw and Moscow. Since the April 1994 Lithuania-Poland agreement on friendship and cooperation, the bilateral ties between the two countries have gained considerable momentum. The two countries have seen a growth in bilateral trade, an increase in the number of joint ventures, and a reduced waiting time for freight transport at border checkpoints. They have strengthened cooperation on defense, forming a joint Polish-Lithuanian battalion that participated in international peacekeeping operations and in NATO's PFP program. Other new agencies have included a joint Inter-Parliamentary Assembly, an intergovernment coordinating committee, and a Lithuanian-Polish Presidential Committee. At the initiative of the two countries' presidents, on September 5–6, 1997, Vilnius hosted a conference dedicated to "Coexistence between Peoples and Good-Neighborly Relations as Guarantor of Security and

Stability in Europe." Eleven heads of state (from Lithuania, Poland, Belarus, Bulgaria, Hungary, Latvia, Moldova, Romania, Finland, Ukraine, and Estonia), as well as the Russian prime minister, attended the conference.

The decision by the presidents of Lithuania and Poland to invite President Lukashenko to the conference gave rise to controversy. Sentiment shifted from rejection to support as a result of the accomplishments of the conference, statements by its participants, and the numerous bilateral meetings that occurred between heads of state. Algirdas Brazauskas, president of Lithuania, summed up the basic sentiments of the participants regarding Belarus:

> Belarus is still going through what is not an easy time of establishing and affirming its statehood. It is very important that such processes take place in a democratic manner, with due respect for the universally recognized standards of the freedom of the individual, assembly, and the press. We, being its closest neighbors, are highly interested in it and we discuss it candidly and in a well-wishing way. Ignoring universally recognized principles always strikes back at the state and its citizens. I am also convinced that isolation of any country does not promote the emergence of democratic standards in it.[31]

As for Lithuania's relations with Russia, few issues remain unsolved. The Russian-speaking population of Lithuania enjoys the full gamut of civil rights. In October 1997, top officials from the two countries signed a border agreement in Moscow. Even statements by certain Russian politicians and their recommendations to refrain from ratifying the border agreement with Lithuania because of Russia's claims to the Klaipeda seaport seemed to target primarily an internal audience and are unlikely to cause real problems. Lithuania has legally formalized its borders with all its neighbors. This achievement should have a positive impact on future negotiations about its membership in the EU.

Sufficient progress in Lithuanian integration with major Western institutions is, however, still lacking. Lithuania failed to make the list of countries invited to negotiations on membership in NATO at a July 1997 meeting of the leaders of NATO countries in Madrid.

Also in July 1997, Lithuania failed to get recommended for EU membership by the Commission of the European Union after an intergovernment conference in Amsterdam. Lithuania's integration into the EU appears to depend above all on economic factors and on the harmonization of its laws with EU norms, as well as on the willingness of the EU to expand. Lithuania's membership in NATO depends primarily on the political will of the alliance and its willingness to overcome Russia's resistance to expanding NATO.

LITHUANIAN-BELARUSIAN RELATIONS

Lithuania and Belarus recognized each other's independence in December 1991, although the formal agreement to establish diplomatic relations took another year. In 1992–1993 they maintained a low profile in bilateral relations and failed to achieve any major breakthroughs. During those two years both countries concentrated more on their own pressing problems, such as the withdrawal of Russian troops from Lithuania and the removal of nuclear missiles from Belarus, applications for membership in various international institutions, and the establishment of diplomatic relations with dozens of countries.

Even though the Belarusian leadership at that time included representatives of progressive political forces such as the BPF, it maintained a rather unenthusiastic relationship with the leaders and politicians of Lithuania. The reason in part was that some members of the BPF began speaking about historical Belarus as being the Grand Principality of Lithuania and hinting at Belarus's historical right to annex the Vilnius area, including the capital city of Lithuania.[32]

Bilateral contacts did pick up speed in 1994. In July of that year, President Brazauskas attended the celebration of the fiftieth anniversary of liberation of Belarus from Nazi occupation, and the chairman of the Lithuanian Seimas attended the inauguration of President Lukashenko. In February 1995, Lukashenko paid an official visit to Lithuania and signed two important treaties: "Cooperation and Good-Neighborly Relations" and "The State Border between the Lithuanian Republic and the Republic of Belarus." For the first time in history, the two countries had a border that they both recognized in a legal document. The border demarcation commenced in 1996 after the parties exchanged ratification papers. Demarcation work slowed in 1997, however, because of a lack of financing, especially in the area allocated to Belarus.

Between 1994 and 1996, Lithuania and Belarus consolidated their trade relations by signing agreements on international trucking, guaranteed pensions, simplified border-crossing procedures for residents of border areas, and economic and trade cooperation. As a result bilateral trade more than doubled during those two years to $450 million. Lithuania's exports grew particularly rapidly, hitting the $342 million mark in 1996, but declined slightly in the first six months of 1997.[33] The traffic of Belarusian goods through the Klaipeda seaport grew even faster, registering a staggering tenfold increase over the same two-year period.[34] These positive trends do not guarantee that economic relations will not be suspended in the future. The first signs of a reversal in these trends came in the second half of 1997, and the internal Belarusian political scene and the Russian financial crisis continue to hamper positive economic developments.

The presidents of Lithuania and Belarus discussed the status of their bilateral relations at the September 1997 Vilnius conference. Issues of vital interest to both sides included an agreement on the readmission of refugees, Belarus's transfer of exports through the Klaipeda seaport, sales to Belarus of surplus power from Lithuania's Ignalina nuclear power plant, and terms of transit through Lithuanian territory from Belarus to the Kaliningrad region, as well as through Belarus between Lithuania and Russia. Unfortunately, the two sides have not yet achieved tangible progress on any of these issues.

The top priorities for Lithuania are to strengthen controls at its Belarusian border and to sign an agreement on the readmission of refugees. A vast number of Asian refugees have entered Lithuania from Belarus, using it as a corridor to Western Europe. Another factor prompting Lithuania to press for tougher procedures at the Belarusian border is the EU's requirement that its associate members reliably control their eastern borders. The same requirement applies to Lithuania's intention to obtain non-visa status for admission to the EU countries. President Lukashenko, aware of the problems experienced by Lithuania, has nevertheless stalled a refugee readmission agreement, arguing that it would be better to sign a tripartite agreement between Lithuania, Belarus, and Russia. Apparently the same rationale has slowed demarcation work at the Belarusian segment of the joint border, although official explanations cite a lack of funding as the reason.

Another instrument used by Belarusian authorities to influence Lithuania's foreign policy is the choice of ports on the Baltic Sea for future Belarusian exports and imports. Belarus can choose between Klaipeda (in Lithuania), Ventspiels (in Latvia), and Kaliningrad (in Russia). If Belarus opts for Kaliningrad, it would need to obtain long-term guarantees and secure favorable terms of transit via Lithuania or Poland. In the context of a market economy and democratic institutions, the choice of ports should be driven by economic considerations and not by the current methods of government in Belarus. Nevertheless, Lukashenko currently has the power to route Belarus's exports through the port of his choosing, and his choices are sure to have a significant economic impact on the Baltic ports that are already competing for their economic future.

Belarus may also create a host of problems for Lithuanian trade with Russia. Most of this trade passes through Belarusian territory. Lithuania has the ability to reroute its trade with Russia through Latvia, but this route would raise the costs, even if only marginally. Once again, Moscow's position needs to be taken into account, since it can influence decision making in Minsk. Most of Russia's transit to the West goes through Belarus, a fact that gives Lukashenko leverage over Moscow's policies. Although that leverage is rather limited, given Belarus's economic dependence on Russia, it still is a factor that needs to be considered.[35]

This analysis of Lithuanian-Belarusian relations suggests that they are to a large extent interwoven with the interests of Russia, Poland, and, to a smaller degree, Latvia and Ukraine. Russia's enclave in the Baltic Sea territory, the Kaliningrad region, will play a considerable role in the future of Lithuanian-Belarusian relations. One indication of that role was the adoption by the Russian Federation in September 1997 of a federal program to create a special economic zone in the Kaliningrad region for the period 1998–2005.[36] It is too soon to discuss regional cooperation in a narrow scenario (Lithuania, Poland, Belarus, and Russia) or even in a broader scenario (the entire Baltic region). The Neman regional cooperation project (involving the border areas of Poland, Lithuania, and the Kaliningrad region) is still at an embryonic stage. Broader regional cooperation between Russia, Latvia, Lithuania, Poland, and Belarus will be influenced by the position of the EU, since the two Baltic republics and Poland are seeking membership in the EU and are likely to clear their actions with Brussels. This is not to say that such cooperation has no prospects whatsoever. Rather, the level of Belarus's involvement will largely depend on its foreign and domestic policies. Alternatively, the EU countries, just like Belarus's neighbors, are hardly interested in fully isolating Belarus or in seeing the Belarusian economy take such a deep dive that it might trigger large-scale social upheavals. That scenario would directly affect the security of Belarus's neighbors and the stability of the Baltic and Central European regions, as well as the rest of Europe.

BELARUSIAN POLICY AS A FACTOR IN REGIONAL SECURITY AND STABILITY

An attachment to the January 1997 law on National Security of the Lithuania Republic, entitled "The Fundamentals of National Security of Lithuania," defines the key national security provisions of Lithuania's foreign policy. The attachment cites the following risks to Lithuanian national security: obstruction by other countries of efforts to obtain international security guarantees, the presence of foreign military potential near Lithuanian borders, foreign military transit through Lithuania, illegal immigration, and an influx of refugees. Since most of these risk factors come from neighboring countries, Lithuania is paying priority attention to developments in Russia and Belarus. Surprisingly, the statement fails to include good relations with neighboring countries as a key foreign policy objective.[37] Such an objective was, however, expressed in the annual report of the president of the republic, who, under the Lithuanian Constitution, determines and, together with the government, implements the country's foreign policy.

Political developments in Belarus, as well as foreign policy statements by its president and other officials, are a cause of concern among its neighbors and the rest of Europe. As early as 1995, Lithuania took notice of a Russian Strategic Center report called "Conceptual Provisions of a Strategy for Counteracting the Principal External Threat to the National Security of Russia," which argued that Russia and Belarus had the right to reclaim Klaipeda and the Vilnius area.[38] In 1996, Poland and Lithuania were stunned by an initiative between Yuri Matochkin, governor of the Kaliningrad region, and President Lukashenko for an extraterritorial railway corridor between Belarus and the Kaliningrad region through the territory of Poland and Lithuania.[39] Lukashenko later admitted that such a decision would require consultations with the governments of Poland and Lithuania.[40] However, statements coming from Russia only caused additional worries about the Kaliningrad region in the Baltic capitals and in Warsaw. One statement came from Yegor Stroyev, chairman of the Council of the Federation of Russia, in his address to the Supreme Soviet of Belarus in April 1996. Stroyev insisted that Russia and Belarus had a common interest in strengthening the Kaliningrad region, as Russia might find itself under pressure from external forces such as NATO and the Baltic nations.[41]

Although Belarus did not resort to such measures after Poland joined NATO in March 1999, the possibility of Belarus undertaking such measures exists. Several deputies in the State Duma of the Russian Federation believe that the process of uniting Russia and Belarus into a single state will turn the Baltic states into an enclave bordering the Kaliningrad region to the west and Belarus and Russia to the south and the east. In the view of a number of Russian deputies, such a development would help influence the policies of the Baltic states and bring pressure on them in terms of their transit requirements. Such statements by Belarusian and Russian officials of course do not foster trust between the Baltics and Belarus.

NATO enlargement and Lithuanian aspirations to join NATO further complicate relations with Russia and Belarus. In the spring of 1996, Belarusian defense minister Maltsev stated that if Poland were to join NATO, Belarus might be forced to redeploy troops closer to the Polish border.[42] In support of his colleague, Pavel Grachev, then Russian defense minister, said that Moscow was closely monitoring possible Polish and Lithuanian admission to NATO. If the two countries did join NATO, Russia's response could include the creation of a "powerful Russian-Belarusian military grouping" in Belarusian territory.[43] In May 1997, President Lukashenko again stated that Belarus needed a military alliance with Russia.[44]

It should be also noted that the three Baltic states, whose aggregate population of 8 million is close to that of Belarus (10 million), have only a 15,000-strong armed force at their disposal. The Belarusian armed forces have 113,000 personnel, as well as top-level equipment and materiel.[45] Lithuania has expressed a well-justified concern about the grouping of Russian troops in the Kaliningrad region. Under an agreement with Vilnius, Russia transits civil and military goods and personnel to Kaliningrad through Lithuanian territory. Finally, the Kaliningrad city of Baltiisk is the main base of the Russian Baltic fleet. All these factors increase Vilnius's concerns.

The Russian Federation's February 1997 statement entitled "Long-Term Concept for the Baltics" calls for encouraging regional economic integration and speaks of the indivisibility of security for the nations of the Baltic region.[46] The latter obviously refers to Russia's objection to Lithuania, Latvia, and Estonia joining NATO, although the right to choose allies and means of achieving national security freely is provided for in a 1991 Lithuania-Russia treaty, as well as in similar treaties Russia signed with Latvia and Estonia the same year. The Russian concept with regard to Lithuania and the other Baltic states, in spite of a series of mutually acceptable provisions, does not constitute an effective security instrument for all the parties. An unstable and undemocratic Belarus will pose less of a threat to stability in its home region and all of Europe if several of its neighbors become members of what is essentially a defensive alliance among democratic nations.

FUTURE SCENARIOS

There is no current or near-term future threat to the security and independence of Lithuania and the other Baltic states. But in view of developments in the Balkans and in the Russian north Caucasus, it is too soon to argue that the danger has disappeared for good. Internal political developments in Belarus, the progress of Belarusian-Russian integration, and Minsk's foreign policy all strongly suggest that Belarus is among the few European nations whose future policies are difficult to forecast. A spokesman for the Lithuanian foreign ministry, speaking at an October 1997 conference in Prague on enlarging NATO and the EU, outlined two possible scenarios for Belarus.[47] Under the first scenario, the EU and Belarus maintain their current positions while Belarus's isolation increases, as Lukashenko builds an increasingly rigid authoritarian regime and exacerbates the internal political situation in Belarus. Under the second scenario, the EU adjusts its position after Lukashenko announces an early parliamentary election and amends the constitution. Belarus is then given a chance to participate in European processes and institutions.

The second scenario can only become a reality with the help of the EU and Belarus's neighbors, especially Russia. It is hard to say how far Belarus's neighbors are prepared to go to facilitate such a scenario. It would require coordinated policies and teamwork on their part, for which there is as yet no precedent. From Lithuania's point of view the isolation of Belarus from common European processes does not serve its interests. Despite diametrically opposed foreign policy preferences, Lithuania and Belarus maintain pragmatic relations. Unfortunately, these bilateral relations are being hampered by their different approaches to human rights and freedom of the press and by the lack of agreements on long-term economic cooperation.

The situation in Belarus may not follow either scenario to the letter. Most likely, it will incorporate elements of both. If so, in the short and medium term Belarus will continue to be a source of regional instability and a concern for Lithuania and its other neighbors.

NOTES

[1] Michael Urban and Ján Zaprudnik "Belarus: A Long Road to Nationhood," in Ian Bremmen and Ray Taras, eds., *Nations and Politics in the Soviet Successor States* (New York: Cambridge University Press, 1993).

[2] For a solidly argued and interesting analysis of the emergence of Belarusian national identity and the Belarusian nation, see George Sanford, "Belarus on the Road to Statehood," *Survival*, vol. 38 (Spring 1996), pp. 131–53.

[3] A. Kulakauskas, in *European Dimension: Good Neighborly Relations and Lithuania Society, Proceedings of the Vilnius Conference* (Vilnius: Pradai, 1997).

[4] Michael Urban and Ján Zaprudnik, in *European Dimension: Good Neighborly Relations and Lithuania Society, Proceedings of the Vilnius Conference* (Vilnius: Pradai, 1997), p. 113.

5   *Eta-Elta* (Estonian Information Agency-Lithuania Information Agency), June 1, 1996.

6   Ibid.

7   *Interfax-Zapad*, August 15, 1996.

8   *Baltic News Service*, September 1, 1996.

9   *Interfax-Zapad*, September 11, 1996.

10 *Baltic News Service*, September 25, 1996.

11 *Belapan* (Belarusian News Agency), October 16, 1996.

12 *Documents of Parliamentary Assembly of the Council of Europe*, vol. 3, document N7701 (Strasbourg: Council of Europe, 1997).

13 "Belarus cour constitutionnelle," *Bulletin de jurisprudence constitutionnelle*, vol. 4 (1996), pp. 33–44.

14 *Interfax-Zapad*, October 18, 1996.

15 *Baltic News Service*, November 14, 1996.

16 *Itar-Tass*, November 25, 1996.

17 *Interfax-Zapad*, November 25, 1996.

18 Ibid.

19 *Itar-Tass*, January 13, 1997.

20 *Itar-Tass*, November 20, 1996.

21 *Belorusskaya delovaya gazeta*, October 16, 1997, p. 4.

22 O. Manayev, in *European Dimension: Good Neighborly Relations and Lithuania Society, Proceedings of the Vilnius Conference* (Vilnius: Pradai, 1997).

23 *Belorusskaya delovaya gazeta*, October 16, 1997, p. 4.

24 *Diena*, November 12, 1997.

25 *Interfax-Zapad*, June 29, 1995.

26 Irina Kobrinskaya, *Russia and Central Eastern Europe after the "Cold War"* (Moscow: Carnegie Moscow Center, 1997), p. 102.

27 *Itar-Tass*, July 28, 1997.

28 *Belapan*, August 12, 1997.

29 *Itar-Tass*, May 22, 1997.

30 See Kobrinskaya, *Russia and Central Eastern Europe after the "Cold War."*

31 Remarks by Algirdas Brazauskas, president of Lithuania, at the conference, European Dimension: Good Neighborly Relations and Lithuania Society (Vilnius, September 5, 1997).

32 *Narodnaya gazeta* (Belarusian Popular Front publication), May 27, 1993.

33 Data provided by the Statistics Department of the Lithuanian Republic.

[34] Ibid.

[35] "Lietuva ir jos kaimynai" (Lithuania and its neighbors) in *European Dimension: Good Neighborly Relations and Lithuania Society, Proceedings of the Vilnius Conference* (Vilnius: Pradai, 1997), p. 162.

[36] *Rossiiskaya gazeta*, October 21, 1997.

[37] Parliament of the Republic of Lithuania, (Vilnius: Valsty Bes Zinios), January 8, 1997, p.16.

[38] *Baltic News Service*, October 20, 1995.

[39] *Baltic News Service*, February 28, 1996.

[40] *Baltic News Service*, March 4, 1996.

[41] *Baltic News Service*, March 23, 1996.

[42] *Interfax-Zapad*, April 10, 1996.

[43] *Interfax*, May 14, 1996.

[44] *Itar-Tass*, May 22, 1997.

[45] *Itar-Tass*, February 22, 1997.

[46] *Dipkurier*, no. 3(53) (February 1997), p. 12.

[47] D. Trinkunas, "Belarus, Russia and Europe. An Immediate Neighbor's View," paper presented at the conference, Expansion of NATO and the European Union: Challenge to Confidence-Building, East-West Institute (Prague, October 10–11, 1997).

5
Belarusian-Russian Integration and Its Impact on the Security of Ukraine

Hrihoriy Perepelitsa

The emergence of Belarus as an independent state on the political map of Europe has considerably modified Europe's geopolitical landscape. Belarus sits at the crossroads of the military and political interests of key neighboring states and even the major powers of Europe. It has had a sizable impact on the internal developments of its immediate neighbors and on the balance of forces in Eastern Europe.

Belarusian influence is a result of its geopolitical situation, not its size or economic potential. It is situated halfway between the northern and southern subregions of Eastern Europe and between Russia and the Europe of NATO and the EU, a junction that explains its vast geopolitical and military importance. It is defined in part by its ability to act as a link among the three highly dynamic subregions of Europe:

- The first of these is comprised of the Central European nations, such as Poland, the Czech Republic, and Hungary—nations seeking to integrate themselves into Western political/military/ economic structures. Belarus is a crucial neighbor of this subregion and forms a key transportation corridor between Central Europe and Russia. Nearly 70 percent of Russia's exports to Europe pass through Belarus. Without access to this route, Russia would find itself economically and geopolitically isolated from Europe.

- The second subregion, to the immediate north of Belarus, comprises the North European region of Scandinavia and the Baltic Sea states. The three Baltic states of Lithuania, Latvia, and Estonia have been vigorously integrating themselves into this northern region. By looking north to Scandinavia and west to Germany and Poland, the Baltic states make plain their intention of seeking full-fledged membership in all European structures.

- The third subregion, to the south of Belarus, is the Black Sea area, a fast-growing zone of economic cooperation. Many states in this subregion would like to foster closer ties and links with Northern Europe. This ambition is embodied in the notion of a formal Baltic–Black Sea mechanism for cooperation, announced by former Ukrainian president Leonid Kravchuk. In any such mechanism, Belarus would be a key actor, whether to facilitate or complicate cooperation between north and south. The idea of a Baltic–Black Sea confederation of Lithuania, Belarus, and Ukraine was once put forward by an earlier generation of Ukrainian statesmen and thinkers, chiefly Mikhailo Hrushevsky and Stepan Rudnitsky, and then was revived by President Kravchuk in the early 1990s. Belarus's strong pro-Russian attitude, however, has considerably damaged this particular vector of Eastern European integration.

Belarus therefore finds itself in a geopolitical field defined by the interaction along four external vectors: north, south, east, and west. The Baltic states, Poland, Ukraine, NATO, the EU, and Russia will all exert their influence on Belarus and be affected in turn by Minsk's response. The relative strength of developments on these vectors will also help shape Belarus's foreign policy priorities.

The Russian Federation is and probably will remain the strongest influence on the domestic and foreign policies of Belarus. Because of Belarus's geopolitical location and its geostrategic importance, Russia assigns high priority to Belarus. The territory in question constitutes a sort of a springboard that, depending on the particular military-political objectives being pursued, can turn Belarus into a modern day *cordon sanitaire*, a nuclear-free zone and a zone that counters NATO enlargement, or a zone of expanded external pressure and influence. The military presence of any foreign country in Belarus makes it possible for such a country to put pressure on Ukraine, the Baltics, Poland, and Russia itself—for the simple reason that the shortest route from the West to Moscow cuts through Belarusian territory. In that sense Belarus serves as Russia's natural shield, one that has repeatedly prevented or at least delayed military expansion from the West. Its geographic location has always made Belarus hostage to whatever differences Russia may have had with the West, and for this Belarus has paid a high price. Belarus lost 3 million people (out of a population of 10 million) during World War II alone. Control over Belarus has long been seen as the key to control over Eastern Europe as a whole, and Belarus has always ended up in the midst of East-West military-strategic rivalry.

Which aspect of Belarus's geopolitical position is most important depends on the perspective from which it is evaluated. From the north-south perspective, Belarus is most valuable as a security zone. Strengthening the north-south vector helps solidify Belarus's independent foreign policy course and reduces the chance of resumed confrontation between Russia and the West. Certain political forces in the West, as well as in the Central European countries, tend to view Belarus as a buffer zone, protecting Central and Western Europe against relapses of Russian expansionism.

From the Russian perspective, Belarus's military-strategic significance depends on which model of military-political relations between the West and Russia prevails. The three most likely models are the following:

- *Russia exerts limited military-political influence on Central Europe.* Since the Central European nations joined NATO in 1999, this scenario could only occur if NATO eventually withered as the key security institution in Europe. Such a scenario does not appear likely. NATO seems, for example, to have withstood the challenge of Kosovo. Moreover, even if the preconditions were in place, implementation of this model would require both the deployment of powerful Russian or Russian-Belarusian military forces near the Polish and Lithuanian borders, and the absence of a similar military force in Poland and the Baltics. Given the current weakness of Russian forces, such a deployment does not seem very likely in the near future.

- *Russia uses Belarus as a region to counteract U.S. and Western influence in East-Central Europe.* This model is possible if Russia, unhappy with the post-Madrid compromise with NATO, attempts a more confrontational strategy toward the West.[1] This strategy would inevitably result in Russia's construction of a western defense barrier from the Baltic to the Black Sea, consisting of the Kaliningrad region of the Russian Federation and Belarus, along with attempts to include Ukraine and Moldova in the structure. Belarus would be the principal component of such a defense line, since it is the centerpiece of this axis and shares a border with Poland, NATO's newest member, on the forward line of the collective defense system of the Atlantic alliance. The presence of a powerful military force in Belarus would enable Russia to maintain a certain balance of forward-based forces relative to NATO.

- *Russia exerts military-political dominance over the Commonwealth of Independent States and the Baltics.* This model becomes possible if Russia reaches a consensus with the West that recognizes, officially or unofficially, Russia's dominance in the post-Soviet space, and that views the CIS countries as a zone of Russia's vital interests. In this scenario Belarus plays the role of "model vassal," since it serves as a testing ground for working out various approaches to military-political reintegration of the CIS countries into Russia's sphere of interest.

The Russia-NATO Founding Act of 1997, if it holds and develops according to plan, essentially limits Russia's immediate choice of a security model to the last one. The potential role of Belarus, given its highly developed military infrastructure, is, however, similar regardless of the particular model. Belarus is home to Russia's first line of early-warning missile attack systems. An example is the Russian military facility in Baranovichi. Belarus also boasts having a key Russian naval communications center and a ramified network of military airfields, all in good working order and well equipped. The problem, however, is that the Russian Air Force is far inferior to that of NATO, making any serious development of a confrontational strategy problematic in the near term.

THE SECURITY INTERESTS OF UKRAINE

As far as Ukraine is concerned, none of the above models meets its security interests. The impact of Belarus's geostrategic position on Ukrainian security has been reflected in Ukraine's defense concept and military doctrine. Ukraine's Soviet legacy includes individual components of the forward strategic defense line. While these were the most powerful components of the Soviet defense posture, in Ukraine's case they are located in the western parts of the country, facing what the Soviets regarded as the main threats, but not what Ukraine might face today.

Ukraine has articulated a new defense concept in its Program for Reforming and Building the Armed Forces of Ukraine until 2005.[2] A basic assumption of the program, and of Ukrainian security policy as a whole, is that Ukraine will remain outside any military bloc or alliance. The country's limited military potential, however, makes it impossible to set up multiple lines of defense in all directions. Therefore one of the goals of Ukraine's defense policy is to identify the key strategic directions on which to concentrate the bulk of its defense potential. Such directions will be determined based on an evaluation of its probable enemies, the disruption that restructuring might cause to the existing balance of forces, and an assessment of the most vulnerable parts of Ukrainian territory. Because Ukraine does not see any country as a military enemy, and because the balance of forces in the vicinity of its borders does not pose an immediate military threat, the criterion of Ukraine's territorial vulnerability is emerging as the most important.

In previous wars, the gravest danger to Ukraine's security and defenses came from the north. The first government of newly independent Ukraine was toppled by Bolshevik troops attacking from Bryansk in 1918. A second offensive was launched against the fragile Ukrainian state from the area of Gomel (now part of Belarus). Nazi troops mounted their offensive from the same direction in 1941 and were able to encircle a group of Soviet forces in the vicinity of Kiev. In the past, the northern direction was preferred because of the minimal depth of offensive action required to seize the capital of Ukraine: from that direction the distance between Ukraine's border and Kiev is a mere 90 kilometers. From this perspective, Ukrainian defenses appear to be most vulnerable from the direction of Belarus. Recognition of the importance of that particular direction was one of the reasons for the formation of the Northern Operational Territorial Command, a third military-administrative unit in the Ukrainian armed forces at the operational-strategic level.

Undoubtedly, an independent Belarus does not threaten Ukraine. But Belarus's geopolitical choice will determine whether or not its territory will be used to bring military pressure on Ukraine, as has happened in the past. Given its current geopolitical situation, Ukraine would benefit most from a nonbloc, neutral Belarus. Hence Kiev naturally looks with suspicion at the military consequences of Russian-Belarusian integration.

FROM NONBLOC STATUS TO ALLIANCE WITH RUSSIA?

As with Ukraine, Belarus's 1990 Declaration of Sovereignty stated that its ultimate foreign policy objective was neutrality and a nonbloc status. The neutrality model that Ukraine, Belarus, and, subsequently, Moldova originally opted for was one of "instrumental neutrality." It involved no rigorous international legal obligations and granted vast freedom of action, including involvement in collective security systems. This model by and large reflected the newly independent states' reaction to the collapse of the bipolar security system.

Generally, neutral nonbloc status is sought by countries whose independence and sovereignty already have a rock-solid platform. The formal status ratifies existing conditions that provide the neutral country with the means to achieve national security. To the CIS nations, however, declaring neutrality and a nonbloc status became a way of achieving sovereignty. It could not be viewed as a mature statement of national security and foreign policy strategy. Yet even in their initial formulations Ukraine and Belarus differed in their respective approaches to neutrality and the avoidance of military blocs.

From the beginning, Ukraine's embrace of neutrality and nonbloc status was an expression of its policy toward Russia, not NATO. Kiev assumed that Russia, being the legal successor to the USSR, would not easily give up its military-political claims to Ukraine. Russia regularly sought to secure Ukraine's adherence to the Tashkent Collective Security Treaty of 1992 and to bilateral agreements on military cooperation. Ukraine's nonbloc principle has enabled it to avoid all such entanglements with Russia or the CIS. In addition, nonbloc status better than any other accommodates the domestic political situation in Ukraine, in which different regions still harbor different geopolitical orientations. Nonbloc status thus serves the interest of internal political stability as well.

For Belarus, to the contrary, the nonbloc and neutral status had a narrower, more transient, and tactical nature. Belarusian leaders saw the declaration of neutrality and nonaffiliation with military blocs as a way to constrain NATO and prevent pro-Western and pro-NATO sentiments from gaining ground among the Belarusian public. Belarus's communist elite also used nonbloc status as a way to insulate itself from the democratic processes under way in Russia.

Strong pro-Russian sentiments among the Belarusian public, however, forced the national leaders to abandon the country's neutrality and nonbloc status soon after it was declared and to move quickly toward a closer relationship with Russia. The change in Belarus's foreign policy was made, above all, for economic reasons. The most hard-core opponents of Belarus's nonbloc status were the managers of the military-industrial complex, who had considerable influence with the national leadership. More than 100 defense factories in Belarus needed a market. Military production in Belarus depended on Russian-made components, making an eloquent case for closer military-political ties with Moscow. The Belarusian military, too, kept pushing for the alliance, aware that the nation's military industry could meet only 3 percent to 5 percent of the Belarusian armed forces' requirements in armaments and materiel.[3] In 1993, Stanislau Shushkevich, the first leader of independent Belarus, yielded to pressure from industrialists and the military and reluctantly agreed to let Belarus join the Tashkent Collective Security Treaty.

The expected growth of military orders from Russia never took place, although the pro-Russian stance came to prevail and dominate the politics, economy, society, and culture of Belarus. Elected president in 1994, Aleksandr Lukashenko came to personify and embody that trend, as he proposed a model of profound political, military, and economic integration with Russia.

The complete dependence of the Belarusian economy on Russian oil and gas, and the absence of hard currency in Belarus, made integration almost a must. With barter as the principal form of trade, Belarus was unable to reach outside the CIS framework for markets. In the mid-1990s, Belarus failed to convince Russia to subsidize 50 percent of its oil exports to Belarus and to reschedule Belarus's huge debt in exchange for increased deliveries of farming and industrial products from that country. Bilateral negotiations in 1994 demonstrated that Russia would only write off the $1.5 billion worth of

Belarus's debt if Belarus were to fully reintegrate itself into the Russian Federation.[4] To prevent social upheaval and economic collapse, Lukashenko accepted the Kremlin's rules of the game, a step that resulted in the signing of the Union Treaty by Belarus and Russia in the spring of 1997.

BELARUS'S ROLE IN RUSSIA'S REINTEGRATION POLICY

When he came to power in 1994, Lukashenko found Belarus in a difficult economic situation. He had two options to pursue to maintain Belarus's highly developed economic base and social stability. One was comprehensive market reform, which would reorient Belarus's economy toward the West and weaken its dependence on Russia, a course similar to that adopted by the Baltic republics. The other option was to make few changes in the economy and to climb to a priority position in the CIS by reestablishing, to the extent possible, the economic ties that had existed under the once unified economic regime of the USSR.

Lukashenko's choice was predetermined by Belarus's complete economic dependence on the CIS nations, above all Russia. Belarus depended on that market for 70 percent of its raw materials, 90 percent of its energy needs, 80 percent of its imports, and 90 percent of its exports.[5] Lukashenko's policy of integration was highly popular, supported by 90 percent of the population in some polls. Eventually this policy also came to coincide with a revival of Russia's reintegration desires. To take significant steps toward integration, the Belarusian leadership had to fit its needs into the framework of Moscow's reintegration plans.

In his foreign policy strategy, Lukashenko has thoroughly exploited the ideas of pan-Slavism, laying claim to the role of unifier of the Slavic world. These ideas are based on the symbols of Slavic brotherhood, the Slavic triangle of Belarus-Russia-Ukraine, a single pan-Slavic state, or the great power symbols of a restored USSR. As he called on Ukraine to join the Belarus-Russia union during a visit to Kiev in May 1997, Lukashenko noted, "God has so ruled and destiny has so determined that we have set our sights very high lately, and people have begun to talk about us as a commonsense-driven republic capable of implementing Slavic unity. . . this is our burden that we have to carry; we must try and glue back together the great Slavic world."[6] Lukashenko limited his definition of the Slavic world to the CIS borders, however, never mentioning that at least half of that world lay to the west of his country's borders.

Whereas Ukraine adhered to the strategy of acting as a bridge between Russia and the West, Belarus tried to play the role of a bridge between Ukraine and Russia. Where Ukraine is seen as a key factor of European stability, Belarus could be referred to as a key factor of the CIS integration. Yet neither Belarus nor Russia can be happy with the current integration processes in the CIS. Hundreds of agreements and accords signed within the CIS framework never went beyond the paper on which they were written. Since 1990, the turnover of goods among the CIS countries has dropped significantly because of basic differences in the way CIS countries approach relations among post-Soviet countries. Russia and, more recently, Belarus view the commonwealth as a stepping stone on the way to a single state, or a substantially integrated union. The other CIS members see the commonwealth as a form of "civilized divorce" and a way to put interstate relations on an equitable, mutually beneficial basis.

These two views are diametrically opposed. Russia has claimed the key positions in all CIS structures, virtually subordinating the other countries to its national interests and essentially seeking to recreate a single state on the basis of the commonwealth. The resulting encroachment on the interests of the other CIS members has prompted them to deepen bilateral and multilateral cooperation with each other and beyond the borders of the CIS. At least three different processes are taking place within the CIS at present: (1) the reintegration that Russia vigorously lobbied for; (2) disintegration in response to the first process; and (3) an integration intended to strengthen bilateral cooperation at the interstate level. The third trend leads to the emergence of regional power centers other than Moscow, a phenomenon that Russia sees as a threat to its security and domination.[7]

The union of Russia and Belarus embodies both reintegration and integration. Such processes lead to the formation of supranational structures. Russia needs a supranational structure to bring the CIS nations into the embrace of its own statehood. Belarus needs a supranational structure as a formal mechanism for manipulating Russia's governmental institutions in its own interests.

The creation of supranational structures dominated by Russia means changing the relations of dependence currently existing in the CIS to relations of subordination that paradoxically would derail the commonwealth or, at the very least, strengthen the disintegrative tendencies within it. It is no accident that most of the CIS leaders have reacted coldly to the Belarus-Russia partnership. Ukraine's President Kuchma stated, for example, that "unification of countries at different levels within the CIS is nonsense. It is a road to the collapse of the commonwealth."[8]

Advancement of reintegration and integration processes in Belarus-Russia relations will take place within the framework of confederation-federation. Russia's strategic objective is to incorporate Belarus as a subject of the Federation. Some in Russia would like to see unification lead to the creation of a single federated state.[9] Many in the Russian foreign policy community support the idea of Belarus joining Russia as a new subject of the Russian Federation, or as six separate subjects (corresponding to Belarus's six regions).[10] The Belarusian leaders, however, will not give up sovereignty to the point at which they lose complete authority in their own country. Hence they opt for a confederation.

THE 1997 UNION TREATY OF RUSSIA AND BELARUS

Currently, the most promising form of Russia-Belarus unification is the confederation that has been formalized as the Belarus-Russia union. The name of the union does not refer to Russia as the Russian Federation. Is this omission meaningful? Creation of a confederation on the basis of or within the Russian Federation would result in the disintegration of the confederation itself, as well as in the collapse of the Russian state, because *oblasts* and autonomous regions within the Russian Federation would demand a similar confederate status.

What has Belarus gained from being in the union? In the short run it has gained concrete economic support for its failing economy. This support includes Russia's continued acceptance of Belarusian manufactured goods, often through barter arrangements, the management of Belarus's energy debt, the development of joint infrastructure, unified transport and energy systems, an integrated communications and information system, and joint research and technological programs. In exchange, Belarus is obliged to apply to its other trade partners the same foreign trade treatment, customs tariffs, and nontariff regulations as Russia does. With regard to Ukraine, such regulations would tie Belarus to Russia's lead, should Russia adopt discriminatory trade measures in its dealings with Ukraine.

Belarus must also coordinate its policies with Russia if it is to make use of the economic potential of the union and create an environment for the activities of Russian transnational corporations and financial-industrial groups. Such coordination inevitably leads to the preservation of Belarus's structural dependence on the Russian economy. By looking exclusively toward Russia and honoring the provisions of the Union Charter, Belarus will eventually isolate itself from international economic relations, trends, and structures. It is worth noting, however, that in most cases advanced and state-of-the-art technologies are not to be found in Russia these days, but elsewhere.

In the military-political area, Belarus could in theory count on the union to help develop and pursue joint military purchases, ensure deliveries of arms and materiel on the basis of those purchases, and create a unified system of technical support for the nation's armed forces. There is little hope, however, that such support will be forthcoming from the arrangement. The Russian defense ministry, like its Belarusian counterpart, is strapped for cash and unable to subsidize the military needs of Belarus. In addition, the Belarusian military-industrial complex is only a fraction of Russia's. Where, in the past, Ukraine's 700 military works accounted for 18 percent of the USSR's military output, Belarus had a mere 100 defense plants whose share in overall military production accounted for a tiny one percent.[11] Russian industry has long learned to get along without this input. It is now more in the interest of Russian manufacturers to keep their government's declining support for defense production to themselves.

In legal terms, Belarus has achieved—on paper—equality with Russia in the union's bureaucracy. Decision making in the Supreme Council currently operates on the "one state-one vote" principle.[12] Nonetheless, the powers of the national governments and parliaments far exceed those of the supranational agencies. There is also the matter of resources and capabilities, an area in which Russia exceeds Belarus's potential many times over. Should decisions made by the Supreme Council fail to meet Russia's interests, Russia will simply ignore them. Still, the union of Belarus and Russia tends to cast in concrete a certain structure of international relations in the post-Soviet space and to define the development prospects of the former Soviet republics.

Only time will tell in which direction these relations will go. It is most likely that the union will strengthen centrifugal forces in the region. The CIS will continue to transform itself into an even more amorphous entity, while the union of Belarus and Russia will be even more short-lived than the commonwealth. Russia does not stand to benefit from stronger supranational agencies in the union, as they may invite resentment on the part of the subjects of the Russian Federation. A weakening of the authority of supranational agencies will make the union even less effective than the CIS. Hence, further modification of the union will be by the steady transfer of functions and powers from the Belarusian state to Moscow, something that has already occurred in the area of military policies.

ECONOMIC RAMIFICATIONS OF THE UNION

The union also has economic ramifications. The specifics of the developing market economy in Russia are determined in part by the heritage of its imperial civilization, its vast deposits of natural resources, and a still powerful military-industrial complex. Given this combination of important factors, national capital is being formed on the basis of traditional export-oriented production of raw materials and defense industries, to the detriment of an intensive development model involving technical restructuring of civilian industries and agriculture.[13]

Russian economic development is rapidly narrowing to a focus on the domestic market, prompting Russia to export its raw materials and weaponry primarily to its former trade partners, particularly to the nearby, but relatively closed, markets of CIS countries. Such exports are only competitive within an artificial CIS monopoly that inflates the demand for Russian products and handicaps the economic progress of the other CIS countries. Access to these external markets is best ensured through Russia's military-political domination and restoration of its imperial-style relations with the CIS nations. As Boris Yeltsin clearly told the heads of state at a CIS meeting in March 1997, "we do not want anybody's domination in the former USSR, especially in the military-political sphere. We do not want any states to act as buffer states."[14]

The last statement referred mainly to Ukraine and Belarus. Ukraine, the largest consumer of Russian energy, imports 30 percent of all Russian gas exports (57.2 billion out of 196.5 billion cubic meters).[15] Even today the Russian energy corporation Gazprom has a tangible impact on the domestic and foreign policies of Ukraine. Belarus, for its part, is attractive to Russia as a route for the raw materials it sells to European markets. Over the past two years alone, this route has earned Russia $1.5 billion in profits, far in excess of the total Belarusian debt written off by Moscow.[16]

MILITARY ASPECTS OF RUSSIAN-BELARUSIAN INTEGRATION

As Russia fails to accomplish its objectives in the CIS exclusively by economic means, it employs political and military-political means to reintegrate those countries into the safety of Russian statehood. Such policies enjoy popular support in Russia, appealing to nostalgic sentiments favoring restoration of the Soviet Union and recovery of Russia's great power status. In this view the most important attribute of great power status would be to restore the "natural borders" in the framework of the former USSR, or at least allow complete Russian domination within those borders. Vitaly Tretiakov, editor of the influential *Nezavisimaya gazeta*, makes this aspect of Russian policy plain:

> One of the objectives of Russia's geopolitical game plan that is never mentioned by official politicians, let alone diplomats, but that is always implied, is as simple as can be: Russia today is a nation with artificial borders. What is artificial gravitates toward a natural state, and the natural state can be achieved either by increasing territory or by losing it. Two graphic examples: it would be natural for Russia both to lose the Kaliningrad region and to bring on board the Crimea and the left-bank Ukraine. . . . But that cannot be done simultaneously. The question is, which of the processes will start sooner?[17]

This candid quote indicates that the period of ultimate and irreversible separation of the periphery of the Russian Empire from its nucleus is not yet over. Moreover, a strong tendency is evolving toward restoration of the empire in the form of military-political hegemony of the nucleus over the periphery. So far three stages for such restoration have been outlined: (1) the military presence of Russia in the CIS countries and joint protection of the borders of the former USSR; (2) the Tashkent Treaty on Collective Security; and (3) the creation of bilateral military alliances. The long-term plans apparently include the creation of a single military organization within the framework of a unified state.

It is a known fact that a foreign military presence performs external and internal functions. The external function is to protect one's military ally against external aggression. The internal function, in contrast, is to control the ally and its domestic situation. As for the presence of Russian troops in the CIS countries, only the border guards of the Russian Federation perform—to a certain extent—the external function. The main objective of Russian troops stationed in the CIS countries is to control the territory and the internal political developments of the host countries, and to shape the foreign policies of national leaders in line with Russia's national interests. Depending on the nature of such interests, Russian troops may stabilize or destabilize the situation in the host country, pushing it toward an even more rigid type of military-political dependence, that is, the Tashkent Treaty on Collective Security. A case in point is the situation in Georgia and Azerbaijan.

Elements of Russia's military presence in the CIS countries include use of the military infrastructure facilities of the CIS by or in the interests of Russian troops, peacekeeping operations, joint protection of borders, and joint handling of military and military-political problems. Russia's military presence in the CIS nations is intended to prevent them from entering into alliances and blocs with other nations and at the same time to "encourage the intentions of the Tashkent Treaty members to come together into a defense alliance based on common interests and shared military-political objectives."[18]

The Tashkent Treaty on Collective Security has not become an effective security system for the signatories. No single conflict, either within member states or between them, has been resolved completely. One of the key reasons is that Russia sees the treaty as a mechanism to strengthen its military-political domination of the member states and has repeatedly attempted to transform the Tashkent pact into a defense alliance. That transformation has taken place in the following stages:

- Originally the Tashkent Treaty was to follow the Warsaw Treaty model. The alliance was to have consisted of central and national agencies in command of the coalition forces, governed by a joint staff. The alliance's main goals were to contain aggression in times of peace and to rebuff aggression in times of war. In the event of aggression against any signatory to the treaty, all the other signatories were to help rebuff it. It soon transpired, however, that the alliance, while accommodating the large-scale interests of Russia, failed to cater to the military-political interests of the other signatories, which were primarily regional in nature. The withdrawal of Uzbekistan and other members in 1999 demonstrate the treaty's inherent flaws.

- The second stage of the treaty's evolution was the reconstruction of its structures on the regional principle. The defense alliance was to consist of several regional security systems and responsibility zones: Eastern Europe, Caucasus, Central Asia, and East Asia. A coalition of forces would be formed in each of the regions, reporting to the united command in the region. The scheme lacked viability and coherence and was bound to compromise centralization and coordination.

- Finally, Russia set about implementing a third stage—the creation of military alliances based on a highly differentiated selection of the most loyal strategic allies. This approach produced the military alliance between Belarus and Russia, formalized in the Union Treaty. The parties agreed to undertake joint measures to prevent threats to each other's sovereignty and independence, to coordinate military restructuring and the improvement of their respective armed forces, to use existing military infrastructure jointly, and to pursue coordinated border policies and joint programs on border issues.[19] The Belarusian and Russian defense ministries approved the draft of a joint military policy to implement these agreements. The common military policy is intended to create a system for armed protection of the union and to ensure the two nations' military security in their part of the world. The two countries plan to form a military structure made up of a regional grouping of Belarusian and Russian forces and a command and control body. The joint task force will be used for common purposes, agreed upon in advance. The two countries' defense ministries intend in the coming years to switch to joint strategic and operational planning.

Obviously, if implemented, the policy will turn the territory of Belarus into a forward-based military-strategic springboard for the Russian Federation, similar to its role during the Soviet period. The Belarusian Soviet Socialist Republic was the most militarized zone of the former USSR, with one soldier for every 43 civilians, in contrast to the 1 to 98 ratio of soldiers to civilians in Ukraine and the 1 to 634 ratio in Russia.[20]

The 1996 revisions on the CFE Treaty limit Belarus to 1,800 tanks, 2,600 armored personnel carriers, 1,615 artillery pieces, 260 combat aircraft, and 80 attack helicopters. Efforts to build up the combat potential of regional forces are likely to consist of deploying medium- and short-range missiles to the theater, allowing Russian air forces to use Belarus's airfields, redeploying Russian forward-based forces if necessary, enhancing the air defense forces of Belarus with a Russian contingent, and conducting joint reconnaissance missions.

Much attention will go toward maintaining the military infrastructure left over from the Soviet period and toward improving access to and use of such infrastructure for airlifting Russian troops. Belarus has twelve military airfields and twenty-three missile bases at its disposal. Russia has about 100 airfields with concrete runways, including 65 in European Russia, although 40 percent of them are in need of repair.[21] Availability of the Belarusian airfields would thus open up vast opportunities for maneuver during operational missions of the union's joint air force. Indeed, the Russian and Belarusian air defense troops have gone on joint combat duty. Russia's contribution includes units from the Moscow Air Defense Military District and the Air Defense Army, which are deployed in Russia's northwest.

In late April 1997, Russia and Belarus held joint air force exercises whose chief objective was to restore the skills involved in the redeployment of air groupings in Belarus. Several military experts offered bold forecasts that "it [was] possible within a very short period of time to deploy in Belarus a joint Belarusian-Russian air grouping capable of counteracting the NATO air groupings."[22] Speaking about the joint exercises, General Pyotr Deinekin, commander in chief of the Russian Air Force, said, "Undoubtedly, we cannot but think about confrontation. From the military perspective, advancement of NATO to the east is aggression, but so far without the use of arms."[23] The general's remarks confirm that the military alliance of Belarus and Russia is clearly anti-NATO in nature. Its mere existence, however, poses threats to Ukraine as well.

THE IMPACT OF INTEGRATION ON UKRAINE

Ukraine opposes the creation of any new military blocs, especially in proximity to its borders. The creation of a Belarusian-Russian military bloc not only brings military confrontation back to Eastern Europe but also significantly increases Russia's military-political hegemony over the CIS countries. During its dialogue with NATO, which culminated in the signing of the Founding Act in May 1997, Russia considerably strengthened its military-political position by securing its military presence in Ukraine for at least another twenty years (the May 1997 Black Sea Fleet Agreement) and by developing a military alliance with Belarus.

As compared with the other military blocs, the Russian-Belarusian alliance provides for a high level of centralization and integration. In the language of Article 3 of the Union Charter, the alliance suggests "a consistent movement towards a voluntary association of the member states of the Union."[24] A structure therefore has evolved for stage-by-stage restoration of Great Russia within its natural borders in the framework of the commonwealth. Of course, Belarus and Russia, just like Poland, Hungary, and the Czech Republic, are free to enter into any alliances or unions. In fact, the president of Ukraine stated that, "it is the right of the Belarusian and Russian peoples to enter associations. And we, being neighbors, must respect that right."[25] However, such associations should be formed without damaging the security of neighboring countries.

The danger of this model, geared for the restoration of Russia's great power status, is that Russia may begin to apply it to the other CIS members—most likely, and first, to Ukraine. President Yeltsin has already announced an initiative to get the other former Soviet republics to join the union of Belarus and Russia.[26] Obviously, now that Minsk has signed up, Moscow will seek to expand the unification process by prodding the other Tashkent Treaty signatories to

move up to the level of Russian-Belarusian military-political relations and by encouraging Ukraine to sign the treaty. In August 1997,
Igor Sergeyev, Russia's defense minister, visited Kiev primarily to
convince Ukrainian leaders of the need to accede to the Tashkent
pact and to join a common defense space with Russia. President
Lukashenko has also been active in enhancing the Belarusian-Russian union. In Kiev in May 1997, he repeatedly noted that he "would
very much like Ukraine to join the union between Russia and
Belarus."[27] These attempts to involve Ukraine in the Belarusian-
Russian unification have generated added challenges to Ukraine's
security.

The creation of the Belarusian-Russian union indeed brought
about highly noticeable, albeit short-lived, signs of destabilization
of the internal political situation in Ukraine. Left-wing forces mounted an unprecedented campaign for changes in the country's foreign
policy and for accession to the Belarusian-Russian union, while
Ukraine's parliament was frequently bogged down in a battle of
foreign policy resolutions. Leftist forces also conducted a broad-
scale anti-NATO propaganda campaign both inside and outside the
parliament. Following in the footsteps of the State Duma of the
Russian Federation, 170 deputies of the Supreme Council of Ukraine
created an anti-NATO bloc in 1997. The anti-NATO campaign
peaked when deputies of the Supreme Council and political forces
in the Crimean Peninsula attempted to frustrate the international
war game, Sea Breeze-97. This effort was intended to discredit
Ukraine and make the country, which had just signed a Charter on
Special Partnership with NATO in July 1997, appear to be an unrelia-
ble partner to NATO alliance members. However, Sea Breeze-98
took place with much less controversy and resistance.

Russian-Belarusian unification has had some indirect positive
implications for Ukraine. First, the idea of a Slavic union, lobbied for
by Lukashenko and the Ukrainian Communists, nudged secessionist
sentiments out of the minds of the Crimean leadership within
Ukraine, considerably weakening the influence of the separatist
forces. Second, the campaign for Ukraine to join the Belarusian-
Russian union clearly revealed that certain political forces wanted
to involve Ukraine in a confrontation against NATO. Third, after
Russia made a defense alliance with Belarus and obtained the right
to lease the Crimean seaport of Sevastopol, Ukraine found itself

virtually surrounded by Russian troops, with the exception of a segment of its western border. This massive Russian presence created strong resistance within Ukraine to such pressure.

UKRAINIAN AND BELARUSIAN DIFFERENCES ON NATO

Kiev's position on NATO is as drastically different from Moscow's and Minsk's positions as its policy toward post-Soviet integration is. As described by President Kuchma, Ukraine seeks "friendly and mutually beneficial relations with NATO." Unlike Belarus and Russia, Ukraine sees NATO expansion as an element in the adaptation of the European security structure to new conditions, not as a threat to its national security. Ukraine also believes that the process of NATO expansion cannot happen overnight: after admission of the early candidates, the NATO expansion should continue. NATO's openness to cooperation with other countries, as well as to incorporation of new members, should remain one of its defining principles.

The European integration process should assign an important role to building relations and deepening cooperation among the new European democracies. This multidirectional process will inevitably bring completion to general European integration. NATO expansion is an important component of that process. On the basis of this approach, Ukraine signed a Charter on Special Partnership with NATO, committing itself to an expanded relationship with NATO.

Belarus has followed Russia's foreign policy lead, choosing a more confrontational model for its relationship with NATO. Minsk has expressed its complete opposition to NATO's expansion to the east. In Lukashenko's words, this opposition is "not only the view of the leadership of this country but, above all, the position of the Belarusian public, 90 percent of whom strongly reject the expansion of the North Atlantic bloc."[28]

Russia, unlike its Belarusian ally, was busy bargaining for a special military and political role in Europe at the same time that it was counteracting NATO. Moscow created a mechanism for influencing NATO decision making to uphold Russia's interests, including legitimization of its military presence in the CIS. Belarus adopted a stance of out-and-out rejection of NATO expansion, which left it in an uncertain relationship with the Atlantic alliance and without any international security guarantees whatsoever. Belarus will likely have to make do with whatever the NATO-Russian Joint Council provides and may eventually choose to negotiate its own agreement with NATO—although the best time for such a policy was before the 1997 NATO summit in Madrid, not after. There appears to be no sense of urgency in Brussels about a NATO-Belarusian partnership.

There is a certain asymmetry built in to the NATO-Russian relationship. Russia succeeded in obtaining a NATO promise not to deploy its troops or nuclear weapons in the new member states. Russia, however, is free to make use of the military infrastructure of the former USSR in the CIS countries and is deploying forward-based forces there.

Even more uncertain is whether Eastern Europe will see the deployment of nuclear weapons or become a nuclear-free zone. At a 1995 conference on renewal of the NPT, Belarus suggested creating a nuclear-free zone in Eastern Europe. Ukraine was the first to support the initiative because, as a nuclear-free country, it is interested in denuclearizing its neighbors and the region as a whole. The first practical step toward a nuclear-free zone in Eastern Europe could come in the form of a joint Ukraine-Belarus statement declaring the territory of both countries free from nuclear weapons. Moscow's response to such a nuclear-free zone initiative, however, remains a major question. Minsk obviously clears its initiatives with the Russian foreign ministry, and so far Russia has supported the initiative. But Russia's primary concern has been to ensure that no nuclear weapons are deployed in the new NATO member states. Should the nuclear-free zone fail to include the new NATO members, Russia is likely to oppose it. According to Vladimir Orlov, a prominent Russian expert on nuclear non-proliferation, "the creation of a nuclear-free zone made up only of Ukraine and Belarus would run counter to Russia's interests; at least, it would run counter to the hypothetical calculations of a 'power adequate response' to NATO expansion in the form of deployment of tactical nuclear weapons in Belarus."[29]

To accommodate Russia's demands, the NATO member states reaffirmed in the NATO-Russia Founding Act that they "do not have intentions, plans, or reasons to deploy nuclear weapons in the territories of new member states and have no need for changing any aspect of the structure of the NATO nuclear forces or NATO's nuclear policies, nor do they foresee any need for doing so in the future."[30] But the Founding Act includes no such language on Russian nuclear intentions in Belarus.

Russia's caution in undertaking similar commitments can probably be attributed to the fact that, from the military-political point of view, it would benefit from deploying tactical nuclear weapons in forward areas, given that it is considerably inferior to NATO in conventional forces. Experts of the Russian Research Center of the Committee of Scientists for Global Security note that, in the context of its economic crisis and limited capacity to equip its armed forces with new weaponry, Russia will only be able to ensure its security through reliance on nuclear weapons, both now and in the fairly distant future.

OUTLOOK FOR RELATIONS BETWEEN UKRAINE AND BELARUS

Kiev's early response to Belarus-Russia unification included public efforts to distance itself from the process as well as to limit Ukrainian-Belarusian dialogue. Ukrainian leaders realized that, if the union were realized, Ukraine's bilateral security issues with Belarus would no longer be under Minsk's control but would be decided in Moscow. Ukraine thus decided to act to resolve outstanding issues with Minsk, before it was too late. One such issue was the delimitation and demarcation of the Belarusian-Ukrainian border. Delimitation was put on a fast track and completed in April 1997. On May 12, 1997, during a visit to Kiev by President Lukashenko, the two countries signed a Ukraine-Belarus Treaty on the State Border, which allowed them to start demarcation work.

Next came an attempt to enhance bilateral economic cooperation. When the two presidents sat down to the negotiating table in the Belarusian city of Gomel, near the border with Ukraine, the two sides made progress on joint environmental work and economic cooperation between the border regions, to the benefit of both. Ukraine's continued interest in an independent and fully sovereign Belarus meant that Kiev tried not to leave Minsk alone with Moscow, while the Belarusian president used his dialogue with Kiev to increase his leverage vis-à-vis Russia. Despite a certain amount of progress, economic cooperation between Ukraine and Belarus trudges along at a slow pace and at a low level, while military cooperation remains one of the narrowest bottlenecks in the Belarusian-Ukrainian relationship. There are virtually no contacts between the two countries' defense ministries, with the exception of a few working meetings over the past four years on barter trade in components, repairs of armored equipment, and reconciliation of aeronautical charts.

Despite these limitations, Kiev appears to have found the right formula for a relationship with Minsk—to develop a bilateral political dialogue with Belarus while building up regional political cooperation within the Warsaw-Kiev-Vilnius-Minsk quadrangle. With such a policy, Ukraine is both encouraging a more independent Belarus and hedging its bets, should such a Belarus disappear.

NOTES

1 The NATO conference in Madrid that defined the terms of enlargement took place in 1997.
2 S. Markiv, "Ukraine Adopts Military Reform Program," *Jamestown Monitor Prism*, vol. 3, no. 3 (March 21, 1997).
3 *Narodna armia*, September 11, 1996.
4 *Politika*, February 5, 1994.
5 George Sanford, "Belarus on the Road to Statehood," *Survival*, vol. 38 (Spring 1996), pp. 83, 131–53.
6 *Vseukrainskiye vedomosti*, May 13, 1997.
7 *Nezavisimaya gazeta*, April 5, 1997, p. 2.
8 *Vseukrainskiye vedomosti*, April 2, 1997.
9 *Nezavisimaya gazeta*, May 22, 1997.
10 *Nezavisimaya gazeta*, April 22, 1997. It needs to be stressed, however, that the financial crisis of August 1998 significantly reduced the enthusiasm of many Russian policy makers and politicians for a union with Belarus, as the costs of the union would put an additional burden on the sorely troubled Russian economy.
11 *Narodna armia*, September 11, 1996.
12 "Ustav Soyuza Belarusi i Rossii" (Charter of the Union of Belarus and Russia), *Rossiiskaya gazeta*, May 24, 1997.
13 *Nezavisimaya gazeta*, May 28, 1997.
14 *Nezavisimaya gazeta*, April 5, 1997.
15 *Den*, July 15, 1997.
16 *Nezavisimaya gazeta*, April 22, 1997.
17 *Nezavisimaya gazeta*, May 21, 1997.
18 *Nezavisimost*, October 4, 1995.

[19] "Ustav Soyuza Belarusi i Rossii."

[20] Sanford, "Belarus on the Road to Statehood," p. 84; *Krasnaya zvezda*, March 15, 1997.

[21] *Nezavisimoe voennoe obozrenie*, no. 15, April 19–25, 1997.

[22] Ibid.

[23] Ibid.

[24] "Ustav Soyuza Belarusi i Rossii."

[25] *Vseukrainskiye vedomosti*, May 14, 1997.

[26] *Nezavisimaya gazeta*, January 15, 1997.

[27] *Vseukrainskiye vedomosti*, May 14, 1997.

[28] Ibid.

[29] "Osnovopolagayushii Akt o Vzaimnix Otnosheniyax, Sotrud-nichestvo, i Bezapasnosti Mezhdu Rossiiskoi Federetziei i Organi-zatsiei Severoatlanticheskovo Dogovora" (Founding Act on Mutual Relations, Cooperation, and Security between the Russian Federation and the North Atlantic Treaty Organization), *Nezavisimaya gazeta*, May 28, 1997.

[30] *Politika chas*, no. 5, 1996, p. 32.

6

The Place of Belarus on Russia's Foreign Policy Agenda

Vyacheslav Nikonov

The relationship between Russia and Belarus is unique in many respects and includes both vast opportunities and serious problems. Russia-Belarus relations are being cultivated on a different basis than relations between Russia and other CIS countries. In a number of areas the relationship is more advanced and less dependent on third parties' positions. But it is also relatively politicized and reactive to changes in domestic politics. While Belarus by no means constitutes an antidemocratic exception among the former USSR republics, it happens to be the only CIS country with which Russia has made human rights a top priority on the bilateral agenda.

In both Russia and Belarus, the issue of promoting bilateral relations, unlike other international issues, is an important factor in internal political debates and is of great interest to the public in the two countries, whose populations have few reasons to treat one another as ethnically different. Their historical, ethnic, and cultural commonality is quite obvious. Economic ties play a major role in bilateral relations, a testament to the former high level of economic integration between the two countries.

Belarus is the world's only country ready to maintain an allied relationship with Russia, as provided for in a Union Treaty signed by the two nations in 1997. Yet, the Union Treaty notwithstanding, bilateral relations have failed to achieve the scope and tone sought by both countries. The treaty provides for a form of integration that falls far short of the bar set by the EU in its integration process. Subsequent internal political events have slowed implementation of the treaty, leaving experts to talk about a crisis in Belarus-Russia relations and about their unpredictable future.

THE BELARUSIAN CONTEXT FOR BILATERAL RELATIONS

Following the breakup of the USSR, Belarus, like the other former Soviet republics, witnessed a debate on the appropriate nature of integration both within the CIS framework and with Russia. From the beginning, Belarus was more pro-integration than any other former Soviet republic. Belarus's policy of rapid rapprochement with Russia was a major factor in Aleksandr Lukashenko's victory in Belarus's first presidential elections, held in 1994. For the next two years the policy enjoyed unwavering support from the majority of parliamentary party factions and public groups.

The key opposition forces, the Belarusian Popular Front (BPF) and its ally, the Belarus Association of Servicemen, proposed, as a counterbalance to Russia, a Baltic–Black Sea community of nations, and a pro-Western and anti-Russian stance. By late 1994, other alternative concepts had emerged, including the notion of Belarus as a bridge between East and West. This proposal won the support of the right-wing and Communist factions in the parliament. In the fall of 1995, Stanislau Bogdankevich, leader of the right-center United Civil Party, urged Belarus to stay away from all unions and alliances.

The public revealed its sentiments in a May 1995 referendum, which asked Belarusians whether they "support the actions of the president of the Republic of Belarus toward economic integration with Russia." An overwhelming 82.4 percent answered "yes." Lukashenko's public approval ratings remained high in the wake of the April 1996 signing of a treaty creating a Community of Sovereign States between the two nations.

Dramatic changes in the internal balance of forces in Belarus occurred in the summer of 1996. The local Communist and Agrarian parties joined the anti-Lukashenko coalition, signaling a new spiral of confrontation between the president and the opposition. The novelty of the new stage was that, while previously the parties had differed on the issue of integration with Russia, this time around the opposition turned pro-Russian. Obviously it was a mere tactical ruse on the part of the anti-Lukashenko political establishment—the subject of Russia-Belarus unification became a key ideological mechanism widely used by the parties in the political and informational tug-of-war surrounding constitutional reform. The Communist Party of Belarus, which in August–November 1996 took over the helm of parliamentary and public opposition to the president, referred to the Russia-Belarus unification process as a top priority policy objective. When the Communists formed a coalition with certain extremely right-wing anti-Lukashenko opposition forces, however, they greatly diluted the public's perception that the president's opponents sought deeper integration with Russia. The president and his supporters quickly took advantage of this shift, so that most ordinary citizens came to view closer ties with Russia as the president's policy more than the Communists' policy.

The constitutional crisis in Belarus put Russia's leaders in a sensitive position. On the one hand, Moscow gave clear signals that it was not pleased with Lukashenko's unconstitutional moves. On the other hand, the president of Belarus did nothing that his Russian counterpart had not done in the fall of 1993 while still enjoying complete support in international public opinion. Having sent tanks to rip apart his own parliament, Yeltsin would hardly have been on solid moral ground pressuring Lukashenko to abandon his plan to amend the constitution through a referendum.

The constitutional reform in Belarus, based on the outcome of the November 24, 1996 referendum, produced a moderately authoritarian regime with a super-presidential form of government. The Kremlin's assessment of these events was generally negative, yet highly reserved, compared with the West's reaction. Moscow's restraint should be attributed to the fact that, in its CIS policies, Russia is forced to proceed not so much from European democratic standards as from the realities of the CIS. With this in mind, the referendum did not put Belarus far behind the other newly independent states in terms of political practices. Moscow would have applied a double standard had it laid serious blame at Lukashenko's door for violating democratic freedoms.

The new and tougher regime in Belarus had various implications for the Russia-Belarus relationship. On the one hand, the new Belarusian government might be more amenable to a closer relationship with Russia, considering Lukashenko's commitment to the idea of integration and the complete ouster of opposition forces from the republic's government structures. On the other hand, the new regime might discredit the integration process in the eyes of reform-minded forces, cause Russia to be accused of encouraging authoritarianism, generate fears for the future of democratic reforms in Russia itself, and set a highly unfavorable public relations background for future efforts at integration.

The constitutional reform created a much more visible divide between the pro- and anti-integration political forces in Belarus. The principal anti-integration forces in Belarus are the BPF, the United Civic Party, the Belarusian Social-Democratic Gromada Party, and such public groups as the Belarusian Language Association (named after Fransisk Skorina), the Union of Belarusian Poles, the Belarusian Student Association, the Belarusian School Association, and the Worldwide Association of Belarusians, known as Batskuscina. While numerically insignificant (with the exception of the BPF), all these organizations are well organized and increasingly influential among intellectuals, especially those based in Minsk. Many newspapers and weeklies, including *Narodnaya Volya, Svaboda, Imya, Beloruskaya gazeta, Nasha Niva, Pagonya, Byelorusskaya Maladyozhnaya, Zgoda,* and *Gramadzyanin,* have adopted the goals of these organizations. These organizations have also benefited from the support of the Russian media, primarily the ORT and NTV television channels. This support is particularly important in Belarus, considering that Russian television is on the air five times more than Belarusian television stations. Until Lukashenko's crackdown on foreign foundations in 1996–1997, the opposition also drew on the support of more than twenty foreign foundations active in Belarus.

The steps toward a Belarus-Russia union taken in early 1997 against the backdrop of Lukashenko's crackdown on internal opposition increased the activity of anti-integration forces in Belarus. The BPF, again leading the opposition, launched a series of street rallies in February 1997. As forces opposed to the president's regime (which the opposition claimed had been "imposed with Moscow's consent") gained momentum, the anti-president and anti-Russian rhetoric blended, and the opposition gained support among urban intellectuals and young people.

Among the main pro-integration forces in Belarus are the government and its agencies, the leadership of the Federation of Trade

Unions, the Communist Party, the Agrarian Party, the Liberal-Democratic Party, the Movement for Social Progress and Justice, the Party of All-Belarus Unity and Concord, and the Belarusian Patriotic Movement. President Lukashenko's hostility toward the leading political parties, however, including those that support integration and that only recently did a massive job of educating the public about the need for integration with Russia, makes any discussion of unity among pro-union forces irrelevant. In addition, the left-wing forces have split beyond repair, following their unnatural alliance with anti-president right-wingers and nationalists.

The Belarusian "party of power" that Lukashenko relies on brings together, in the first place, regional and capital city-based government officials, the president's appointees, top-level managers, and representatives of "the president's vertical line." In other words, the party of power controls the economy more than it constitutes a public and political force that shapes public opinion. The local government and economic elites—reluctant to relinquish power and end up "under Moscow's control"—are generally cautious about lessening differences with Russia.

Lukashenko's personal pro-integration enthusiasm dwindled after the referendum and constitutional reform (which made him the only real political force in Belarus), as a result of powerful shots fired at him by the Russian government and media. Lukashenko's visit to Moscow in March 1997 removed some of the misunderstanding and clarified the two countries' positions. In particular, Minsk made clear that it was prepared for gradual transformation of the association of Belarus and Russia into a union, the introduction of common citizenship, the formation of a series of bilateral agencies, and movement toward a single currency. Minsk agreed to these developments on the condition that the Belarusian president would play an appropriate role in decision making in the supranational bodies and, along with the Belarusian elite, would maintain his basic powers within the country. This position was recorded in the draft Union Charter.

Public debate about the Union Charter in April and May 1997 put Belarus-Russia relations to a serious test. The substance and tone of coverage by the Russian media (television, primarily) was not favorable to Lukashenko and was, at times, insulting toward the Belarusians. Discussion of the draft charter became so heated that many experts predicted an immediate political and psychological split in the government and intellectual elite of both countries.

A split was avoided, however, and in May 1997, Presidents Luka-shenko and Yeltsin signed a draft Union Charter. Polls indicated that 80 percent of the Belarusians supported the idea of the union but wanted Belarus to maintain its state sovereignty. The Belarusian electors, as well as members of the Belarusian elite, are apprehensive, though, that some of Russia's problems (wage arrears, high prices, and crime) may be exported to Belarus as a result of establishing the union. They also fear that Russia's criminalized capital assets may be used to buy Belarusian assets through privatization pro-grams. In the summer of 1997, Minsk authorities arrested correspon-dents from the Belarusian bureau of Russia's ORT television station for their strong criticism of the Lukashenko regime. This had a strong negative impact on bilateral relations, bringing them to a short temporary halt.

RUSSIAN ATTITUDES TOWARD INTEGRATION WITH BELARUS

Opinion polls in Russia indicate that public opinion favors a closer-knit relationship between Russia and Belarus. The Union Treaty was supported by more than 80 percent of Russians. Opinions on this issue come as close to a consensus as those on any other issue on Russia's agenda. Still there is not total agreement among the elite on issues of integration. To the contrary, Russia-Belarus relations have become a focal point of internal political debate, taking on a serious edge when the draft Union Charter was discussed in the spring of 1997. The debate revealed four principal approaches that are still relevant today: moderate pro-integration, anti-integration, full-fledged restoration of the USSR, and democratic super-integrationism.

The *moderately pro-integration approach* prevailed as the Union Treaty between Belarus and Russia was drafted. Critical support for the union came from part of the so-called party of power, including, and above all, Boris Yeltsin. Other supporters included the former prime ministers Viktor Chernomyrdin and Yevgeny Primakov, the senior management of Russia's fuel and energy complex, the corres-ponding industry ministers, the "power" ministers, and the foreign ministry. Support also came from factions in the Duma known as "Our Home is Russia" and "Russian Regions," and such influential politicians as Yuri Luzhkov and General Aleksandr Lebed, as well as most of the leaders of the constituent entities within the Russian Federation.

The moderate pro-integration group enlisted the support of various Russian media, including *Nezavisimaya gazeta, Trud, Rossiiskaya gazeta,* the radio station Mayak, television channels 3 and 5, regional publications, and regional television and radio studios. Moderate supporters of integration campaigned for early signing of the Union Treaty as an open-ended document that would evolve as Russia and Belarus drew closer together. To them, integration was a process that needed an early head start. They claimed that a relatively favorable context existed for rapprochement between the Russian Federation and Belarus: many of the original economic ties between the two countries had survived, and there was mutual interest in building them up. The policy of rapprochement enjoyed public support in both countries, catered to the intentions of the nations' leaders, and meshed with the purposes of most political parties and movements.

According to the advocates of integration, a closer relationship with Belarus is basically in Russia's national interest, bringing with it a number of geopolitical and, in the longer run, economic advantages. Supporters of integration see the possibilities for a stronger Russian position in Central Europe, satisfactory solutions to the issues of advancing transport routes and energy transmission lines from Russia to the rest of Europe, and expansion of the common economic space. Belarus's semi-authoritarian political regime is seen as a serious, but by no means insurmountable, obstacle to closer relations between the two countries (just as the existence of one-man power regimes in certain autonomous Russian entities does not prevent them from being part of the Russian Federation). The differences in the economies of Russia and Belarus could be gradually evened out as a result of implementation of the Union Treaty, while without the treaty, the differences in the two economies would only grow. Meanwhile, human rights issues could be more successfully tackled in the context of integration.

Without considering long-term integration plans (for instance, the totally impracticable creation of a single state), moderate proponents of integration supported a "one plus one" association in the form of a union between Russia and Belarus, that is, a mechanism that could deepen integration and still respect the sovereignty of both partners. In their opinion, the time factor, at least in the medium term, does not favor unification because every practical step for bringing the Russian Federation and Republic of Belarus closer results in an outcry from anti-integration forces within the two countries and elsewhere.

The second most influential approach to Russia-Belarus relations is the *anti-integration approach.* This group received its most prominent government support from then deputy prime minister Anatoly Chubais and has been treated sympathetically by some federal government agencies (the economy ministry, the finance ministry, and some parts of the Central Bank, the State Tax Administration, the State Property Committee, and the State Customs Committee). This group relies on the more popular media, such as Channels 1, 2, and 4 on national television, the newspapers *Izvestia, Moskovsky Komsomolets, Segodnya,* and several others.

Opponents of integration reflect a whole array of forces (each driven by its own considerations) opposed to closer Russia-Belarus relations, including:

- liberal economic quarters that still believe that the former Soviet republics present a burden for the Russian economy

- various democratic forces that are not opposed to the concept of unification, but that unequivocally reject dealing with the current Belarusian leadership because of its authoritarian nature, and

- forces within the Russian bureaucracy, primarily in the federal center, that are apprehensive about having to compete with their Belarusian counterparts once the latter gain access to the inner workings of Russia's government.

Consistent political opposition to integration has been mounted by Yegor Gaidar's Democratic Choice of Russia and Grigory Yavlinsky's Yabloko in the Duma that—in this situation—speak from liberal economic and political positions. The anti-integration forces among the Russian elite argue that unification with Belarus will deal a blow to the Russian economy, given that genuine economic integration is impossible anyway because the economic systems of Russia and Belarus differ today more than ever before.

Opponents of integration argue that, in the event of unification, Lukashenko will head the new single state—a difficult argument to buy because unification of the two states is not on the agenda. They also argue that formation of supra-national bodies is unconstitutional in the Russian Federation, that both countries will lose their sovereignty, that the constituent republics within the Russian Federation may be tempted to press for even greater autonomy, and that the governing bodies of the union will be used to tip the balance of forces at the top level in Russia. Critics of integration place particular emphasis on Belarus's poor human rights record, the illegitimacy of the Belarusian parliament, and therefore, the illegitimacy of its ratification of the Union Treaty.

The Communists and the nationalist opposition support a third approach, something more ambitious than integration or even union: they seek *full-fledged restoration of the USSR*, with union between Russia and Belarus as a first step. This group also relies on the bureaucracies of the Communist Party of the Russian Federation and the Liberal-Democratic Party, their parliamentary factions, the Power to the People faction, and the Agrarian faction in the Duma. In terms of media support, they count on their own publications, such as *Pravda, Sovetskaya Rossia, Pravda Zhirinovskogo,* and a number of independent media outlets. The group includes Gennady Zyuganov, the Communist leader, Gennady Seleznyov, speaker of the State Duma, and Vladimir Zhirinovsky, leader of the Liberal-Democratic Party, and others.

The restoration-seekers see the Belovezh Agreements of 1991, which put an end to the USSR, as legally invalid and argue that Russia and Belarus have never ceased to be parts of a single state. They support the Union Treaty and accuse Yeltsin of being reluctant to create a single state with Belarus, pointing to a "fifth column" within the Yeltsin government that has allegedly been undermining the process of unification.

The restoration-seekers prefer the Belarusian economic and political model to the Russian model. They see early unification with Belarus as part of an effort to counteract NATO expansion to the east. Restoration proponents have some serious advocates in the Parliamentary Assembly of the Union, which has already voted for the red flag with the sickle and hammer emblem and for the USSR national emblem as the state symbols of the Belarus-Russia Union. While the Parliamentary Assembly's decisions have no legal force, restoration seekers can still inflict serious damage on the integration process by discrediting it in the eyes of the public, who are far from enthusiastic about any prospects for reemergence of the USSR.

The fourth approach could be summed up as *democratic super-integrationism*. It has been structured around the "Unity" movement led by Nikolai Gonchar, a deputy in the State Duma. The movement, formed in July 1997, has been campaigning for a referendum on unification and actual inclusion of Belarus as a subject of the Russian Federation or as six additional provinces. According to its proponents, super-integration would speed up democratic and market reforms in Belarus and dethrone Lukashenko. At the final stage of discussion of the Union Treaty, certain leaders of the republics within the Russian Federation who were critical of union with Belarus, such as Mintimer Shaimiyev, Ruslan Aushev, and Murtaza Rakhimov, took a similar position.

The 1997 arrest in Belarus of correspondents from the Belarusian bureau of Russia's state-run television station, ORT, enabled the anti-integration forces to go on the offensive, and their influence grew visibly, counterbalanced only with the appointment of Yevgeny Primakov as prime minister in August 1998. Rank-and-file Russians had a highly negative reaction to the arrest of Russian television reporters in Belarus. According to the Public Opinion Foundation, a mere 10 percent of the Russian population supported the actions of the Belarusian authorities. By September 1997, Lukashenko's approval ratings had plummeted to a paltry 9 percent, while a staggering 54 percent said they did not trust him. (His approval ratings were never high: in December 1996, only 17 percent of those polled approved of his policies, 23 percent did not trust him, and 42 percent had difficulty answering the questions.) Nonetheless, Russians' support of the very idea of a union with Belarus remained virtually unchanged despite the arrests.

INTERNATIONAL ASPECTS OF INTEGRATION

Originally Belarus gave less priority to its European policies than any other Central or Eastern European country. A vast majority of the population and political elite in Belarus does not identify strongly with Central and Eastern Europe. Instead, it still feels nostalgic about the days of the USSR and remains pro-Russian.

Belarus first registered its commonality with the other countries of Central and Eastern Europe in the preamble of the June 23, 1992 Polish-Belarusian Treaty on Good-Neighborliness and Friendly

Cooperation by acknowledging the "ethnic and cultural proximity of the Polish and Belarusian peoples." In July 1994, Belarus obtained associate membership in the Central European Initiative,[1] allowing the country's representatives to attend meetings of its working groups on transport, energy, and the environment. Belarus attended the meetings, sending the prime minister and foreign minister as observers. In the fall of 1994, during a visit of the speaker of the Belarusian parliament to Poland, the issue of Belarus joining the Central European Visegrad Group, as well as the Central European Agreement on Free Trade (CEFTA) was raised. The possibility of the Baltics, Romania, Ukraine, and Belarus joining CEFTA was discussed at Poland's initiative by member countries at a November 1994 meeting in Poznan.

Shortly after his election as president, Lukashenko spoke of his intention to establish clearly Belarus's position in Central and Eastern Europe and to give higher priority to Europe in Belarus's foreign policy. Lukashenko noted that the "republic intends to fly with two wings, as it were, that of the West and that of the East," and to base its relationships on pragmatism or "on interests, first of all, economic." He nevertheless emphasized that

> . . . we are prepared for mutual cooperation with all countries. However, our top priority is, of course, Russia. After all, at this point in time, 75–80 percent of our exports and imports are hooked up with Russia. Such realities are not to be ignored. Not that we could realistically target any other markets either: the world market has long since been carved up and nobody in its Western segment is anxious for us to arrive.

The Belarusian foreign ministry also stated its intention to balance better the nation's policy along the West-East axis while continuing to treat relations with Russia as its top priority. Other important foreign policy objectives, according to the foreign ministry, were to enhance ties with Ukraine, Poland, Lithuania, and Latvia. Belarus demonstrated its commitment to these goals by keeping a higher profile in Central and Eastern Europe. Even as a customs union between the Russian Federation and the Republic of Belarus was being signed in January 1995, the Belarusian and Polish prime ministers conferred in Brest, reaching agreement on economic issues. The issue of oil deliveries was also dealt with in January, in a bilateral Russia-Belarus agreement giving Belarus access to energy resources at prices almost matching domestic Russian prices, in exchange for duty-free transit through its territory.

Shortly afterward Lukashenko paid official visits to Latvia and Lithuania. During a February 1995 visit to Vilnius, he discussed Belarus's possible contribution to the construction of an oil terminal in the city of Buting and a pipeline to the Novopolotsk refinery. According to Lukashenko, these projects would provide Belarus with an alternative source of energy and "freedom of economic maneuver." He made it clear, however, that he was opposed to Russia's exclusion from the project.

Western nations place low foreign policy priority on Belarus compared with the priority they give Central and Eastern European countries and other former Soviet republics. Europeans have noted the slow emergence of democratic institutions in Belarus and put the Republic of Belarus at the bottom of the waiting list for membership in the Council of Europe. Germany was the only Western nation to develop economic ties of any significance with Belarus.

Relations between Belarus and its Western neighbors are being aggravated by NATO's expansion to the east, seen as a negative development by both Belarus and Russia. The April 1996 agreement signed by Russia and Belarus creating a Community of Sovereign States did not raise serious concerns in the West, however. The West saw it more as a propaganda ploy used by the two presidents to accomplish short-term political goals—helping Yeltsin get reelected and supporting Lukashenko in his squabble with the Belarusian parliament.

After Lukashenko disbanded the parliament and toughened his political regime, the West grew increasingly critical of Minsk's policies and the Belarus-Russia rapprochement. Based on observer missions to Minsk in December 1997, the Organization for Security and Cooperation in Europe (OSCE) and the Council of Europe demanded that the outcome of the December referendum be reviewed. Meanwhile, the U.S. State Department recommended that American businessmen refrain from doing business with the current Belarusian regime and that they move their investments to neighboring countries.

The transformation of the Russia-Belarus Community into a union in April 1997 did generate controversy in the West. While the U.S.

State Department never saw a big difference, the European Parliament expressed a high level of displeasure in its April 10 resolution, which called for ratification of the Union Treaty to be postponed until democratic institutions evolved in Belarus.

At the same time, it would be wrong to say that the West fully shut the door on contacts with official Minsk. Contacts at the institutional level continued, with Poland and Ukraine frequently acting as intermediaries between the West and Belarus. According to several Polish politicians, complete international isolation of Belarus would be counterproductive. In the words of a high-ranking official of the European Commission, "Poland has long been trying to convince the West not to give up its efforts to draw Belarus into its sphere of influence. Poland has suggested carrot and stick treatment for Minsk as the only possible solution."

Relations between Belarus and the external world worsened considerably in 1998, following Lukashenko's demands that foreign ambassadors abandon their residences in the Drozdy governmental complex, ostensibly for planned building repairs. In the scandal that followed, Moscow unsuccessfully attempted to convince Minsk that its action was counterproductive and thereafter preferred to consider the incident an internal affair of Belarus.

In spite of the country's growing international isolation, an IMF mission began work in Belarus in November 1998. This mission did not rule out the possibility of rendering emergency financial aid to Belarus on the condition that it begin moving forward with market reforms. These talks continued in December 1998, a positive sign.

The CIS adopted a fairly neutral response to the Russia-Belarus union, with the exception of the irritation shown by the presidents of Kazakhstan and Ukraine. Their irritation was largely attributable to the fact that the union between the Russian Federation and Belarus and their plans for single citizenship would encourage large numbers of ethnic Russians in Kazakhstan and Ukraine to pressure their own governments into integration with Russia. Moreover, Kiev feared that a closer relation between Russia and Belarus might weaken Ukraine's economic positions, above all because Russian pipelines would no longer need to go through Ukraine to reach Western markets.

Russian political experts, both those favoring and opposing the Russia-Belarus rapprochement, agree on most of the positive and negative implications of that process for the Russian Federation. Russian analysts have identified the following advantages of a closer relationship with Belarus:

- direct access to the borders of the Central European region, that is, Belarus as a window to Europe

- removal of the potential threat of a so-called Baltic Sea–Black Sea belt that could isolate Russia

- additional leverage for influencing Russia's relationship with Ukraine

- a stronger position for Russia's dialogue with Poland and, to a lesser degree, its dialogue with the Baltics

- an active role model for further rapprochement in the pro-integration nucleus of the CIS (Russia, Belarus, Kazakhstan, Kyrgyzstan, and, possibly, the entire commonwealth)

- overall strengthening of Russia's position in the international political arena as a result of Russia's ability to complete successfully such a large-scale undertaking as formation of a union with an independent neighbor

- optimization of Russia's overall strategic situation vis-à-vis the West

- improvement of the situation around the Kaliningrad region

- additional room to maneuver within the CFE Treaty, and

- new opportunities for improving Russia's air defenses and anti-missile defenses.

The negative international implications, according to Russian analysts, include the possibility of a number of nations adopting individual or coordinated policies to neutralize Russia's newly acquired advantages. The main components of such policies may be:

- faster expansion of NATO (in military, more than political, terms) to the Central European nations and the creation of a forward-based infrastructure. (It should be noted that influential Russian politicians and experts do not view the Russia-Belarus rapprochement in the context of NATO expansion; in their opinion the parties to the union have diverse national interests requiring their integration, the future of NATO notwithstanding.)

- Polish-Ukrainian and Polish-Lithuanian rapprochement, as well as further consolidation of the Baltics, both trends that narrow Russia's room for maneuver

- increased Western interest in Ukraine, resulting in efforts to undermine the Russia-Ukraine partnership model

- increased differences between Russia and the West. (While Western nations are bound to a certain extent by their previous statements to accept Russia-Belarus integration if accomplished through democratic procedures, they nevertheless may try to mobilize their allies to prevent such unification or, subsequently, to split up the union of Russia and Belarus.)

- indirect economic pressure by the West in the form of a continued reduction of financial aid to Russia and continued refusal to provide financial and economic assistance to Belarus's economy, using the pretext that if Russia has the resources to perform large-scale political measures, it should not count on international aid.

In the opinion of Russian analysts, most of these negative tendencies are already a reality and will continue to be irritants in the future, even without any Russia-Belarus integration. On the whole, however, Moscow assumes that the West will not risk open confrontation if Russia forges closer links with Belarus. Rapprochement is viewed as a process that, while not serving the interests of the West, is fairly predictable and natural, considering the similarities between the Russian and Belarusian peoples, and it invokes an analogy with the recent reunification of Germany.

INTEGRATING ECONOMIC AND TRADE POLICIES

Since becoming independent, neither Russia nor Belarus has ever seriously questioned the need for close economic, military, and political integration. The interest in economic integration springs from their strongly interconnected economies. Belarus had been among the most advanced Soviet republics and, by Soviet standards, possessed high-tech production facilities, highly skilled labor, and a ramified infrastructure. It was home to advanced and large-scale specialized companies putting out finished products, while components, materials, and fuel arrived primarily from Russia. Belarus was a long-standing supplier of meat and dairy products, potatoes, and flax, while remaining strongly dependent on Russia for supplies of a few items such as fodder grain.

Economic integration with Belarus promised Russia a number of obvious advantages:

- a larger domestic market
- the ability to use Belarus's highly advantageous geographic and economic position and its well-developed transport and foreign trade infrastructure to advance common economic interests
- access to a reliable transport corridor for shipping goods to the West, especially gas and, subsequently, oil
- guaranteed deliveries of vital supplies to the Kaliningrad region, and
- restoration of old and creation of new production ties between Russian and Belarusian industrial entities.

One important prerequisite for integration has been a comparable level of economic development. After the breakup of the USSR, Belarus ranked first among the CIS republics in per capita GNP and third in industrial output, food production, and light industrial output. The subsequent crisis in the Belarusian economy largely resulted from the rupture of former economic ties, reduced deliveries of Russian oil (by 1993 oil deliveries had shrunk to one-third of their 1990 levels), discontinued production of outdated technology, and slashed military production. These factors worked together to reduce Belarus's GDP by 36 percent from 1992 through 1996. Russia's GDP dropped by 38 percent for similar reasons during the same period. Because of the different structure of the decline, however, average income in Russia was almost double the Belarusian figure. Nonetheless, Belarus was able to pay wages and salaries without delays, to keep prices at lower levels, and to avoid the dramatic income stratification that occurred in Russia.

Russia has remained Belarus's principal trading partner, accounting for 52 percent of its foreign trade. Belarus relies fully on Russia for its oil and gas consumption. In the 1990s Belarus received from Russia, on average, 70 percent of its ferrous imports, more than 50 percent of its cement, about 80 percent of mineral fertilizer, almost 100 percent of its industrial wood, 100 percent of trucks, 70 percent of tractors, and 100 percent of its grain-harvesting combines.

From Russia's perspective, Belarus is a meaningful foreign trade partner, but not a top priority. Belarus accounts for 4 percent of Russia's overall foreign trade. A serious incentive for bilateral trade was provided by the 1995 Customs Union of Russia, Belarus, and Kazakhstan, and by the abolition of customs duties. Within two years Russia's exports to the other members of the Customs Union grew by 40 percent (less real export revenues, because some of Russia's export receivables remained unpaid).

Many provisions in the Customs Union agreement have yet to be implemented, however, and the system of foreign trade regulation in Belarus has yet to be coordinated with Russia's, as provided for when the Customs Union was formed. Although customs tariffs on four hundred items were unified in March 1997, differences remained in the customs duties on sixteen items, in the taxation of excise goods (sixty groups of goods), and in customs clearance fees. No single value-added tax exemption on imports of production equipment has been established yet, and there is a long "to-do" list remaining. Considerable differences also remain in Russia's and Belarus's preferential trade regimes regarding the list of countries, goods, and level of benefits.

The lack of coordination between the regulatory frameworks of the two countries, when the common customs zone was formed, encouraged illegal importation of alcohol, tobacco, and other excise goods. In 1996, illegal alcohol imports through Belarus cost Russia an estimated 6,000 billion rubles. To address this situation, Belarus introduced mandatory licensing of alcohol imports as of January 1, 1997. Belarus, for its part, also suffers from hidden damages as a result of imports through Russian territory. It is still unclear how the members of the Customs Union will participate in international trade, if they join the World Trade Organizations at different times, with Kyrgyzstan being the first to join.

Russian entrepreneurs have mentioned that the investment environment in Belarus is reasonably favorable, primarily because of the almost total lack of competition in the local capital market. The most widespread form of Russian investment in Belarus is joint project development and financial-industrial groups. As a result of the increasingly statist nature of the Belarusian economy, however, certain restrictions slow the growth of investment and full-scale economic integration.

The policy of economic integration of the Russian Federation and Republic of Belarus included a set of measures to coordinate the legislation and economic policies of both nations. As stated in Article 4 of the April 2, 1996 agreement on the Community, Russia and Belarus "as of late 1997 shall synchronize the stages, schedule, and depth of economic reform, and create a single regulatory basis to remove any interstate barriers and obstacles." Although Belarus started bringing its finance, budget, trade, and other legislation in line with Russia's as early as 1993, considerable differences remain in the regulatory frameworks of the two countries.

President Yeltsin has repeatedly noted that the two countries must conduct reform at similar speeds, otherwise there cannot be any integration. The official Belarusian press has suggested that Moscow came up with the idea of "reform synchronization" to avoid making real moves toward integration. In April 1997, however, the Supreme Council of the Association of Russia and Belarus approved a program of synchronization of economic reform. There has been little progress on implementing the program. The Belarusian economy is still being managed on the basis of government programs. Under the current privatization schedule, 70 percent of the companies will not be denationalized until 2000. By late 1998, just over 20 percent of the country's enterprises had been privatized, most of them small businesses. Meanwhile, the government continues to regulate the prices of a large number of goods.

There are differences between the two countries' budget policies, as well as their budget revenue and expenditure structures. In Russia the revenues of the consolidated budget account for 27 percent of GDP, while in Belarus they exceed 50 percent of GDP. The principal rates of the value-added tax and the profits tax are similar, but Belarus has many more taxes, excise goods, and tax breaks and exemptions than Russia. The Belarusian budget provides for much more significant expenditures on social programs and support for the economy. The two nations' policies of covering the budget deficit differ dramatically as well. Until August 1998, Russia relied primarily on external and internal borrowing, while in Belarus the budget deficit is credited directly by the National Bank.

Although Belarus features relatively strict exchange controls, including restrictions on currency purchases, these have failed to keep the Belarusian ruble stable. Experts have attributed the early

1998 aggravation of the crisis in Belarusian currency markets to the government's policy of maintaining an unjustifiably high exchange rate for the national currency through administrative measures. While certain shifts toward a more liberal currency market in Belarus are taking place, there is still a long way to go before an economic agent can freely buy foreign currencies at the local currency market.

The financial crisis that crushed Russia in August 1998 had serious repercussions for the Belarusian economy. The anti-crisis measures developed by the Belarusian government remain statist. They include an expansionary monetary policy, indexation of working capital, crediting of the budget deficit, direct financing of the economy (in particular, housing construction and key production facilities), netting of mutual arrears, and debt restructuring to solve the problem of delayed payments.

In Russia many private enterprises and banks have weakened, and the government has started to take care of state food reserves and to discuss plans to support local producers. As the liberal newspaper *Izvestia* stated on October 17, 1998 (exaggerating the facts to some extent), "the breakdown of inconsequential Russian reforms has turned our economy back to the status that the Belarusian economy never left."

In Belarus the opposite trend has occurred. The financial crisis stimulated faster reforms, a fact that became obvious in the gradual liberalization of the national currency rate and the canceling of government price controls on a large group of items, including energy. Financial troubles in Russia have thus destroyed some barriers that stood in the way of economic integration of the two countries.

Differences in their economic mechanisms continue to invalidate all attempts at unifying the national monetary systems, however. After the two countries signed a monetary agreement in April 1994 (which still awaits implementation), integration of their monetary systems became a subject of a divisive political debate. Belarusian industrialists and bankers on the whole have hailed the idea of a single ruble zone. They are attracted to the idea of common prices for energy and raw materials within the common ruble zone, removal of many barriers to Belarusian exports, and mobilization of additional hard currency resources for economic restructuring. The Belarusian opposition, conversely, stated clearly that unification of the two monetary systems would be equivalent to Belarus giving up its independence.

The concept of monetary union also came under strong fire from liberal-monetarist Russian economists and politicians. They argued that the mechanism of a ruble zone, including hidden price subsidies, would be used to transfer a sizable chunk of Russia's GDP to Belarus and that, as a result, implementation of the agreement would place a heavy burden on the Russian budget and produce yet another inflation spiral. In late February 1995, the Russian government issued a statement declaring monetary union a matter for the future. In December 1998, it was agreed again in principle to attempt such a currency union in 1999.

In 1996 the Belarusian government invited the Russian government and central bank to start negotiations on linking the Belarusian ruble to the Russian ruble and on mutual convertibility of the two currencies in their respective domestic markets. In early March 1997, the Central Bank of Russia and the National Bank of Belarus signed an agreement to phase in a market-based exchange control mechanism in Belarus, that would bring its exchange controls more in line with Russia's. The agreement provided, in the long term, for transactions at the internal currency market rate of the partner country, including access to bidding at currency exchanges. By the end of 1997, the commercial banks of the two countries were to be able to freely convert their balances in Russian or Belarusian rubles in corresponding accounts in the banks of the partner country into third-country currencies, including hard currencies. The central banks of both countries intended to pursue a single policy of setting the exchange rates of their national currencies. In August 1997, however, the Central Bank of Russia suspended its negotiations with the National Bank of Belarus indefinitely, because the latter had failed to honor any of the provisions in the March 1997 agreement.

In December 1998, Lukashenko renewed negotiations with Victor Geraschenko, chairman of the Central Bank of Russia, in the hope of supporting the Belarusian exchange rate and allowing Belarus to pay for Russian goods with Belarusian rubles. Geraschenko reacted cautiously, however, and both sides instead agreed to prepare a plan for the gradual establishment of a common currency system to begin in 1999. Little, however, has been accomplished since then.

MILITARY INTEGRATION ISSUES

Both Russia and Belarus have a clear interest in military and military-technical integration. Belarus has assumed obligations to ensure the collective security of CIS members within the Tashkent Treaty framework, and has entered into a number of bilateral agreements on military cooperation with Russia. In July 1992, Belarus and Russia agreed to coordinate military activities and set forth principles for mutual technical and logistical support for the armed forces and for the training of officers at military education establishments. They also agreed to bilateral cooperation in the military economy, in the material and technical support for the armed forces, in social and cadre problems, and in research programs.

Removal of Russia's nuclear weapons from Belarus became a serious avenue of cooperation. Removal of tactical nuclear weapons was completed in April 1992. In May 1992, Belarus signed the Lisbon Protocol providing, in part, for the dismantling of eighty-one SS-25 ICBMs. In February 1993, Belarus ratified START-I and acceded to the Non-Proliferation Treaty. Russia supported Belarus's proposal for a nuclear-free zone that would include Belarus, Ukraine, and the Baltics. Withdrawal of Russian nuclear forces was complete by late 1996.

Military-technical cooperation was effected in accordance with a special agreement signed in October 1993, based on interaction in the areas of development, production, supplies, maintenance, and repair of arms and military technology. Belarus manufactures few, if any, finished military products, and its military production relies on cooperation with the Russian defense complex. Currently 180 Russian defense works maintain production ties with 120 entities within the Belarusian military-industrial complex. Many Belarusian military works still hold monopolies in the CIS markets.

Russia's defense interests were taken into account in bilateral agreements signed in 1995 covering various military facilities located in the territory of Belarus—the Baranovichi complex (an early warning missile attack radar) and the Vileika naval low-frequency radio station (part of a submarine tracking system). Under the agreements, Russia would continue to use these facilities for twenty-five years.

After a visit by the Russian defense minister to Minsk in December 1995, the sides signed eighteen documents expressing their intentions to boost cooperation within the common military-strategic space, to engage in cooperative military production and standardization of armaments, and to use defense facilities jointly. The parties signed three protocols covering specific areas of interaction: (1) on regional strategic planning within the Tashkent Collective Security Treaty; (2) on joint combat duty of air defense forces and weaponry within the unified air defense system of the CIS member states; and (3) on the main avenues of bilateral military cooperation between the air defense troops of Russia and Belarus.

Under the Union Treaty, Belarus and Russia have agreed, if necessary, to take joint measures to prevent threats to either party's sovereignty and independence, to coordinate military buildup activities, to use military infrastructure jointly, and to cooperate on border issues. Military cooperation is being hampered, however, by Belarus's independent policy of selling Russian-made arms to Sudan, Yemen, Iran, Iraq, China, Vietnam, and other countries. A good example of the problems these sales have caused is the scandal involving the delivery of MiG-29 fighters from Belarus to Peru. Components and maintenance guarantees were originally to be supplied by MAPO, the Russian manufacturer, which only learned about the transaction after the fact. Naturally, MAPO refused to be involved.

Minsk is prepared to engage in close military cooperation with Russia, but its Russian counterparts are concerned about their own internal military reform and slashed military expenditures. Nevertheless, military cooperation remains the most advanced area of Russian-Belarusian relations.

POLITICAL INTEGRATION

The actual level of political integration between Belarus and Russia remains a mystery. The main principles and objectives of the union are fairly abstract and have no concrete mechanisms to rely on. The implementation record thus far is poor. The interstate bodies brought into existence by the 1996 Community Agreement and provided for by the 1997 Union Treaty create a detailed but poorly functioning political infrastructure.

The future of Russia-Belarus integration depends largely on how quickly the two nations and their leaders leave behind the crises in their relationship that began to brew after the signing of the Union Treaty. The vendetta between Lukashenko and the Russian press has prompted Yeltsin to take an increasingly tough position on the observance of journalists' rights in Belarus. Nor is mutual understanding in any way promoted by the Belarusian president's occasional attacks on "opponents of integration within the Russian government," who allegedly have prevented implementation of the agreements. Direct cooperation between Belarus and some of Russia's regions angered Yeltsin, who virtually ordered Lukashenko not to operate in Russia other than through the Kremlin. This problem was settled in 1998, and with Moscow's approval Belarus has concluded partnership agreements with sixty out of the eighty-nine regions of the Russian Federation.

Nonetheless, the deeper the tensions in the Belarus-Russia relationship, the more difficult it becomes for both presidents to save face. Supporters of the union in the Russian government have been working to resolve the impasse and to establish practical cooperation. In the fall of 1997, an upsurge of diplomatic activity culminated in the release from police custody of Pavel Sheremet, head of ORT's Belarusian bureau, a step that removed a major irritant from bilateral relations. The Primakov government radically downgraded the human rights issue but was itself too distracted by internal problems to heal the political rifts.

The Russia-Belarus union is based on the principles of "sovereign equality of the member states" and, in the long term, seeks consistent movement toward a voluntary association of the member states on the basis of free expression of will by their peoples. Citizenship in the union is seen as a way of achieving a greater degree of unity, but the charter provides only for quasi-citizenship: for instance, a citizen of one country can vote in another country's elections only up to the municipal level.

Important objectives and goals, such as the coordination of positions and actions when dealing with common political issues, coordination of national legal environments, and formation of a common legal environment, have yet to get off the ground. Russia has no effective leverage to advance "promotion of democracy in the Union, and observance and protection of the rights and basic freedoms of the individual and citizens," as provided for in the charter. This lack of leverage continuously creates friction in the Moscow-Minsk relationship.

The Supreme Council of the Union, comprised of the two presidents, the prime ministers, and the speakers of both houses of parliament, went for months without a single meeting. Its first meeting took place in January 1998, when two main issues were discussed: coordination of foreign policy and the budget for the union. The 1998 budget was approved in the amount of 585 million rubles (65 percent contributed by Russia, 35 percent by Belarus). The two sides plan to finance thirty joint programs in the fields of industry, agriculture, customs and frontier infrastructure, and science and culture. The 1999 union budget was increased by 100 million rubles, but given the devaluation of the ruble, it actually represents a decline in real terms.

Under the Union Treaty, the Parliamentary Assembly of the Union, comprised of thirty-six delegates from each of Russia's and Belarus's top legislatures, meets twice a year and has authority to pass legal acts that have the status of "legislative recommendations." The first meeting of the Parliamentary Assembly showed it to be dominated by left-wing and pro-communist forces and lacking in constructive ideas. The experience could hardly convince Yeltsin of the need to accelerate "the creation of conditions for the transformation of the Parliamentary Assembly into a representative and legislative body elected directly by citizens" as provided for in the charter.

The standing Executive Committee of the Union, with its sizable bureaucracy, is busy doing routine work that has little influence on the nature of political relations and public opinion in either country. Planned meetings of the Supreme Council of Russia and Belarus were delayed several times in 1998 because of Yeltsin's health problems.

During the Russia-Belarus summit of December 1998, both presidents managed to agree only on "auditing the performance" of implementing previous agreements and presidential decrees on integration. On the completion of his visit Lukashenko declared that he had submitted to Yeltsin proposals to strengthen the alliance. A week later, the specifics of these proposals were outlined in a Declaration of Further Unification of Russia and Belarus, signed suddenly by Yeltsin and Lukashenko. That document expressed their firm intent to continue a gradual movement toward voluntary association in the union, while preserving the national sovereignty of both countries (whatever that may mean).

By mid-1999, an Agreement on the Union State was to have been designed and submitted to referenda in both Russia and Belarus. By a time not specified in the declaration, the union's governing bodies, common budget, and mechanisms of joint policy making in the spheres of international affairs, defense, and security will be formed. Yeltsin and Lukashenko plan to unify economic and civil legislation and to create a common tax zone and monetary system. The declaration stresses the importance of protecting human rights and liberties in the union in accordance with universally recognized principles of international law. Obviously, as liberal forces gain strength in Russia, the chief opponents of integration will increasingly be put on the defensive, and the possibilities for mutual rapprochement will grow accordingly.

NOTES

[1] The Central European Initiative (CEI) was established in 1989. Since then it has significantly expanded its membership. It aims at European integration and supports member countries that are not yet EU members, but that are seeking EU membership. It also seeks to enhance regional cooperation.

7

Belarus in U.S. Foreign Policy

Robert Legvold

In U.S. foreign policy, Belarus occupies the worst of two worlds. On the one hand, it exists in the largely forgotten recesses of memory. Among top policy makers it captures little regular attention and in the U.S. Congress and media almost none at all—except, from time to time, for the anger of a handful of senators. On the other hand, what there is of U.S. policy toward Belarus resembles rather curiously U.S. policy toward hostile communist regimes during the cold war. Because the Belarusian government responds in kind, relations between the two countries have slipped from an unassuming start at the time of Belarusian independence in 1991 to an odd echo of a now dead age.

How did this happen? Why has this relationship above all others between the United States and the states of the former Soviet Union taken on such an embittered character? In what follows, I address not only these questions but also the undulations in U.S. aims and approaches toward Belarus since independence in 1991. Because Belarus is not a marginal, but a potentially crucial, factor in Central European security, I also offer thoughts about the adequacy of U.S. policy and make suggestions for ways that it might be adjusted to address better the Belarusian challenge.

Comparing current U.S.-Belarusian relations to those in cold war times is not simply exaggeration for effect. In important respects, the relationship has taken on characteristics from the past. First, the policy of each country toward the other rests on a basic suspicion that leadership on the other side embraces values basically at variance with its own, pursues objectives threatening to its interests, and frequently acts in bad faith. Second, each leadership at moments permits itself to engage in a level of recrimination similar to the sharp language of the earlier period. The Belarusian president accuses the United States of trying to destabilize his country,[1] while spokesmen for the U.S. government complain about the destruction of democratic aspirations in Belarus and President Lukashenko's "expanding dictatorship."[2] Third, the relationship is regularly marred by incidents characteristic of the earlier era: on the Belarusian side, by expulsions of U.S. diplomats for attending anti-government demonstrations; on the U.S. side, by granting political asylum to Belarusian dissident politicians based on their "well-founded fear of persecution were [they] to return to [their] country."[3] Fourth, and most important, the United States now deals with Belarus chiefly by using a combination of carrots and sticks (mostly sticks), an approach closely paralleling U.S. policy toward Soviet allies during the cold war. Belarus, too weak to use carrots and sticks in its dealings with the United States, substitutes the same hard shell of indifference to American importuning as Warsaw Pact countries once did fifteen years ago.

TRACING THE EVOLUTION OF RELATIONS

On February 4, 1993, the Belarusian Supreme Soviet ratified the START-I treaty and the Lisbon Protocol by an overwhelming margin and, later the same day, Belarus's status as a non-nuclear power under the nuclear Non-Proliferation Treaty. This was the high-water mark in U.S.-Belarusian relations. Belarus had been the first of the former Soviet republics to give up nuclear weapons. Unlike Ukraine and, more feebly, Kazakhstan, it did so without attaching conditions. Three months earlier, in November 1992, the parliament had already committed the country to a future without nuclear weapons and to a schedule for removing them twice as fast as was called for by the START agreement.[4] To the United States, whose overriding concern in the months after the collapse of the Soviet Union was to short-circuit the proliferation of nuclear weapons to any post-Soviet state other than Russia, Belarus had done the single most important thing it could.

Moreover, Belarus had taken this decision as part of a distinctly benign foreign policy conception. By the original Declaration of State Sovereignty of July 1990, adopted a year and a half before the Soviet Union came apart, the country had committed itself to "neutrality," "nonparticipation in military blocs," and a non-nuclear status. Stanislau Shushkevich, speaker of the parliament and head of state, vigorously embraced these ideas. They were given substance by the apparent large-scale reductions in conventional military power called for by Paval Kazlouski, the new minister of defense, when he arrived in office in April 1992. Kazlouski, to the applause of Washington, wanted to junk the massive, heavily armored, offensively oriented forces left on Belarusian soil after the demise of the Soviet Union, and to replace them with a force half the size, lighter, and more defensively postured.

If the new Clinton administration did not lavish praise and rewards on Belarus as one might have expected, maybe it was because it had difficulty warming up to a regime that seemed dominated by a traditional Soviet *nomenklatura*, and that harassed, rather than incorporated, the most liberal political elements in society.[5] In January 1994, President Clinton visited Belarus, largely as a tribute to the country for helping to solve the nuclear problem. But he came and left within the day, betraying the relative unimportance that the administration attached to the country. He also learned firsthand of the regime's political conservatism. Having assumed that a visit to Kuropaty to honor the victims of Stalinist terror would be a natural gesture in post-Soviet Belarus, the administration was taken aback when Belarusian officials resisted the idea, preferring that the president focus on the Monument of Victory of the Soviet People in the Great Patriotic War.[6]

In fact, long before Clinton arrived in Minsk, a significant turn of events in Belarus had begun to erode the basis for U.S.-Belarusian relations, although at the time it went largely unnoticed in Washington. On March 18, 1993, Viacheslau Kebich, prime minister and a rival of Shushkevich, delivered a speech attacking both the feasibility and wisdom of pursuing a neutralist course and exhorting Belarus to join the other CIS states in a collective security arrangement. He also defended the idea of seeking an economic union of the Slavic core: Belarus, Ukraine, and Russia, plus Kazakhstan.[7] Soon after, on April 9, 1993, despite the heated opposition of Shushkevich and the democratic opposition, the Supreme Soviet voted decisively to adhere to the Tashkent Treaty on Collective Security of May 1992.

Although the path to a genuinely effective collective security organization would be blocked by great obstacles, and the idea of an economic union would stagger forward only in bits and pieces over the next several years, in the spring of 1993, Belarus was making a fateful choice. Until then, the formal premise of its foreign and security policy had been neutrality and nonalignment, but with a variety of alternative choices still open. A sizable part of the political elite clearly preferred explicit alignment, even re-integration with Russia, and for them the formula of neutrality and nonalignment was phrase-mongering. Others, mostly on the democratic left, but with Shushkevich's sympathy, advocated an entirely different course—one that would align Belarus with Poland, Romania, Moldova, Hungary, the Baltic states, and Ukraine in "a belt of neutral states," a kind of *cordon sanitaire*.[8] The vote on April 9 not only buried this option—admittedly an option with limited prospects, since Poland and others were already seized with the notion of joining NATO—but also ended any meaningful pursuit of neutrality and nonalignment.

From a U.S. perspective at the time, the Belarusian decision to tie its security to Russia raised no particular problems. True, to the extent that it contributed to a Ukrainian sense of isolation and of incipient encirclement, it made management of U.S.-Ukrainian and U.S.-Russian relations somewhat more awkward, but beyond that Washington found little reason to object, and it said nothing in public or private. What did disturb Americans, however, were the political trends within Belarus that led to the decision. Support for it came from the People's Movement of Belarus, a bloc formed from old-line communist groups, the Union of Officers of Belarus (a hardline, pro-Russian organization of military officers), the leaders of defense industries, and a variety of pan-Slavic organizations. The triumphant vote within the Supreme Soviet and the apparent indifference, maybe even sympathy, of the public underscored Belarus's drift back to a dominant political ethos at least as conservative, if not more so, than in the Soviet period. All signs pointed in the direction of tough sailing for economic reform, a limited advance toward democracy, and the marginalization of Western-oriented liberal elements within society—indeed, the marginalization, as well, of the one leading politician with some appeal for Western governments, Stanislau Shushkevich.

When the Supreme Soviet ousted Shushkevich as speaker just two weeks after Clinton's brief visit to Minsk in January 1994, the conservative trend appeared to be deepening, and the U.S. State Department publicly expressed the Clinton administration's regret over the dismissal. The regret doubtless had much to do with the not-altogether-accurate impression that Shushkevich had been done in by, to quote Zyanon Poznyak, the leader of the Belarusian Popular Front, a "communist coup d'état."[9] Moreover, because Kebich, the protagonist of Russian-Belarusian integration, appeared to be the beneficiary of Shushkevich's fall from power, U.S. newspapers began to suggest that henceforth Belarus would be "less an independent state and more a virtual protectorate of Russia."[10]

While the descent to the friction-ridden relationship of the moment has some roots in this earlier period, its primary stages occurred later and as the result of a qualitatively different spiral of events. In retrospect these stages are not difficult to identify, particularly the decisive one in the fall of 1996. The dynamic lying behind them, however, is less obvious.

GETTING FROM THERE TO HERE: THE RISE OF LUKASHENKO

In June 1994, the first round of elections were held for the newly established position of president of Belarus. Contrary to most early predictions, the winner of the July runoff was Aleksandr Lukashenko, a parliamentarian who had made his reputation as head of the Supreme Soviet's anti-corruption commission. Lukashenko had used this position to level corruption charges against most major political figures in the country, including several other presidential contenders and Mechyslau Hryb, the new speaker of the parliament—accusations that the head of the Belarusian KGB characterized as "too cheap even for a primitive political provocation."[11] This background scarcely served to build U.S. confidence in the new president. To make matters worse, Lukashenko's earlier attacks on Shushkevich had been key to the case made against the former speaker, and he arrived in office with the support of "Belarus" and a cluster of conservative, sometimes anti-Western political groups. Nor could the cognoscenti in Washington have been reassured by the judgment of the liberal Moscow press comparing Lukashenko to Vladimir Zhirinovsky and warning of the boost his election would give to Russia's own antidemocrats.[12]

Still, it would be a mistake to assume that, with Lukashenko's election, the United States suddenly moved to a different level of concern over Belarus's dimming democratic prospects or dwindling commitment to economic reform. On the contrary, the new president's first actions stirred hopes that he intended to accelerate the process of economic reform. In July he announced the government's intention to abolish subsidies on meat, bread, and other basic commodities. He freed the price of vodka. In early August the cabinet decided on measures to protect U.S. direct investment, to be submitted to the parliament during its upcoming session. Far from sounding like a stalking horse for Russian imperialism, in his first public interviews Lukashenko emphasized the impracticality of reconstituting the USSR and stressed the need to find a formula honoring national independence.[13] After his first meeting with Yeltsin, on August 3, 1994, his earlier trumpeting of monetary union with Russia subsided, replaced by a frank admission that Belarus, with an inflation rate eight times that of Russia, was simply not ready to attempt a merger.[14]

Moreover, even Lukashenko's heavier-handed moves against opponents were not conspicuously different from past practice. He did not invent crackdowns on public demonstrations and the arrest of their organizers, or the harassment of radical democratic elements. His predecessors, both in the Soviet era and after, had repressed strikes and other organized actions against the government, most recently in mid-February 1994, when the so-called Belarusian Strike Committee had drawn several thousand people to the streets to protest Shushkevich's removal and to demand Kebich's resignation. U.S. policy makers disapproved, but not with an intensity that matched their reaction to the repression in, say, Uzbekistan, or that led them to shun the Belarusian leadership as they did with Uzbek president Islam Karimov during this period.

Belarus, however, had the ready-made basis for a protracted, slow-rolling political crisis, and Lukashenko's authoritarian personality gradually ignited it. During the first two and a half years of independence, legislators had labored assiduously to avoid elections.[15] The creation of the presidency and Lukashenko's victory in the country's first national election greatly increased the parliament's vulnerability by highlighting its lack of popular legitimacy. What until that point had been a continuous, but relatively even, struggle for power between the executive and legislative branches soon turned into a deadlier contest. In May 1995 parliamentary elections were held at last, nearly a year after the presidential elections and six months later than originally planned. An indifferent public elected only 119 deputies out of 2,348 candidates to a 260-seat body. The old parliament, scheduled to expire the previous March, refused to step down. The new parliament could not convene. Lukashenko, increasingly at loggerheads with the old parliament, capitalized on the confusion to impose his will on a widening range of economic and political issues. By the time the situation was clarified in a further round of legislative elections the following November, the president's autocratic style was in full flower.

During this somewhat bizarre phase, it was not clear whether the U.S. administration blamed Lukashenko for the sad state of Belarusian politics or had begun to fear his imperious leadership. None of the senior figures in Clinton's foreign policy team commented publicly. Within their own councils, however, the administration's misgivings were mounting. Lukashenko was increasingly viewed as a "bad actor," capricious and authoritarian. Under his leadership, economic reform had not received a new impulse and, in most respects, continued to lag behind other European post-Soviet states, including Ukraine after Leonid Kuchma's election (by chance, on the same day Lukashenko won in Belarus). In March 1995 privatization, which had scarcely begun, appeared to be derailed by the president's decision to suspend the work of the investment funds managing voucher bids. In April, when two hundred masked police set upon eighteen BPF deputies who had organized a sit-in in the parliament to protest Lukashenko's actions, the alarm bells were suddenly loud and clear for U.S. diplomats in Minsk.[16] A month later, at the time of the parliamentary elections, Lukashenko roused large numbers of voters to support referenda in favor of restoring the Soviet-era emblem and flag in Belarus, integrating economically with Russia, placing the Russian language on a par with the Belarusian language, and adding to the president's power over parliament.

These public mobilizations seemed all the more ominous in American eyes because they occurred as Lukashenko began veering in more sharply anti-Western directions. Russian leaders by now were well aroused against plans to expand NATO into Central Europe, and the Belarusian president yielded nothing to them in his own criticism of the idea. In February 1995, he suddenly announced that he had ordered a halt to the dismantling of conventional arms required by the 1990 Treaty on Conventional Forces in Europe (CFE) because Poland and Lithuania's move toward NATO posed a threat to Belarus.[17] There followed a week or so of confused explanations from Belarusian officials insisting that Belarus had no intention of jeopardizing the CFE Treaty and that the destruction of weapons had stopped because the government had run out of funds. The president, however, never explicitly reversed himself and continued to link the decision to the danger of an "imbalance of forces" that would arise were NATO to expand eastward.

In May the message grew shriller. After the May 26 CIS summit in Minsk, at which Ukraine turned a deaf ear to Lukashenko's entreaties to unify the Slavic core, the Belarusian president lashed out at the Western powers for blocking integration among the post-Soviet states.[18] The IMF, he said, stood ready to punish Ukraine by cutting off credits were it to weaken in its opposition to CIS integration. In Washington, Lukashenko was beginning to sound like the anti-Western right wing in Russia—only he was in power, and they were not. To top things off, on September 12, 1995, the Belarusian air defense shot down a team of American air balloonists who had strayed over Belarusian territory. The government, while expressing regret, refused to accept responsibility.

During this period the Clinton administration began to distance itself from the regime. Senior foreign policy officials stopped traveling to the country and by spring 1995 had consciously decided to avoid Minsk in their trips to the region until the Belarusian leadership changed its ways. In June 1995, Coit Blacker, the National Security Council staff member responsible for CIS affairs, did go to Minsk, where he met with Lukashenko in a low-key attempt to see if the deterioration could be stemmed. The initiative, however, stirred little interest at higher levels of the administration and raised few expectations. When Lukashenko came to New York in October 1995 for the fiftieth anniversary of the United Nations, he arrived knowing—contrary to his earlier hopes—that there would be no meeting with the U.S. president. Washington was unwilling even to offer him a session with a senior member of the administration.[19]

Had this been where matters came to rest, it is doubtful that U.S. policy toward Belarus would have hardened to the degree that it has. Matters did not come to rest here, though. If February 1993 and Belarus's ratification of the NPT represented the high point in post-independence U.S.-Belarusian relations, early 1997 was the first of two low points. In late February the U.S. government took the extraordinary step of expressly downgrading the relationship, accompanied by a stinging rebuke of the Lukashenko leadership.[20] "We have informed the Belarusian government," the document said, that "policy-level contacts" will now "be infrequent" and at a level "commensurate with U.S. objectives."[21] These, U.S. government spokesmen made plain, were increasingly limited. In the words of State Department spokesman Nicholas Burns, the two countries cannot have normal relations when "there is so much that divides" them.[22] Two weeks later he repeated the point and promised that "we'll have very limited dealings with them." From then on U.S. policy toward Belarus was to be one of "selective engagement."[23]

The chain of events leading to this sour démarche is more complex than it might seem. On the surface, the decisive cause was the November 1996 referendum in Belarus and its aftermath. Decreed by the Belarusian president in August 1996, the referendum summarily abandoned the constitution adopted in 1994 and substituted other provisions that vastly strengthened the powers of the presidency and substituted for the recently elected parliament a new body largely of the president's creation. Washington's justification for its new arms-length policy made much of the referendum, its "undemocratic character," and the degree to which democratic principles and respect for human rights had been jeopardized since.[24]

Without question, Belarus's apparently sharp authoritarian turn in the fall of 1996 played a critical role in the hardening of U.S. policy. But ultimately the particular force of the U.S. reaction was the result of the convergence of two other deepening trends. First, it was not simply democracy that seemed threatened; in the year and a half before the referendum, hope of serious economic reform had evaporated, and Belarus appeared fated to remain among the most laggard of the post-Soviet economies. Lukashenko (and his government) received most of the blame for this state of affairs from the international community and eventually even from within his own entourage.[25] The Belarusian president often mixed promises of economic reform with pledges to preserve the benefits of the Soviet economic order, including the collective farm system. The government's blueprint for social and economic development to the year 2000, announced in early 1996, featured heavy state intervention in markets, mixed forms of property, tightly constrained provisions for privatization, and the continuation of many traditional monopolies. In December 1995, IMF Chairman Michel Camdessus warned the Belarusian prime minister that his government's failure to meet stabilization targets, interference with the central bank's currency and credit policies, lack of progress on privatization, and indifferent enterprise reform now jeopardized the release of the next tranche of a $300 million standby credit.[26] A few weeks later the IMF cut Belarus off. This conspicuously disapproving step, plus increasingly critical assessments of the investment climate filed by the U.S. embassy in Minsk, greatly reinforced the general impression in Washington that Belarus was headed in the wrong direction *both* economically and politically. This impression constituted the other half of the administration's defense of its new policy of selective engagement.

The Americans were not the only ones whose reactions at both levels now hardened noticeably. In June 1996, the Parliamentary Committee for Foreign Affairs of the European Community urged that the provisional trade agreement with Belarus, laboriously negotiated the year before, be suspended, as much because of human rights abuses as economic obstacles.[27] Thus, even before the November referendum, a broader consensus was emerging among Western powers that Belarus was falling by the wayside as new states struggled to escape their Soviet past. After the referendum in January 1997, even before the change in U.S. policy, the Council of Europe's Parliamentary Assembly dropped Belarus from guest status because of the undemocratic, indeed illegal, nature of the referendum and because the new presidentially appointed parliament was without legitimacy.[28] In March, NATO's North Atlantic Assembly froze relations with Belarus for the same reason.

The downward spiral in U.S.-Belarusian relations, however, was driven not by two but three interlocking dimensions. At the same time that U.S. officials grew increasingly disenchanted over trends within Belarus, their unhappiness over the course of Belarusian foreign policy also mounted. In somewhat obscure ways, the roots of the problem lay in the unfolding Russian-Belarusian relationship. From the start of Belarusian independence, the country's political elite had favored extensive integration or re-integration with Russia. In 1993, the country's national security was tied to Russia's, and by the end of the year the two leaderships had agreed in principle to forge a monetary union. Lukashenko had long been a critic of the December 1991 decision to dissolve the Soviet Union and an advocate of Russian-Belarusian integration. By early 1996, the two sides announced what was ostensibly to be a far-reaching merger of the two societies.[29]

The Clinton administration claimed not to object in principle to Russian-Belarusian integration. Coit Blacker, when in Minsk in the summer of 1995, stressed that the United States fully accepted that, "the character of mutual relations between Russia and Belarus must be defined by these states themselves."[30] Yet, as the talk of integration intensified, the administration's suspicions grew apace. One can only guess that Washington's misgivings stemmed primarily from a feeling that integration as conceived by the Belarusian leadership had too many elements of the old Soviet relationship and, worse, that it fostered the least constructive tendencies in each country's foreign policy.

In the summer of 1996, for example, to U.S. consternation, Lukashenko appeared to endorse a wild-eyed accusation by Viktor Ilyuskin, a hard-line Communist deputy in the Russian Duma, that from Warsaw the CIA had begun implementing an elaborate plot to destabilize Belarus, using extremist Ukrainian nationalists and Belarusian subversives. The Belarusian media, now fully responsive to the president's desires, gave wide circulation to the claim, and Lukashenko implied in television statements that he thought there might be something to it.[31] On his own, some weeks later, he then charged U.S. and British diplomats with offering money to his domestic political opponents, prompting the U.S. embassy to demand an explanation from the foreign ministry.

More seriously, the more Lukashenko stressed Belarus's attachment to Russia, the more readily he and his subordinates seemed to take radical positions on issues dividing their country from the United States. Thus, in January 1996, the Belarusian president upped the volume in the argument over NATO expansion by warning that his country might, if these plans went forward, want to retain Russian nuclear weapons in Belarus. Three months later, deputy foreign minister Valery Tsepkalo repeated the threat, suggesting that the withdrawal of strategic missiles might end and that tactical nuclear weapons might be reintroduced.[32]

By February 1997, U.S. discontent in all three spheres had reached a breaking point. The administration announced that it would avoid dealing with the newly established parliament and Constitutional Court and would instead seek wider contact with "democratic elements in Belarus, the independent media, and non-governmental organizations."[33] No further insurance or financing from the Overseas Private Investment Corporation (OPIC) would be extended; the Business Development Committee would lower its profile; and the Export-Import Bank would offer no more support. Agency for International Development assistance would be channeled only to the promotion of democratization, the protection of human rights, humanitarian assistance to Chernobyl victims, and the promotion of private enterprise and an independent media. And, as a final chastising gesture, the U.S. government would encourage U.S. investors to stay clear of Belarus and explore opportunities in other, more promising nearby countries.

For the rest of 1997 and early 1998, the relationship stagnated. U.S. officials talked regularly of "the drift toward presidential dictatorship and the suppression of personal freedom of speech and assembly."[34] Little formal intercourse between the two countries took place. Trade scarcely rose above $100 million annually. Through the spring of 1998, under pressure from the Congress and U.S. labor unions, the Clinton administration wrestled with a decision to remove Belarus from the list of countries eligible for special trading privileges. Direct foreign investment, only a drip before, now virtually stopped. In early 1998, after more than a year of futile efforts to gain access to the abandoned launch pad facilities of the now-removed SS-25s, the company contracted by the U.S. government to aid with their destruction packed up and left. Few U.S. officials traveled to Belarus, and no senior official any longer bothered to mention the country in speeches and testimony devoted to the newly independent states.[35]

THE NADIR OF U.S.-BELARUS RELATIONS

Short of an open confrontation, it seemed difficult to imagine how the U.S.-Belarus relationship could descend to a lower level. Then, in June 1998, in a bizarre step, the Belarusian authorities informed the twenty ambassadors with embassies in Drozdy, an area of Minsk surrounding the presidential residence, that they would have to move out. Allegedly the reason was to repair electrical and sewage facilities. In fact, Lukashenko had decided that he wanted the area cleared of foreigners and the eviction, despite fuzzy talk about its temporary nature, was to be permanent.[36] The United States and countries from the European Union regarded the action as a violation of the Vienna Convention and a further instance of authoritarian caprice. Late in June they pulled out their ambassadors and slapped a no-entry order on all senior Belarusian officials wishing to travel to their countries. Thus began a nearly year-long "sewer war," during which the Western powers made it plain they had no further time or patience for the Lukashenko regime. By February 1999, the EU states reached a partial accommodation with Belarus (they would move embassies, but with Belarusian compensation), the travel ban was lifted, and ambassadors made ready to return. The United States seemed to be moving in the same direction after a State Department delegation traveled to Minsk in early March, but the crisis surrounding Kosovo then intruded.[37] U.S.-Belarusian relations remained frozen.

Until the Drozdy affair, while the United States had severely curtailed dealings with the Belarusian government, in accord with the new policy of February 1997, less was done to punish Minsk than originally threatened. The trickle in U.S. foreign investment resulted more from conditions within Belarus than from an explicit effort on the part of the U.S. government to drive investors away. In November 1997 Mikhail Marinich, head of the ministry of foreign economic relations, arrived in Washington on an official visit intended to explore ways of reinvigorating economic relations between the two countries. On the eve of the visit, Marinich met with Daniel Speckhard, the new U.S. ambassador in Minsk, who assured Marinich that he regarded "the improvement of the business climate as one of his most important tasks."[38] OPIC was not writing political risk insurance in Belarus, but not because the administration had forbidden its activities as threatened in the February statement of policy. Rather, it was because of an unsettled OPIC claim against the Belarusian government.

In June 1998, when relations sank still lower, the last remnants of government-to-government cooperation ceased, and the U.S. ambassador was called home. Not much cooperation was left to cut, but cut it was: a Department of Defense joint contact team intended to facilitate greater openness within the Belarusian military ceased; so did educational and exchange programs for government officials as well as financing for Belarus's participation in the Partnership for Peace program.[39] Separately and for reasons that had more to do with the poor investment climate, in June Motorola abandoned its plans for a joint venture, and a few weeks later Ford's joint venture halted automobile production. Short of a formal break in relations, the relationship could scarcely have been more desiccated.

As the regime's isolation from the United States and Western Europe grew, a subtle and malign new stage occurred in the evolution of Belarusian foreign policy. Lukashenko continued to mouth the idea of a balanced policy—in his phrase, a "multi-vectored" policy—directed West as well as East, but the formula now seemed mere cant.[40] The East, always acknowledged as having priority, took on the quality of Belarus's only option. In this context, Belarus began to seek out the outcasts of international politics—Iraq, Iran, and extremist nationalists in the Republic of Yugoslavia, North Korea, and the like. In them Lukashenko found counterparts who resented U.S. policy every bit as much as he did, that were as ready as he was to assail the demands made by the United States on his country, and that, for this reason, eased his sense of isolation and reinforced his sense of self-righteousness. As he said on Iranian television in February 1999 in praise of Iran's clear stand on sovereignty, "Iran does not yield to pressure and is not afraid of anyone."[41] Countries such as Belarus and Iran should join with Russia and China in creating a counterbalance to the United States. In this spirit he pledged that Belarus was "prepared to sell Iran everything it needs."

U.S. OBJECTIVES AND STRATEGY

During Belarus's first two years of independence, it was difficult to identify a broad, let alone coherent, set of U.S. objectives. Instead, the United States pursued a single, decisive concern—namely, removing first the tactical nuclear weapons deployed in Belarus and second the eighty-one SS-25s. Before Belarus gained independence, the Bush administration preoccupied itself with ridding Belarus of tactical nuclear weapons, seen as a particularly perilous part of the European nuclear balance. After independence, the focus shifted to preventing the emergence of new nuclear-possessing powers among the successor states.

The United States obviously hoped that Belarus, like all the other former Soviet republics, would commit itself to a democratic, market-oriented future, and it was prepared to help the country move in this direction. But here Belarus, like many of the other post-Soviet states, remained something of an afterthought. Russian democracy and market reform constituted the inspiration and focus. Beyond the rather perfunctory commitment to democratization and the consuming concern with nuclear weapons, Washington had few, if any, other specific objectives in Belarus.[42]

Later, the list of U.S. objectives would grow, but largely from negative impulses. That is, the greater the number of problems in the relationship, the more complex the U.S. agenda became. Promoting Belarusian democracy may not have been a separate, compelling part of the original U.S. agenda, but dealing with its demise formed a critical part of the subsequent agenda. Worrying about Belarus's place in an evolving Central European context was not on the minds of U.S. policy makers in 1991 and 1992, but coping with the difficulties Belarus posed for Poland, Ukraine, and others when acting in league with Russia was very much an issue in 1996 and 1997. Along the way, the essentially constructive interaction leading to the elimination of nuclear weapons was replaced by the far less auspicious focus on preventing Belarus from aiding Iran with its nuclear program.[43] And the initially limited U.S.-Belarusian arms control agenda was much complicated after 1994 by Minsk's fitful implementation of the CFE agreement and its separate set of demands in the 1997 adaptation of the treaty.

Amid this more ramified and troubled agenda, the U.S. effort to discourage Belarus's retreat from a democratic option assumed pivotal importance. It is important to understand why. More is involved than simply the general tendency of the United States to make human rights a policy concern when dealing with other governments, and more than the Clinton administration's renewed emphasis on the issue when it came to office. Clinton and his people altered policy to accommodate human rights concerns not merely toward Belarus, but toward countries from China to Haiti and a number of places in between, including Uzbekistan and Azerbaijan. In addition, congressional politics guaranteed that human rights issues would be an unavoidable part of U.S. policy, particularly with the election of a Republican majority four months after Lukashenko assumed the presidency.

By 1995 an economy-minded U.S. Congress had already begun to whittle away at funding under the Nunn-Lugar legislation, a portion of the defense budget set aside to assist the post-Soviet states dismantle their nuclear weapons. Belarus was not the only (nor even the primary) inspiration for the cutbacks, but its increasingly unfavorable human rights record stiffened the resolve of the legislators eager to find reasons not to spend money on the post-Soviet states. Two years later Belarus was the only, and quite specific, target of action. On March 21, 1997, one day after the latest public demonstration in Minsk and subsequent round of arrests, a State Department spokesman announced that additional Nunn-Lugar support would be suspended, a step that halted the remaining $39 million earmarked for nuclear cleanup in the country.[44] The program, he said, required that recipients be certified for human rights compliance, and the State Department could no longer make that claim before the Congress. On April 3, leaders of the (U.S.) Commission on Security and Cooperation in Europe (CSCE) sent a letter to Lukashenko sharply criticizing his government's actions during the past three months.[45] Two of the signers, Senators Frank Lautenberg (D-N.J.) and Alfonse D'Amato (R-N.Y.), had a few weeks earlier introduced into the Senate a concurrent resolution calling on the Belarusian leadership to meet its human rights obligations under the Helsinki Act.[46]

Although only a handful of House and Senate members were actively engaged on these issues, they would have had no trouble rallying majorities among their essentially passive colleagues, giving the administration good reason to suspend Nunn-Lugar assistance, even if it had preferred to keep nuclear and human rights issues separate. If the administration could not or would not overcome congressional opposition to assistance for Azerbaijan, where Caspian Sea oil gave it compelling reasons to do so, there was no chance that it would risk a conflict with Congress over policy toward Belarus.

Ultimately, however, the reason domestic developments within Belarus came to assume such a decisive role in U.S. policy was altogether more profound. A fundamentally new dynamic was at work in post–cold war Europe, and Belarus was not above its influence. Because democracy had become a critical foundation of modern international relations in Western Europe, Europe's major powers were not willing to admit post-socialist societies into their midst unless they met this standard. More than this, the West Europeans and Americans had come to believe that democracy—including respect for human and minority rights—constituted an important source of international stability and, therefore, of European security. As a result, they consciously and systematically used the entire architecture of West European institutions—from the Council of Europe to NATO—and the desire of East and Central European states to be a part of it, as leverage for promoting democracy in these states. Where the prospect of early membership in NATO and the EU did not exist, as in the case of Russia and Belarus, Europe's democracies relied on other institutions, such as the OSCE, to foster the link between democracy and security. Because this premise lay so close to the core of Western foreign policy concepts, no East European state, from Albania to Estonia, escaped its influence.

The United States, of course, had other aims for its relations with Belarus than discouraging a new authoritarianism, but none of these stood on its own. Until the post-1996 deterioration in relations, for example, the United States sought to increase the opportunity for profitable U.S. investment in the country. As late as May 1996, the U.S.-Belarusian Business Development Committee held its second meeting in Minsk and planned a series of steps to aid U.S. business activity in Belarus.[47] A few weeks earlier a U.S. Chamber of Commerce office had been established in Minsk. Throughout this period, the U.S. embassy in Belarus devoted a good deal of its time and energy to promoting economic ties between the two countries. And in July, James Collins, then the U.S. ambassador-at-large to the CIS states, arrived in Minsk to discuss various joint activities contributing to a better business climate.[48] Nearly all of this activity, however, came under a cloud when the political environment deteriorated in early 1997.

The United States had an additional interest in encouraging Belarus to develop an effective export control regime: to prevent the flight of nuclear materials to third parties and the flow of advanced weaponry to what the U.S. regarded as rogue states.[49] But this objective, too, was eventually subordinated to the harder line the United

States took on Belarus's general economic and political evolution. To a lesser extent the same can be said of the remainder of the U.S. arms control agenda with Belarus. After the last SS-25 left Belarus for Russia in November 1996, this agenda was largely reduced to Belarus's part in the CFE regime.

Finally, the Clinton administration had an interest in the nature of Russian-Belarusian integration, although, as noted, the precise character of this interest was not always clear. Provided this integration was something the people of Russia and Belarus wished, Washington saw no reason to interfere. Others had a more critical view, including David Swartz, former U.S. ambassador to Belarus. They objected in principle to what they feared would be the loss of Belarusian sovereignty and regarded the whole idea of re-integration among the post-Soviet states as contrary to the U.S. national interest.[50] Some went further—determined to circumscribe Russia as much as possible, they opposed any alliance or fusion that might add to Russian power.

Even the Clinton administration's more benign position eventually led to reservations over the agreements reached in April 1996 and May 1997. On the surface, these reservations were less over content than process. The administration accepted the right of the two countries to integrate, but not if the leadership of one country moved in that direction by flaunting democratic procedure. Yet again, the issue of Belarus's domestic politics intruded. When asked to comment on the April 1997 Union Treaty between Belarus and Russia, State Department spokesman Nicholas Burns responded that "we are not reflexively opposed to efforts to bring two countries together, but we do believe any such process should be voluntary; that it should reflect the mutual wishes of the peoples of both countries."[51] He then added, "Obviously, we have great respect for the Russian Federation, which is a free and democratic country. It's hard to join those words, however—'free and democratic'—to Belarus."

U.S. officials, however, knew perfectly well that integration with Russia was popular with the great majority of Belarusian citizens and that Lukashenko would have no trouble securing their approval in a referendum. Thus, Burns's comments doubtlessly concealed a deeper level of misgiving. He also said that, if there was to be union between the two countries, the United States favored one that "does not draw new lines in Europe."[52] By this somewhat more revealing formulation, he appeared to be suggesting that the United States' real worry was a union built on an anti-Western basis or in a form impeding cooperation with the West.

Since February 1997, the United States has had an explicit strategy for pursuing this pyramid of objectives. Officials have even given it a name—"selective engagement." By any name it is a strategy of carrots and sticks, with even the carrots used largely as sticks.[53] In the original February 1997 statement the administration asserted that it was not "disengaging from Belarus" nor seeking "Belarus's isolation." Without question, however, it did mean to pressure the regime, to punish it for showing a seemingly growing disregard for democratic practices, and to make it an outcast among European leaderships. This may not have been an attempt to isolate the entire country, but it certainly was intended to make Lukashenko and his colleagues feel isolated. (In this regard, the strategy apparently succeeded. When addressing the parliament in April, the Belarusian president referred to the "international isolation" of his country and claimed that the problem was gradually fading away.[54])

What few carrots the United States kept in reserve were, in the period between February 1997 and June 1998, used as prods, not inducements. Aid, which had been largely turned off, would only flow again if Belarus demonstrated by its deeds its readiness to advance democratic and market reforms. Similarly, the administration held open the prospect that Nunn-Lugar money could resume in late 1997 or 1998, but only if the State Department could assure Congress that Belarus was in compliance with human rights standards. In contrast, in the first three years of Belarusian independence, U.S. aid had been given before the fact, in part on the assumption that various forms of material support, including food assistance, would reinforce the willingness of the leadership to cooperate on the nuclear issue. Then, in the June 1998 clash over the embassy expulsion, the Clinton administration removed the remaining incentives.

U.S. aid had never been large. Through 1996, the United States provided less than $250 million in technical and economic assistance to Belarus, including around $115 million in humanitarian aid, plus an additional $250 million in U.S. Department of Agriculture food assistance.[55] Under the Nunn-Lugar program funding, out of a total of $1.5 billion designated for the post-Soviet states by the end of 1996, Belarus had received less than $80 million. Of the four former

Soviet republics with nuclear weapons, the $120 million that the Department of Defense proposed to spend on Belarus was the smallest share. It was a pattern that generally held in U.S. aid to the new states of the former Soviet Union: Belarus usually ranked last among all twelve recipients, whatever the program. This pattern was true of the Farmer-to-Farmer Program (12 volunteers for Belarus out of 539 to the newly independent states in 1996), the International Science and Technology Centers program ($5 million versus Kazakhstan's $8 million), and Freedom Support grants (17 versus 221 for Russia in 1996). (One of those Freedom Support grants went to Semyon Sharetsky, the speaker of the parliament who, after visiting the United States in May 1996, returned home and delivered an impassioned attack on Lukashenko's threat to constitutional government.) Even in terms of funding from the European Bank for Reconstruction and Development, to which the United States contributed, Belarus's total through September 1996 was just $204 million out of $4.2 billion.[56]

These sums were not large enough to yield much leverage, either as incentives or disincentives. As symbolic displays of U.S. preferences and as modest rewards for good behavior they had their place, but as a means of compelling Belarusian authorities to change a course they had no desire to change, U.S. aid programs were pitifully weak. Even the threat to cut Belarus off entirely gave the United States little leverage, so that when the last lingering forms of cooperation ended in the 1998 confrontation, the gesture scarcely registered. On the contrary, cutting them off entirely in some cases—such as the program to strengthen export controls over nuclear materials— did more to damage U.S. interests than to change Belarusian intransigence.[57]

By its nature current U.S. strategy allows for few other forms of influence. In contrast, until the Drozdy fracas, France, under Jacques Chirac, had preserved the option of appearing ready to advocate Belarus's cause within the EU (while not breaking ranks with European institutions in their condemnation of the November 1996 referendum and its aftermath). The United States, however, has neither the stomach nor the political resources to try to affect Belarusian behavior by holding open the possibility of defending Belarus's security interests within a Central European context or, more generally, by developing for it a Western option. Nor, at the other extreme, can the United States hope to mount a broad-based coalition against a recalcitrant Belarus, such as it has, albeit imperfectly, against Cuba, Iran, Iraq, Libya, and North Korea. The only options have become putting the regime at arms length, rousing the international community's indignation when it acts repressively, penalizing it for dawdling with economic reform, and hoping that changes in the domestic politics of the country will move it back on a more satisfactory course.

A TWO-TRACK POLICY VERSUS SELECTIVE ENGAGEMENT

Anyone faulting the Clinton administration for its present course must take two considerations into account. The first is the state of American politics and their effect on foreign policy, most notably as manifest in the actions of the U.S. Congress. Neither the public nor Congress has the patience or attention span for subtle, complex policies, particularly toward middle and smaller powers. Were the administration to come forward with a less stark, indeed, less harsh policy toward Lukashenko's Belarus, the job of selling it would be formidable. It simply could not be done without a compelling argument and, for reasons to which I will turn in a moment, the administration is a poor candidate to make the argument.

The second reason is Lukashenko himself. Precious little suggests that he would be moved by an alternative strategy. If Russians have trouble getting him to do what they want even when his actions stir their genuine concern (as during the presidential-parliamentary crisis before the November 1996 referendum), or their genuine anger (as with the arrest and detention of Russian television news personnel in the summer of 1997), how can Washington hope to do better? If Belarus's leader feels no special need to indulge his country's closest friends, what could make him bend to the U.S. desires? Three months after signing the 1997 Union Treaty, Yeltsin was fuming over the arrest of Russian journalists saying that Lukashenko "is young and lacks the ability to handle criticism." Such a scene does give a critic of U.S. policy pause.[58]

Lukashenko, it must be recognized, is not simply a vestige of Soviet days, a leader who lacks direction other than from his own autocratic instincts while, when pressured by the outside world, can be counted on to react pragmatically and to adopt a more moderate course. On the contrary, he has a deeply authoritarian streak, with more than a touch of megalomania. On one occasion he supposedly spoke favorably of what Hitler's "firm hand" did for Germany in the 1930s, for "one man cannot be all black or all white."[59] Toward his more liberal opponents he reacts not only with wariness, but with a visceral dislike. He regularly conveyed his loathing of Anatoly Chubais, the reform-minded former Russian deputy prime minister and a critic of Lukashenko. He refers to Russian democrats as "*dermo-kraticheskie*," from a vulgar Russian word for "dung," a revealing characterization doubtless applied to the democratic opposition in his own country as well.[60] With respect to the Western countries, he harbors not merely frustrations over what he sees as unwarranted interference in Belarusian domestic affairs but a conviction that they, with the United States in the forefront, have a deep antipathy toward him and his country. In his own mind he evidently believes his regime is faced not with Western criticism, but Western enmity.

Thus, no U.S. policy toward Belarus should nurse illusions about the challenge to democracy that the Lukashenko regime represents, or the likelihood that a less harsh Western reaction would awaken reform impulses that almost surely do not exist. Nevertheless, one can be utterly unsentimental about the regime and still advocate shifts in the U.S. approach. It all depends on basic assumptions— in particular, how U.S. stakes in this part of the world are calculated.

If the starting point is the assumption that what happens in and around Belarus is of marginal significance to U.S. national interests, then there is little reason to quarrel with current policy. If to this point of view is added the conviction that the Belarusian leadership cannot be influenced, a tough, aloof policy seems about right. Although the United States has little leverage over Lukashenko, it still has reason to maintain its principles, to avoid any impression of coddling post-Soviet regimes that refuse to embrace democracy and market reform, and to make plain to Belarusian elites and others in the region that certain behavior entails a price. Holding the line in dealings with the Belarusians does not prevent the United States from addressing topics of concern, such as Belarusian defense policy or trends in Belarus's relations with Russia. These can be attended to indirectly by focusing on Russia. The easier and better way to influence Belarusian choices in these areas is through the Russians. For the rest, there is simply no reason not to let the regime stew in its own juices. [61]

If the starting point is the basic assumption that Belarus is integral to a crucial political and security environment, one that merges the peace and stability of the post-Soviet space with the peace and stability of East-Central Europe, however, then Belarus ceases to be marginal in the larger scheme of U.S. national interests. In fact, it becomes the hole in a rather important doughnut. How Belarus behaves, the kind of alliance that it seeks with Russia, the degree of its alienation from the West, and the measure of stability within the country all bear directly and critically on the security of its neighbors—Lithuania and Latvia to the north, Ukraine to the south, and Poland to the west.

But if the doughnut itself is not part of one's thinking, there is no basis for the second assumption. In most U.S. circles, and even in the administration, the doughnut is missing. Little thought goes into the linkage between security in the post-Soviet space and security in East-Central Europe. This is not to say that the administration fails to appreciate the Russian dimension as it goes about enhancing Polish, Hungarian, and Czech security through NATO enlargement, or that it ignores the security concerns of the Baltic states and Ukraine. Policy in the post-Madrid period does look to managing the next phases of NATO's development in ways sensitive to the hopes and fears of these countries, while not worsening matters with Russia.

Recognizing the fallout from NATO expansion in the states of the former Soviet Union and attempting to address it constructively is, however, not the same as seeing an integral link between security in the post-Soviet space and security in the remainder of Europe. This linkage stems less from the sentiments of the post-Soviet states toward NATO, the West, and the United States than from the dynamics among these states. If mutual security among them grows, so does security elsewhere in Europe. If it declines, so does security elsewhere.

In this equation the evolution of Russia remains decisive, Ukrainian security is the core problem, and Belarus is the pivot point. For Ukraine, in the worst case Russia constitutes the essential threat, but Belarus in league with Russia converts a general threat into a far more concrete danger of encirclement. Long before any of these possibilities become a reality, its mere specter has a negative effect on security dynamics within the region. For Lithuania and Latvia, how Belarus chooses to define its international role is a vital part of their foreign policy setting. Small states have often been buffeted before by the uncertain gusts in relations between an overshadowing power and a troubled neighbor, as, for example, in relations between Germany and Poland in the interwar period. For Poland, Belarus brings the physically remote issue of Russia into its living room. And let it not be forgotten that Belarus represents for Russia a crucial strategic salient, either as a forward wedge of Russian influence in Europe or as a pathway by which others can threaten its peace of mind.

Belarus, as a result, stands at the center of a series of overlapping circles, each important to the international politics of Europe's eastern half. First and foremost it forms with Russia and Ukraine a critical triangle. Tension along any leg of this triangle would threaten stability throughout the European portions of the former Soviet Union and cast a shadow over neighboring areas to the west. Belarus, either as the footloose object of Ukrainian-Russian competition or as the partner of an aggressive Russia, would be particularly a pernicious factor. Belarus also figures in the Ukrainian-Polish relationship, either as an object of concern or as an interlocutor and, by extension, therefore, also in the German-Polish (or potentially the German-Polish-Ukrainian) relationship. And it plays a role in a Baltic cluster that brings together Lithuania, Latvia, Estonia, Finland, and, at times, Russia.

When thought of in these multiple contexts and as a key variable in each, Belarus takes on a much greater significance to the overall stability of East-Central Europe. Whether seen as the hole in the doughnut or pivot point, Belarus is crucial if European security depends on what happens from the Atlantic to the Urals—and if Western leaders mean it when they speak of a continent whole and at peace. If Belarus does matter this much, then U.S. policy should be calculated accordingly. The trick is to formulate a policy that allows the United States to pursue these larger stakes, without compromising its opposition to anti-democratic and anti-reform actions on the part of the Belarusian leadership.

Given the nature of the challenge, the best alternative almost certainly is a two-track approach. On one track the United States would strive to build a relationship with Belarus to enhance security in East-Central Europe and the former Soviet Union, a relationship that gives the United States a larger role in shaping the international relations of the region. On the other track, the United States would continue to seek ways to nudge Belarus along a democratic, market-oriented path.

Officials in the current U.S. administration would doubtless say that a double-track approach is already in place (or was, at least, until Lukashenko made it impossible with his 1998 power play over embassies in Drozdy). While reacting firmly to offenses the entire West condemns, U.S. officials nonetheless intend to remain engaged in Belarus. They are ready to deal with the leadership on a number of important fronts, including arms control, while at the same time making plain their disapproval of Belarus's human rights record and obstruction of economic reform. "Engagement" represents one track, "selective" characterizes the other—or did, until the summer of 1998.

This argument misses the point. In a genuine two-track policy, one track should not be subordinate to the other. In current U.S. policy all other aspects of the relationship take a back seat to Washington's critical view of domestic developments within Belarus; all are ultimately mobilized to underscore this disapproval. Thus, Belarusian concerns over NATO expansion or thoughts about mechanisms for enhancing European security get a weak hearing because Washington sees no reason to give the Lukashenko regime this respectability. One track was being subordinated to the other when, in 1997, Javier Solana, secretary general of NATO, traveled from Kiev to Central Asia to address concerns over NATO expansion and conspicuously excluded Belarus. When U.S. defense officials make no effort to engage their Belarusian counterparts on military matters, they too are part of the general boycott. Until late 1996, the Poles, Ukrainians, and Belarusians had a regular and productive exchange underway at the foreign minister level, at which point the Poles terminated it, evidently to further enhance their credentials for NATO membership. It would not have crossed anyone's mind in Washington to assure Warsaw that NATO would rather see the dialogue continue. When Belarus, suddenly seeing Russia and Ukraine work out special arrangements with NATO on the eve of the alliance's invitation to Poland, Hungary, and the Czech Republic, scrambled to explore something along the same lines, no one bothered to respond.

Although difficult to accomplish, the two tracks need to be kept separate. Each must have its own integrity. Efforts to work with Belarus in promoting European security (including its post-Soviet sector) should not be halfhearted, dilatory, or second order. This approach implies several changes to current policy. First, Belarus should be treated like Ukraine or the Baltic states as an independent actor in the unfolding diplomacy of European security. Its conceptions of European security and proposals for strengthening it, as well as its critical reactions to others' ideas, should be explored and negotiated seriously. In the end the United States may resist much in the Belarusian position, but engaging Belarus on these issues is an important aspect of a two-track approach. Second, Belarusian defense planning, military cooperation with others, and place in Europe's arms control regimes should be of direct concern to the United States and a subject of continuous discussion between senior defense officials in both countries. Third, Minsk should be put back on the travel itinerary of U.S. policy makers who handle problems of European security. Fourth, the United States should welcome and encourage forums that draw Belarus into a dialogue with neighbors on issues of European security. Sustained bilateral and three-way conversations between and among Belarus, Ukraine, and Poland deserve U.S. support. So, too, do the summits of East European leaders begun by former Lithuanian president Algirdas Brazauskas and his Polish counterpart in September 1997, and to which Lukashenko was invited.

To argue that the first track should be taken seriously assumes that it *can* be taken seriously. It assumes, first, that Belarus is and will remain an independent state and, second, that the current Belarusian leadership cares about the nature of its relationship with other European powers and the United States, despite its current alienation from them. It is far from clear that either of these assumptions prevails among U.S. policy makers. On the contrary, slowly over the past several years the feeling seems to have taken hold that Belarus will not likely endure as a separate state, that processes leading to the country's absorption into the Russian fold are already far advanced. Policy makers find it even more difficult to believe that Lukashenko and his group care about defending Belarus's independence and, therefore, that they have any real stake in ties to the West. Both suspicions should be challenged.

It does not take much firsthand experience in Belarus to sense how rapidly the roots of independence are developing. While the Belarusian sense of nationhood does not reverberate in conspicuous nationalist symbols and sentiments, its quiet, practical manifestations are everywhere, but above all in the attitude of political elites, the trappings of state power, the discourse of intellectuals, and the demeanor of youth. With every passing month Belarus is taking shape as an idea and a daily reality for its people. The widespread sympathy for Russia and eagerness to have special ties with it, particularly in the countryside and among an older generation, should not be mistaken for a readiness to become a part of Russia again.[62] Moscow's elites frequently make this mistake, taking it for granted that forces are leading inexorably to reunification or something very close to it.[63] Perhaps this widely shared view, together with a misreading of Lukashenko's intentions, are what create the impression in the United States that Belarusian independence has neither much substance nor staying power.

In two respects Lukashenko, far from derogating Belarusian independence, appears to be strengthening it. First, and doubtless inadvertently, he and the regime have compromised the idea of integration with Russia among a widening range of politicians, intellectuals, and activists, who now associate it with a regime that for other reasons they reject. No longer is opposition to the submergence of Belarus in a greater Russia confined to a narrow stratum of Belarusian nationalists. Second, from all indications Lukashenko himself has no intention of sacrificing Belarusian independence. Whatever may be his conception of Russian-Belarusian integration, it does not include turning Belarus into Russia's ninetieth subject. In late February 1997, in a speech before the parliament, he said, "Belarus has always been and will be an independent, sovereign state. It will never be a province of another country."[64] If there is to be union, he added a few days later, it would have to be on the basis of "equal republics based on the one-republic-one-vote principle."[65] Whenever Yeltsin begins stressing how soon and on what terms integration will take place or some exuberant group in the Russian Duma casts Lukashenko in the role of governor of a Russian province, the Belarusian president hastens to set the record straight. In January 1997, he said that Belarus would form an alliance with another state, including union with Russia, only on the basis of three fundamental principles: first, that it be an "equal partnership" guaranteeing Belarus's sovereignty and statehood; second, that Belarusian citizens "never be sent to fight outside the country" (a popular stance that long antedated Lukashenko's presidency); and, third, that it be mutually beneficial.[66] Earlier the same day Aman Tuleev, at the time Russia's minister of CIS affairs, had boasted that the two countries would be united by the year 2000.

Lukashenko's critics say that he would merge the two countries in a moment if it served his personal ambitions. But even this charge rests on the assumption that his personal ambitions would only be realized in a union in which Belarus were genuinely equal—and he, the equal of the Russian head of state—or in the still less likely case of an amalgamation that he would come to lead. This is not to say that he is incapable of imagining a turn of events carrying him to power in a genuine Russian-Belarusian union or perhaps even into the Russian presidency. His efforts over the past several years to build direct ties with the Russian provinces can be interpreted in this light, and his public denials of an intention to run in the next Russian presidential election may betray the dreams running through his mind. Still, whatever his imaginings, he gives little sign of wishing to scuttle his country's independence for what remain highly improbable outcomes. Moreover, he knows that the Russian leadership has no interest in integration on his terms, a fact that he regularly and angrily acknowledges.

Similarly, the basic thrust of Belarusian foreign policy toward the West, while increasingly pernicious, does not yet pose an insuperable obstacle to a two-track U.S. policy. Lukashenko has long maintained that Belarus wants to pursue what he calls a "multi-vectored" policy, in which the West forms one crucial vector and Russia and the CIS another.[67] He has never denied that, between the two, Belarus assigns greater importance to the second, but not to the extent that Belarus's stake in Europe and the West in general is without significance. Even as his affirmations of a multi-vectored policy grow hollow, the frustration and annoyance that Belarus's relations with the United States and the European Union are so shriveled come through clearly.

Moreover, among the foreign policy elite in Belarus, including the most senior officials, the recovery of a Western option remains a deeply desired objective. One after another emphasize the impor-tance of developing what a senior figure in the foreign ministry calls the Western "wing" of Belarusian foreign policy. Belarus, they repeatedly stress, does not want a unidimensional policy focused only eastward. Until travel was denied to them in 1998, they spent considerable time justifying their country's policies before officials of West European organizations, all the while conveying the discomfort they felt standing on the outside looking in.[68]

There are good reasons for this stance, beyond the aid and trade benefits that Minsk might hope to secure from the West. First, despite the casual assumptions of Washington, Bonn, and Brussels, Belarus's place in the outside world remains inchoate. Its relationship to the CIS is ambiguous because the future of the CIS is ambiguous. Union with Russia is an idea on paper, but one that falters continuously in practice.[69] At a deeper level the question exists whether either country really wants it. To Belarus's north, south, and west, vital interests are at stake with countries whose future is part of a larger Europe. Even those who may want it, presumably including the Belarusian president, hardly paint a picture of progress. In March 1998, two years into the Union Treaty, Lukashenko complained that "as of today, not a single agreement that we concluded and signed with the president of the Russian Federation and not a single promise made by the government of the Russian Federation has been implemented."[70]

On December 25, 1998, Yeltsin and Lukashenko signed yet another declaration proclaiming steps toward a "union state," this one focused on creating a common budget and currency by the year 2000. Less than a month later, Lukashenko complained that Russia's commitment to the union budget fell far short, typical of politicians who continue to invent every form of obstacle to integration.[71] As a parting shot he added, none too obliquely, "He became a president and does not know what confederation means."

Second, thoughtful Belarusian foreign policy specialists recognize that existing arrangements among the CIS states are not adequate for dealing with potential instability in the region or other security threats and that additional mechanisms, including the Partnership for Peace, may be essential.[72] Third, whatever Belarus's ultimate place in the post-Soviet space, its westward location exposes it to the fundamental processes shaping European politics, an awareness more naturally present among Belarusian foreign policy elites than among their Russian counterparts.

No U.S. policy toward Belarus will be soundly based, however, unless it rests on an understanding that, with or without Lukashenko, Belarus's foreign policy will not resemble that of Ukraine, the Baltic states, or any of the more Western-oriented former Soviet republics. Too many forces are at work dictating that Belarusian foreign policy remain in tandem with Russian foreign policy—that is, respectful of Russian interests and inclined to see trends in Europe in similar ways. Its conception of European security, the role of NATO versus that of alternative institutions, and arms control, as well as its reaction to structures of which it is not a part, will inevitably bear a greater likeness to Russian positions than not. Hence, as a final observation on the first of the two tracks, no matter what the regime in Belarus, success will depend in part on the direction of Russian foreign policy. If Russia continues to value its relations with the West and strives to play a constructive role in promoting European security, a two-track policy toward Belarus can work. If Russia, in anger or frustration, turns its back on the West, the chances of success are slim.

A two-track policy does not mean rectifying one dimension of policy at the expense of the other. Resisting the drift toward authoritarianism in Belarus and encouraging enlightened economic policies on the part of its leadership constitute important U.S. policy objectives. How the United States reacts to the fate of democratic choice in Belarus is not simply a matter of a particular administration's tastes. For the United States to look the other way on this issue would not only invite sharp criticism in Congress and elsewhere, but, more importantly, would also work at cross purposes with the kind of Europe whose emergence is in the U.S. interest. To excuse or minimize steps threatening a democratic future for Belarus would, in fact, undermine one of the fundamental building blocks of European security as conceived by the United States and its allies. To pass over the ill-advised Soviet-style economic palliatives increasingly embraced by the Belarusian government would be to stand by while the country edges toward severe economic trouble, with the attendant risk of internal political instability.

To ease the inevitable tension between the two tracks the United States should weigh carefully the way it pursues the second track. Dual-track policies are in their nature a matter of squaring the circle, and, hence, they need to be constructed with more than the usual attention to nuance. Three suggestions follow. First, for punitive measures to work they need to be well articulated and distinguished from steps whose purpose is not to punish. The West and Western Europe in particular, for example, have a strong intrinsic interest in defending their societies from the harm flowing across poorly policed Belarusian borders. When the objective is to sanction or pressure Belarus because it has failed to do all that it might to control drug traffic, illegal migration, arms exports, and the like, the measures employed should be for that purpose, and not confused with steps taken to deal with human rights abuses.

In the sphere of trade, investment, and finance, the most effective measures are likely to be those directed toward a clear purpose in one realm, say, the development of safeguards for direct foreign investment. Less likely to succeed are vague retaliatory measures for failing to implement a broad-based economic reform, let alone measures sold as a response to political repression. U.S. policy makers should draw careful distinctions for the Belarusians between the impediments their own economic practices place on trade and investment and those imposed by the United States as punitive measures. In guiding the Belarusians toward sounder economic policy, the self-inflicted "stick" of economic failure is likely to work better if reinforced not by the sticks of others, but by "carrots." Confining economic instruments to economic ends means that political aims—such as discouraging human rights abuses—will depend on political means—such as the mobilized condemnation of the European community, pressure through agencies such as the OSCE, and ostracism from organizations for which Belarus fails to qualify, such as the Council on Europe.

Second, U.S. policy makers would be well advised to treat Russia as part of the solution to achieving second-track objectives, rather than as part of the problem. Russia may not embrace the U.S. method for dealing with Lukashenko, but it has scarcely less reason than Washington does to fear the consequences of Belarus's economic insolvency and to care about the state of the regime's internal legitimacy. As Garnett and I argue in the concluding chapter of this book, Russia has played an important and constructive, albeit mixed, role in restraining the Belarusian leadership and in pushing it to respond to the outside community's concerns. Here again, however, the possibility of productive cooperation with Russia depends heavily on the overall state of U.S.-Russian relations.

Third, U.S. censure will be more effective if the United States does not push itself to the forefront of Belarus's critics. In part this is because the Belarusian president operates under the misapprehension that the United States represents his primary problem, that if only the United States would back off, other states would as well. In fact, he is quite mistaken. Nearly the whole of Europe rejects the regime's political course. At the Lisbon OSCE summit in December 1996, Belarus escaped formal censure only because it and Russia held a veto. Lithuania's Brazauskas, in addressing the September 1997 East European summit in Vilnius, encouraged participants to make an issue of the situation in Belarus, although not by using "hard measures" to deal with a "delicate situation."[73] The OSCE, in an effort led by the Europeans, has kept the pressure on Minsk and has successfully negotiated the establishment of an OSCE monitoring group in the country.[74] Under this pressure, Belarus felt compelled to explain itself before the permanent council of the OSCE in September 1997 in Vienna, with all fifty-four members attending. In April 1998, when Lukashenko traveled unofficially to Germany to attend the Hanover trade fair, not only did Helmut Kohl refuse to see him, but Gerhard Schroeder, then the opposition party leader, was publicly rebuked by a foreign ministry spokesman for having lunch with Lukashenko, a breach of formal EU and German policy. In early 1999, a working group from the OSCE's Parliamentary Assembly, comprised of delegates from the smaller European states, arrived in Minsk to explore ways of defusing a mounting political confrontation over attempts to hold presidential elections under the 1994 constitution suspended by Lukashenko in 1996. Thus, Belarus is one case—indeed, almost uniquely so—where the United States could, to better effect, follow the lead of others who have no less of a stake in guiding Belarus back onto a democratic path.

Ultimately this part of the argument rests on two assumptions, neither of which, admittedly, is above challenge. The first is that pressures capable of forcing Lukashenko to change his domestic policies significantly will not soon reach a critical point. True, economic and other crises in the country mount by the month. At some point the frustrations of an increasingly impoverished public may create political opportunities for the opposition, while the mistakes now being made by the leadership, as discussed in the final chapter of this book, will likely have longer-term consequences. True, the ongoing struggle over the constitution has created a focus for the opposition and, for a moment, seemed to draw together otherwise fragmented forces. Despite harassment and arrests, plans did go forward to hold presidential shadow elections in May 1999, as called for by the 1994 constitution, an effort that initially rallied a wide range of opposition figures and dramatized the ongoing question of the government's legitimacy.[75] Because Lukashenko's term under the 1994 constitution expired July 20, 1999, the issue of presidential legitimacy has now been added to that of the government's legitimacy, since Lukashenko did not step down.

Still, there are few signs that Lukashenko sees his leadership in danger or the direction of his policy a failure—notwithstanding the dramatic economic deterioration in Belarus following Russia's economic crisis in the summer of 1998, the increased courage of the opposition that was manifest in the formation of Charter-97 (a broad-based group of intellectuals and public figures modeled on Charter-77, the Czechoslovak human rights organization), and the challenge raised by the move to hold presidential elections. In the course of the May 1999 elections, the opposition again set to feuding, and as a result, this last challenge turned out to be less serious than it otherwise could have been. On the contrary, while Lukashenko's popularity has slipped (he no longer receives positive ratings in the 45 percent range, a starting point far higher than the ratings of his Ukrainian and Russian counterparts), this decline has not translated into active disaffection among any sizable part of the population. Lukashenko handles their growing hardships by a combination of populist gestures (such as a televised meeting with government officials in November 1998 during which he expressed sorrow over Belarusians "becoming poorer and poorer every month," transferred the blame to the officials sitting in front of him, and threatened to have their heads if they did not reverse matters in short order) and of rationalization: Belarus is the victim of nearby economic chaos and Western efforts to break the country's will, perils that would be far more dangerous were it not for his policies.[76] For the most part the gambit works and will likely continue to do so, short of a major economic collapse.

The second assumption complements the first. If Belarus is to get in step with the patterns of change underway in neighboring post-Soviet states—none of which is without failings—such a change is more likely to come about because the leadership slowly realizes that Belarus's place (and security) in a modern European order depends on following their example. There are signs that Belarusian elites, including many within government bureaucracy, are uncomfortable with the growing gap between trends in their country and those in the rest of Europe. As the wages of misguided economic policies accumulate, the limits of the Belarusian-Russian relationship become more apparent. And as the sinews of civil society strengthen, the incentives to make Belarus a part of contemporary European processes will increase, particularly if Russia sees its own future as tied to these processes.

The last point introduces, one more time, the Russian factor: if Russia abandons hope that its future is tied to the broader processes underway in Europe, the second assumption falls. Then Belarus would be torn between the imperative of economic rationalism and the imperative of Russian dependency, a contest that Russian dependency will win. Moreover, even if Russia is not a complication, one cannot be sure that Lukashenko himself will react as many in the bureaucracy would: faced with serious economic instability and shredded dreams of Russian-Belarusian cooperation, his choice could well be a more perfect authoritarianism.

The vulnerability of both assumptions, however, does not undermine the wisdom of a balanced two-track U.S. policy. In such a policy, little is hazarded while much may be gained. I say little is put at risk because the choice is not between a mixed policy of this sort and a clear, decisive policy of unmitigated ostracism and pressure designed to solve the problem by bringing the regime down. Setting aside the question of whether such a policy could succeed, based on previous experience with Cuba, Libya, and Iraq, it simply is not an option. The United States is not ready to deny legitimacy to the Lukashenko government, not the least because its European allies would not follow suit. Between the dueling constitutions of 1994 and 1996, the United States will continue to recognize the 1994 arrangements. But after the expiration of Lukashenko's term under the 1994 constitution on July 21, 1999, rather than withdraw de facto legitimacy by refusing to deal with him, the U.S. will almost certainly press for a reconciliation of the constitutional crisis, and continue to cajole the leadership toward more democratic practice.

Given the limited leverage that a policy of isolation has over Lukashenko's most basic political impulses, it is unclear what advantage the U.S. would forgo by attempting to work this issue more constructively, while simultaneously seeking to draw Belarus into a serious and sustained dialogue over European security. Engagement does not imply muting criticism or welcoming Belarus into political institutions where its actions make it unfit to belong. Nor does it call into question U.S. support for organizations and individuals struggling to preserve Belarus's democratic option. If anything, it calls for bolder, more effective actions on their behalf, such as multilateral programs that provide material support to a now beleaguered independent press. It does entail using what leverage the United States has positively rather than punitively and looking for ways to heighten the regime's sensitivity to the objective consequences of its present course, while adding inducements to turn away.

In truth, the more serious obstacle to this path is on the U.S. side. Dual-track policies, as U.S. policy toward China demonstrates, are complex and time-consuming. They require a careful evaluation of the conflicting stakes in a relationship, a differentiated strategy designed to pursue competing objectives, and an ability to sell the approach to key domestic constituencies. This is a good deal to ask of harried, distracted U.S. policy makers, hampered by an uninformed, uninvolved media and Congress. If, in addition, Belarus appears to be of no compelling importance, the task is still greater. On the other hand, if Belarus is of the significance argued by the authors in this book, to shirk the challenge of fashioning and promoting an optimal policy may yet exact its own large price.

NOTES

[1] The Lukashenko comment was made in a televised comment on September 23, 1996. See Ustina Markus, *OMRI Daily Report*, September 24, 1996.

[2] The U.S. comments are from State Department spokesman Nicholas Burns, April 1, 1997, and his colleague, John Dinger, March 27, 1997.

[3] See Ustina Markus, "CIA Conspiracy in Belarus," *OMRI Analytical Reports* (July 1996).

[4] Ustina Markus, "Belarus Debates Security Pacts as a Cure for Military Woes," *RFE/RL Research Report*, vol. 2, no. 25 (June 18, 1993) p. 69.

[5] See the account of the struggle between the Belarusian Popular Front and the authorities in David R. Marples, *Belarus: From Soviet Rule to Nuclear Catastrophe* (New York: St. Martin's Press, 1996), pp. 116–27.

[6] Conversation with a senior U.S. diplomat who had a central role in planning the president's visit to Belarus, November 28, 1995.

[7] *Zvyazda*, March 26, 1993.

[8] See Shushkevich's version of this approach in an ITAR-TASS report, April 9, 1993. This specific approach and the general idea are discussed in Kathleen Mihalisko, "Belarus: Neutrality Gives Way to 'Collective Security'," *RFE/RL Research Report*, vol. 2, no. 17 (April 23, 1993), pp. 24–31.

[9] *RFE/RL Daily Report*, no. 18 (January 27, 1994).

[10] See Lee Hockstader, "Belarus Drifts Toward Dependence on Russia," *Washington Post*, January 28, 1994, p. A20.

[11] The quote is from KGB chief Henadz Lavitsky, from *RFE/RL Daily Report*, no. 91, May 13, 1994.

[12] See, for example, the editorial in *Nezavisimaya gazeta*, June 28, 1994.

[13] See the interview, "Populisty vse—ot menya do Klintona," (Everyone is a Populist—from Me to Clinton), *Moskovskie novosti*, July 10–17, 1994, p. 10.

[14] Interview on NTV (Moscow), August 7, 1994 in *FBIS Daily Report*, SOV-94-152, August 8, 1994, p. 45.

[15] Linda Edgeworth, Richard Messick, and Ján Zaprudnik, *Pre-Election Assessment of the Parliamentary Elections in Belarus* (Washington, D.C.: International Foundation for Electoral Systems, 1994), especially pp. 8–29.

[16] As one recounted to me in May 1998, the memory of the event still vivid in his mind.

[17] *Interfax*, February 17, 1995.

[18] *Interfax*, May 30, 1995.

[19] Interview with a senior U.S. policy maker, August 25, 1997.

[20] The unusual formal statement is in a *U.S. Information Service Press Release*, February 28, 1997, henceforth referred to as "Belarus: New U.S. Policy."

[21] Ibid.

22 Quoted in K.P. Foley, "Belarus: U.S. Says Divisions Prevent Normal Ties," *RFE /RL Research Report* (March 6, 1997).

23 Nicholas Burns, daily press briefing, U.S. Department of State, March 20, 1997.

24 "Belarus: New U.S. Policy."

25 By late summer, in a session of the Belarus Cabinet of Ministers and Security Council, V.V. Sheiman, secretary of the Security Council, reportedly blamed the government for a lack of progress with economic reform and, thus, for the growing tensions within society. Valery Karbalevich, "Defeat of Democracy," *NCSI East-West Monograph* (March 1997), p. 7.

26 A report on Camdessus's letter was released by *Belapan* (Belarusian news agency), December 15, 1995.

27 See the report by *Belapan*, June 13, 1997.

28 Joel Blocker, "Council of Europe Suspends Belarus Indefinitely," *RFE/RL Research Report*, (January 13, 1997).

29 It was this agreement that sparked a series of public protests in Belarus, arrests of demonstrators, and an outcry from the international community.

30 Quoted in V. P. Vayutovich, "Vsglyad SShA na mecto Belorussii v sovremennom mire and sostoyanie Amerikano-Belorusskikh otnoshenii" (The View of the USA on the Place of Belarus in the Contemporary World and the Condition of American-Belarusian Relations), in E. M. Kozhokina, ed., *Belorussiya: Put k novym gorizontam* (Belarus: The Path to New Horizons) (Moscow: Rossiiskii institut strategicheskikh issledovanii, 1996), p. 167.

31 Andrei Fomin, *ITAR-TASS*, August 1, 1996.

32 Ibid., p. 185. (Tsepkalo later became Belarus's ambassador to the United States.)

33 "Belarus: New U.S. Policy."

34 These are the words of John Shattuck, assistant secretary of state for democracy, human rights, and labor, when introducing the 1997 report on human rights in Belarus, January 30, 1998. See "U.S. Department of State Belarus Country Report on Human Rights Practices for 1997," as published on the internet website of the Department of State: (http://www.state.gov/www/global/human_rights/1997_hrp_report/belarus.html).

35 In December 1997, Stephen Sestanovich, the new coordinator for assistance to the newly independent states, and Edward Warner,

assistant secretary of defense, headed an interagency group that visited Belarus and met with the prime minister and foreign minister, but the encounter appears to have had little effect in either capital.

[36] Lukashenko never explained himself, other than to say that having foreign embassies within a few meters of the presidential residence was abnormal. Some thought he acted out of annoyance over traffic in and out of embassies so near his own office—particularly the U.S. embassy, whose driveway was opposite his own. A more plausible explanation is that he feared that the U.S. embassy from such close range would have an easier time targeting its surveillance technology on activities within his building.

[37] The delegation was led by Ross L. Wilson, principal deputy special advisor to the secretary of state for the newly independent states. He was in Europe to attend the special Ukrainian conference marking the fiftieth anniversary of NATO.

[38] See the U.S. Embassy report of the meeting that appeared on the internet site: (http://www.bisnis.doc.gov/bisnis/cables/971031br.htm).

[39] See the U.S. Department of State daily press briefing of James P. Rubin, July 14, 1998.

[40] See his review before the Collegium of the Ministry of Foreign Affairs, April 6, 1999, as reported by Andrei Makhovskii, "Lukashenko otpravil MID na vse chetyre storony," (Lukashenko Dispatches the MFA [Ministry of Foreign Affairs] to All Four Corners), *Belarusskaya delovaya gazeta*, April 7, 1999.

[41] *Moscow Interfax*, February 22, 1999, from FBIS-SOV-1999-0222, and Valerya Kastsyuhova, *Belarusskaya delovaya gazeta*, February 26, 1999, p. 3.

[42] As noted by a significant Belarusian participant, the failure of the United States to develop a more balanced and comprehensive policy at this point disturbed the Belarusian side. See Sergei Martynov, "Voprosy yadernoi besopasnosti v otnosheniyakh Belrussii i SShA" (The Question of Nuclear Security in U.S.-Belarusian Relations), *Belarus v mire*, vol. 1 (December 1996), p. 90. Martynov, now a deputy foreign minister, was Belarusian ambassador to the United States.

[43] See Irina Grudinina, *Segodnya*, July 28, 1995, p. 9, and Vasyutovich, "Vsglyad SShA na mesto Belorussii v sovremennom mire," pp. 189–90.

44 Nicholas Burns, noon press briefing, U.S. Department of State, March 21, 1997.

45 *Congressional Record*, April 10, 1997, pp. E634–35. The signers were Congressmen Christopher H. Smith (R-N.J.) and Steny H. Hoyer (D-Md.), as well as Senators D'Amato and Lautenberg.

46 *Congressional Record*, March 20, 1997 (U.S. Senate), p. S2718.

47 The committee was led, on the U.S. side, by Jan H. Kalicki, Department of Commerce counselor, and, on the Belarusian side, by Mikhail Marinich, minister for foreign economic relations. (See "Report of the U.S.-Belarusian Business Development Committee," June 3, 1996, on the internet website of the Business Information Service for the Newly Independent States (BISNIS): (http://www.bisnis.doc.gov).

48 While there he gave a relatively uncritical interview to Minsk television. See FBIS-SOV-96-142, July 23, 1996, p. 33.

49 See Suzette Grillot, "Belarus," in Gary Bertsch, ed., *Restraining the Spread of the Soviet Arsenal: NIS Nonproliferation Export Controls* (Athens, Ga.: Center for International Trade and Security, 1996), pp. 31–35.

50 See David Swartz and David Evans, "Belarus: Problems of Integration," Washington, May 1996.

51 Nicholas Burns, daily press briefing, U.S. Department of State, April 4, 1997.

52 Ibid.

53 A senior member of the Department of State, in September 1997, urged me to understand that "selective engagement" was intended to head off far more stringent measures brewing within the U.S. Congress.

54 "Belarus: President Addresses Parliament; Sends Message to Clinton," *RFE/RL Research Report*, April 11, 1997.

55 Derived from Office of the Coordinator of U.S. Assistance to the NIS, *U.S. Government Assistance to and Cooperative Activities with the Newly Independent States of the Former Soviet Union*, FY 1996 Annual Report (January 1997). The $115 million in humanitarian assistance involved mostly private donations ($109 million) (p. 141). The bulk of USDA assistance was in concessional sales under Public Law 480, Title I.

56 Ibid., p. 155.

57 Having reduced or suspended many assistance programs on the grounds of intolerable abuses of human rights in February, the

administration guaranteed that, come the end of 1997, it would not be able or willing to certify Belarus under section 498A(b) of the Foreign Assistance Act of 1961. That act asks whether a potential recipient has "engaged in a consistent pattern of gross violations of internationally recognized human rights or of international law." In the 1996 report, filed in January 1997, the administration had answered: "No. While there have been serious shortcomings in human rights observance (as discussed above), we do not believe that the Government of Belarus is engaged in such a pattern." (Ibid., p. 172.)

58 *RFE/RL Newsline*, August 4, 1997. On July 30, according to *Interfax*, Yeltsin asked reporters to convey to Lukashenko that he was "indignant" over the arrests, and threatened that Russia might even reconsider the recently signed Union Charter.

59 See *Izvestiya*, November 28, 1995, for an account of this interview given to the German newspaper *Handelsblatt* a few days earlier. A presidential press spokesman subsequently denied the quotation.

60 See his interview with Minsk Radio Network, March 17, 1998, as reported in FBIS-SOV-98-077, March 18, 1998.

61 This characterization is of U.S. policy and the senior officials who preside over it, not of the outlook of experts within the U.S. bureaucracy or the U.S. embassy in Minsk, including the two ambassadors who have headed the embassy during the Clinton administration, Kenneth Yalowitz and Daniel Speckhard.

62 A poll taken by the All-Russia Center for Studying Public Opinion (VTsIOM) in March 1998, on the anniversary of the April 1997 Russian-Belarusian Union Charter, revealed that while 64 percent of Russian citizens still considered Russia and Belarus to be parts of one state, only 50 percent of Belarusian citizens thought so. (*Interfax* report, April 2, 1998.)

63 One person who wishes to see Russia and Belarus unified again, but who understands that time is working against the prospect, is Sergei Karaganov. See his interview in *Kommersant-Daily*, April 1, 1997, p. 5: "Either we associate with Belarus or not. When they say that it is necessary to associate, but 'not now, rather later,' this means never. If we do not unite now, we never will. As time goes on, the republics of the former Union are diverging more and more—both economically and politically. In three years the situation will not be more favorable for unification. Rather, it will be worse."

[64] Quoted in Jan de Weydenthal, "Lukashenko Wants Autonomy and Union with Russia," *RFE/RL Analytical Reports*, (February 25, 1997).

[65] Ibid. After the Agreement on Union was signed, Ural Latypov, the Belarusian president's foreign policy advisor, underscored that "the principle 'one state-one vote' means that not a single decision touching the interests of Belarus can be taken without the consent of the Belarusian leadership." (See his interview in *Belarus v mire*, vol. 2, no. 1 [March 1997], p. 41.)

[66] Sergei Solodovnikov, *OMRI Daily Report*, January 23, 1997. He was speaking to the Collegium of the foreign ministry.

[67] See Vayutovich, "Vsglyad SshA na mesto Belorussi v sovremennom mire," p. 171.

[68] See, for example, Belarusian foreign minister Ivan Antanovich's interview in *Minsk Zvyazda*, March 14, 1998, p. 3, most of which focuses on the challenge of unfreezing Belarus's relations with Western Europe's major organizations from the Council on Europe to the EU.

[69] The most recent illustration is the decision of the Russian Central Bank to cut off negotiations with the National Bank of Belarus, because none of what had been promised in March agreements had been done (see *Kommersant-Daily*, August 2, 1997).

[70] On BTK Television (Minsk), March 23, 1998, as reported in FBIS-SOV-98-083, *Daily Report*, March 24, 1998.

[71] Volha Tomashewskaya and Andrey Makhowski, *Belarusskaya delovaya gazeta*, January 22, 1999, p. 1.

[72] See, for example, A. A. Rozanov, *NATO: Problemy transformatsii i rasshireniya* (NATO: Problems of Transformation and Enlargement) (Minsk: Zavigar, 1996), pp. 29–31.

[73] *RFE/RL Newsline*, vol. 1, no. 96, part II (August 15, 1997).

[74] The process was hardly easy. After months of discussions and an agreement in principle to allow the establishment of the office, on July 17, 1997, the Belarusians announced they were breaking off further negotiations, apparently because of a critical report prepared separately by the OSCE. Only in February 1998 was agreement reached and an office set up.

[75] Forty-four members of the rump parliament disbanded by Lukashenko in 1996 voted to organize these presidential elections. This is the parliament recognized by the U.S. Congress and by all

European parliaments except the Russian Duma. The effort was led by Semyon Sharetsky, the speaker of the Thirteenth Supreme Soviet. An electoral commission was appointed, but its chair was promptly arrested. Mikhail Chigyr, Lukashenko's former prime minister, announced his intention to run in the elections, as did two other candidates, including the head of the BPF. Chigyr, too, was arrested. Charter-97, the human rights and pro-democracy movement, threw itself behind the initiative, as did all the opposition parties.

[76] *Moscow Interfax*, November 11, 1998; FBIS-SOV-98-316, November 12, 1998.

8
Conclusion: Dealing With Europe's Reluctant Participant

Sherman W. Garnett and Robert Legvold

Belarus is a European country, but only a reluctant participant in the Europe now defined by expanding political, economic, and security cooperation. Politically, it is the only country of the region to have emphatically turned its back on the democratic and market reforms that have become the European norm. Russian leaders may rail at the IMF, but they continue to seek its support. In contrast, President Lukashenko is proud of his state-managed market. He is unafraid to alter constitutional structures unilaterally or to conduct stage-managed referenda, cultivating an approach to executive power more in keeping with Central Asia than Central Europe. In its security posture as well, Belarus has turned away from Europe to Russia, with Lukashenko regularly calling for Russia, Ukraine, Yugoslavia, and even far-flung Iran or China to band together as a counterbalance to NATO.

Yet, even if not by choice, Belarus is a factor in Europe's emerging security environment. It stands at a vital crossroads where the post-Soviet space meets an expanding Europe. It shares a special geopolitical significance with other such crossroads between the former USSR and the outside world—Ukraine, parts of the Caucasus, Central Asia, and the Russian Far East. These places are the testing ground for new political, economic, and security patterns that will determine the shape and stability of the new political geography of Eurasia.[1]

Belarus occupies crucial territory between Poland and Russia. Poland has now entered NATO and is in line for accession talks with the EU. Within the next five years, Poland will be the forward edge in the region of Europe that is defined by these institutions. Thus, in no small measure, the character of the Polish-Belarusian border will determine the relationship between this institutionalized Europe and the rest of the continent that stretches to the Urals and beyond. This geography alone makes it difficult to isolate Belarus or to see it somehow as a non-European country, even if it shows little vocation for democracy and free markets. Belarus will help define Europe—particularly the stability of institutionalized Europe's new borderlands—simply because of where it is and what it becomes.

As the authors of the preceding chapters have argued, there are at least two ways that Belarus could have a significant impact on Europe in the coming decade without ever participating in the continent's core processes. The first is by consummating a deal with Russia to create a new and integrated commonwealth. The union of the two countries need not reshape the region, but if it became a hostile security outpost to the new NATO, it could significantly reverse the gains already made in the region and in Europe as a whole toward smaller, more stable nuclear and conventional forces.

The second way involves Belarus alone. It depends on the failure of President Lukashenko's regime to provide either prosperity or stability. As the Lukashenko regime falls apart, it would export instability into neighboring Lithuania, Poland, Ukraine, and Russia. Russia in particular would be forced to intervene in the event of serious internal chaos in Belarus, but Belarus's other neighbors could hardly remain aloof. These states would certainly feel the impact of Belarusian failure in the shock waves of political and economic chaos or the flow of short- and long-term migrants.

A U.S. and Western policy designed primarily to reward or punish Belarus on the basis of its political and economic reforms or lack thereof is simply not, in itself, adequate to deal with the impact that this small country could have on its region and on Europe as a whole. A set of policies with a wider horizon, however, cannot avoid the fact of Lukashenko's contempt for European norms or his ability to thwart policies aimed at greater engagement or to use them to his own advantage. This tension is the basic dilemma for U.S. and Western policy toward Minsk. It is a tension these governments rarely acknowledge. Western policy leaders have been content largely to isolate Lukashenko and, as a consequence, the country as a whole. Within the U.S. foreign policy community, Belarus is comfortably placed in the category of outcast state, requiring little thought or effort. The policy of isolation and neglect that results is seemingly justified by every outrageous statement and capricious act by Lukashenko. It is not an approach that meets the needs of the United States' close friends in the region, nor is it likely to promote the stability they require.

Given the richness of the preceding chapters in this volume, it is a daunting task for the editors to offer conclusions about Belarus and its neighbors or to present a single set of policy options that might alter the current standoff between Belarus and the outside world. Although the authors in this volume all stress the need to move beyond the status quo, they do not agree on a single assessment of the problem or a common set of policies. What is offered below is not an attempt to synthesize a common approach from these diverse voices, but rather to present our own response to their rich and varied analysis. Our recommendations seek to bridge the gaps that exist within the region and within Belarus itself, but especially to move analysts and policy makers in the West to see their stake in the future of this forgotten country. They are an attempt to identify potential common ground, a starting point from which Russia, Poland, the United States, Ukraine, Lithuania, and Belarus can perhaps begin to act in a way that lessens Belarusian isolation and strengthens regional stability.

ASSESSING THE RISKS POSED BY BELARUS

The place to begin is with an assessment of the risks. What is the likelihood that Russian-Belarusian integration will occur in a manner hostile to European political, economic, and security trends? How likely is instability within Belarus? We believe that much of Western opinion on both issues rests on analytically thin ice. There is simply not the broad range of policy and scholarly analysis or executive and legislative inquiry into Belarus that exists for Russia, Ukraine, or even the remote but potentially oil-rich states of the Caspian Basin. Much of what does exist presumes the inevitability of Russian-Belarusian integration or fails to look beyond Lukashenko himself when analyzing Belarusian politics. Future analysis of Belarus needs to take into account the factors that create a more complex external and internal environment.

With regard to Russian-Belarusian integration, proponents, opponents, and interested observers alike have yet to recognize the limits and constraints on this process. Although strong general support for integration exists in both countries, the past several years have revealed serious obstacles to consummating the deal. Supporters of the process within the two countries and opponents outside have regularly exaggerated the inevitability and consequences of integration. For them, the weakness of Belarusian state identity and the strength of Russian geopolitical ambitions have made some kind of *Anschluss* inevitable. Despite the long list of bilateral political, economic, and military agreements designed to bind the two states together, what is most remarkable over the last two years is how far apart they remain. Integration faces at least three constraints:

- The first is structural. The political stability and economic prosperity that fuel Western European integration are absent. Even after Russia's August 1998 financial collapse and the appointment of Yevgeny Primakov, a strong supporter of Russian-Belarusian integration, as prime minister, Russia and Belarus remain "out of synch" both politically and economically. Belarus has a closed and backward economy. Monetary union might provide Russia with control over some important assets in Belarus, but such control would be a sustained burden on the still struggling Russian economy. Russia is a far more open society than Belarus, as convincingly demonstrated by Russian-Belarusian disagreements over the shape of the Belarusian constitution in 1996 and the treatment of Russian television journalists in Belarus in 1997.

- The different interests and goals of the supporters of integration are the second major constraint. Lukashenko clearly covets a role on the Russian political stage and sees integration with Russia as one way of assuming such a role. Yet integration is unlikely to occur on terms that Lukashenko wants. The impoverished Belarusian people want the union to provide the same kind of social and economic supports the old system produced.

Russian energy interests want concessions for the pipeline through Belarus to the European market. Perhaps the most important group of supporters—Russian nationalists, communists, and those focusing on the geopolitical advantages of the union—see integration as a means to traditional Russian political ends. They care little for what Belarus wants or needs but seek the aggrandizement of Russian power and influence. Sergei Karaganov, a leading Russian foreign policy commentator, admitted that most Russians think of integration with Belarus as "absorption."[2] President Yeltsin himself spoke on national television in early 1997 of creating "a unified state." Speaking to his parliament in February 1997, Lukashenko vowed Belarus would never become part of a merged state with Russia.

- The third constraint is the opposition to integration generated by the first two constraints. In Russia, economic and political reformers have little interest in adding to Russia's economic burdens or appending a region likely to strengthen communist and nationalist opposition tendencies. In Belarus, the elite that supports Lukashenko and that has reaped economic benefits from sovereignty are jealous of their privileges. They want help from Russia, but they do not want stronger Russian political and economic groups to supplant them. They have insisted on the equality of the union and the sovereignty of its two state members. They and a large measure of Belarusians (as judged by popular opinion) want to limit the military obligations such a union might impose. They do not want Belarusian youth to die in Tajikistan. Belarusian national and political opposition groups have openly rallied against the union, risking arrest and beatings. They, in turn, are but the forward edge of widening public skepticism about the thought of submerging the new reality of Belarus in the old reality of a Greater Russia. Added to these issues is the strong force of divergent interests and the tensions these foster between the two leaderships.

In our view, there are inherent limits on how far the process of integration will go. It is unlikely ever to reach the union that so many in both countries proclaim as their goal and that was reaffirmed in the Treaty on Equal Rights signed by Yeltsin and Lukashenko in December 1998. Each day that passes strengthens the sense of national consciousness among Belarusians—most rapidly among the young, the intellectuals, and those who hold the reins of power and see the advantages that independence has brought. These changes are emerging more slowly in the countryside, among the old, and at the second and third echelons of the communist structures.

Although union or even substantial political integration is not imminent, the two countries remain close. Belarus is economically dependent on Russia, and Russian economic interests are increasingly active in Belarus. Under almost any conceivable circumstances, Russia and Belarus will remain strong strategic and economic partners. In private conversations, Belarusian officials, journalists, and analysts, even from the opposition, stress their country's continued economic dependence on Russia, as well as the strong and deep cultural, linguistic, and historical ties binding the two countries together. Neighboring states and the West in general must begin their approach to Russian-Belarusian relations by recognizing this link, without exaggerating its ability to destroy Belarusian independence.

Granted that the vision of political union is remote, what of the bilateral security relationship? The shape of this security relationship is properly seen as the most important aspect of Belarus's and Russia's growing ties, with the potential to alter the emerging security environment in the region and in Europe as a whole. The two countries have made headway in linking their militaries. They see eye-to-eye on most developments in Europe, especially the undesirability of NATO enlargement. Voices in both Minsk and Moscow, including Lukashenko's own, have regularly characterized Russian-Belarusian security relations as providing the basis for an ambitious set of countermeasures to NATO enlargement, including new Russian nuclear and conventional deployments. Still, although the two countries have expanded their security ties, important limitations on bilateral cooperation remain.

In this volume, Hrihoriy Perepelitsa argues that the Russian-Belarusian security relationship casts an ominous shadow over Eastern and Central Europe. Certainly the rhetorical claims of Lukashenko and senior Russian officials often portray military cooperation as an ambitious and assertive counterweight to what they perceive as the negative security developments in Europe. But the actual pattern of cooperation is more limited and less ominous, although it needs to be monitored over the long term.

The two sides have signed a series of military agreements that commit them to regular staff talks on key defense issues. The air defense forces of the two countries have exercised together and are becoming more integrated. Russia is training key elements of Belarus's future officer corps. Russia also appears to have substantial influence over the personnel policies of the Belarusian Ministry of Defense and other key "power" ministries. Belarusian air defense assets, early warning radar, and other military infrastructure are already part of long-term Russian planning and joint use.

Belarus, however, insists on keeping its forces at home. Lukashenko is as opposed to deploying his soldiers to the far-flung reaches of the old Soviet Union as any other CIS leader. He has insisted on keeping this longstanding restriction on out-of-country deployment as part of any future agreement on bilateral integration.[3] The staffing levels of Russian personnel at early warning and submarine communications facilities within Belarus are strictly capped and regulated by treaty. Cooperation among the border guards of the two countries has deepened, but Belarus has insisted that only its own forces guard its borders with Ukraine, Poland, Lithuania, and Latvia.

Yeltsin, Primakov, and senior Belarusian officials have made it plain that they do not want to deploy Russian ground or nuclear forces in Belarus. The West has an obvious interest in encouraging a reciprocal pattern of restraint between NATO and Poland and between Russia and Belarus, and it is not without allies in pursuing this interest. The relationship itself has not crossed the "red lines" of conventional or nuclear deployments. In fact, there is a rough parallelism between NATO's restraint with regard to Poland and Russia's restraint in Belarus. And there is more: U.S. and NATO officials have a cadre of willing interlocutors in both Minsk and Moscow to help ensure that the pattern of restraint continues. Both Minsk and Moscow see value in the continuation and modification of the CFE treaty. The agreement in its outline, by capping national and foreign-stationed forces and armaments, even reducing forces in the sensitive central region, creates a valuable counter to potentially destabilizing moves and countermoves in the wake of NATO enlargement.

This leaves the problem of Belarusian internal stability. Here conventional wisdom sees a country surprised by independence, ruled initially by a local *nomenklatura* unwilling to reform either political or economic life, and now led by a would-be dictator whose base is in an aging rural population. These judgments are not wrong. Lukashenko's regime is oppressive and likely to be long-lived, but it is not all there is to Belarusian politics.

- First, Lukashenko has created a strongly authoritarian state on a weak base. The kind of political isolation Lukashenko hopes to impose on his country cannot be sustained. He may remain an unchallenged political figure within Belarus, but his state has already been brought willy-nilly into a burgeoning East-West trade. A new gas pipeline is being built through the country. Lukashenko's internal security apparatus may well be strong enough to frustrate his own people, but it cannot shut out the outside world. On many key issues of human rights and democratic process Russia stands closer to the outside world than to the Lukashenko regime, although the post-Yeltsin Russian leadership may well erode this Russian-Western convergence.

- Second, despite the leadership's prideful claims of economic success, its resort to Soviet-style techniques—price controls, state-guided trade, heavily subsidized industry, exchange rate manipulation, and the curtailing of imports—is a dead end. Growth has come at the expense of soaring inflation; controls have caused food shortages reminiscent of an earlier period; and the reorientation of trade toward Russia puts the Belarusian economy increasingly at the mercy of the trends buffeting the Russian economy.[4] As became apparent during the crisis of the Belarusian ruble in March 1998, the Belarusian authorities can insulate their economy from the outside world only to a degree. Sooner or later—sooner if Russia cannot or will not provide subsidized energy prices, congenial markets, and currency support—they will come face to face with the unforgiving discipline of modern international economics.

- Third, Belarus is changing. The current population is still shaped by the attitudes of the old and rural, precisely the groups most nostalgic for Soviet times and most responsive to Lukashenko's mix of populism and discipline. The active opposition in Minsk and in other large cities remains small, but tenacious. The future, however, could belong to the young, especially as Lukashenko's economic illiteracy comes to face to face with global economic realities. The elderly collective farm workers who embrace Lukashenko today are slowly being replaced by a generation that has seen Europe, if only through the mirror of Russian television. They know what they are missing. Lukashenko may successfully delay this generation's encounter with greater political freedom, but he cannot afford to leave them totally outside Europe's prosperity. They want a better life than that offered by the discipline of the collective farm or state factory. They see themselves increasingly as Belarusians and citizens of the Belarusian state. It will take time, but Lukashenko and his successors will have to deal with their political and economic demands. Nor should it be taken for granted that, as Belarus's economic circumstance worsens, Lukashenko will retain his current popularity. There are already signs that the grumbling is increasing even among workers and in the countryside. The president is no longer above criticism. Belarusians are beginning to do what citizens of most countries do when the economy is in decline: calculate that things are getting worse, not better, and conclude that, because Lukashenko has been in power for five years, he bears significant responsibility for their economic plight. If he eventually faces trouble with the population at large or, in the first instance, from trade unions or other organized groups, the Belarusian president may be forced to soften what now seem to be intractable stands. That said, it would also be imprudent to rule out a move toward greater dictatorship as instability grows.

- Finally, the ruling elite that supports Lukashenko has interests of its own that it does not necessarily share with him. Many have gained their current prominence through longstanding positions in the *nomenklatura* and more recent fealty to Lukashenko himself. Yet their long-term interests are not necessarily those of their president. Indeed, while Lukashenko looks to Russia as a larger field for his endeavors, the current generation of Belarusian business and political leaders do not want competition from anywhere, particularly from the new Russian business and political leadership. This difference among the Belarusian leadership is a serious chink in Lukashenko's armor, certainly more serious in the short run than that posed by the opposition in the streets.

Even with this list, however, the basic fact is that Lukashenko dominates both the internal and foreign policy in his country. He looms large over every aspect of current political life. No real political opposition has developed that could openly defeat him. Beneath the inflated totals of his corrupt referenda lies a solid political majority, the same majority that brought him to power in a fair election in 1994. Any policy that seeks to engage this troubled nation will have to reckon with a politically strong and formidable president. It is wrong to underestimate him or to dismiss many of his public statements as bizarre. They do not sound so odd inside Belarus, especially among Lukashenko's core supporters who want order, state intervention, and the benefits of the old system.

RECOMMENDATIONS: A PREFERENCE FOR INCLUSION

The dark and backward side of Belarusian internal and foreign policies is obvious, but the nation and its people are more than the current regime imagines or allows. Belarus's neighbors, as well as the United States, Western Europe, and Belarus itself, need to devise policies that do not ignore or excuse the current stagnation and repression and that are not stymied by them either. In particular, these policies need to be guided by a preference for inclusion of Belarus within Europe as a whole, although this inclusion will require modest goals in the beginning and long-term staying power to overcome Lukashenko's inclination to oppose it or use it to strengthen his own legitimacy.

Such a strategy cannot give Lukashenko a free pass. It will continually be challenged by tension between the near-term desire to keep him at arm's length and the long-term danger of an isolated and unstable Belarus. This tension is inherent in the current situation. Dealing with it is preferable to ignoring it or pretending that it does not exist. The recommendations below do not quarrel with the wisdom of refusing direct political support to the Lukashenko regime and of pressing for a dialogue between the regime and its opposition. But they stress no less the need to remain involved in the country, to foster a serious exchange of views with Belarusian leaders, particularly on issues of European security, and to look for the broadest possible consensus among Belarus's neighbors in formulating a productive policy toward the country. The following recommendations are meant to help guide such a strategy for dealing with Belarus.

1. End Belarusian security isolation. Belarus is at a crucial turning point in defining its long-term security orientation. Given the still uncertain nature of the Russian-Belarusian union and the West's interest in ensuring that any future bilateral relationship takes a course conducive to stability in the region, a policy of isolating Belarus from the larger security environment in Europe is counter-productive. Moreover, it cannot be in the interest of either the United States or Europe to see Belarus rally to the Irans, Syrias, and Cubas of the world, as Lukashenko increasingly has done. The more he is reviled by Western democracies, the more he revels in the pomp and praise that he receives from these states. When he was in Iran in March 1998, his strongest endorsement came from the most reactionary of the Iranian leaders, the Ayatollah Said Ali Khamanei.[5] Throughout the spring of 1999, as the crisis over Kosovo built, Serb politicians gravitated toward Lukashenko and he toward them, and none with greater ease than Vojislav Seselj, the most rabid nationalist among them.

Whether it is China's Li Peng receiving a delegation from the Belarusian parliament (a parliament whose legitimacy the Western powers rejected) or Syria's Hafiz al-Assad painting a picture of Belarus's rapidly developing economic ties with his country, Lukashenko treats such acceptance as proof that his Western critics, not Belarus, stand alone. The danger is not merely that he will come to see this set of states as his country's natural friends, but that he will sanction a broadening military cooperation with them.

Thus, a secondary and indirect reason for pursuing an earnest security dialogue with Belarus is to give its leadership a stake in playing by the rules regulating the transfer of military technology to states seen by the West as potential troublemakers. For all that is wrong in Belarus's relations with the West, it is not a far-fetched objective. There is little to suggest that Belarus has recklessly disregarded the West's efforts to control technology and arms flowing to so-called rogue states. Lukashenko may enjoy stressing his special relations with regimes like that in Iraq, but at the first suggestion that his country might be selling arms to it, he quickly denies any intention of violating UN sanctions on this score.

Lukashenko may spurn a serious discussion of security issues or make himself a dubious interlocutor on most subjects, but this posture scarcely justifies isolating the Belarusian military, particularly at a time when it is formulating the terms of a long-term security relationship with Russia. On this crucial question the United States and the major European powers should think twice before forfeiting their influence. The range of bilateral and NATO-sponsored military-to-military programs, coupled with NATO's announced posture of military restraint in Poland, provides a sound basis for a modest yet sustained security dialogue with Belarus.

The West's security interest in Belarus did not end when the last nuclear weapon left the country in November 1996. Significant portions of the old Soviet military-industrial complex remain in Belarus. Economic decline has inspired a series of arms sales or attempted sales to Sudan, Yemen, Iran, Iraq, China, and Vietnam. The temptation for an alienated regime to export these and other important technologies will remain. Shutting off discussion, technical advice, and material assistance on export controls, for example, makes little sense.

The dialogue between Western and Belarusian militaries must be considerably strengthened. Military-to-military talks need not be thought of as conferring legitimacy on Lukashenko. While various police and intelligence agencies are part of his program to suppress the population, the Belarusian military to date is not. Efforts to bring the emerging Belarusian military leadership into contact with normal Western practices are especially important at a time when the only voices many of these leaders hear on security matters are Lukashenko's or those of their Russian counterparts.

Speaking face to face with Belarusian military and defense officials is a matter of common sense. Even if high-level contacts are to remain limited, lower level ones should continue. The visits of deputy assistant secretaries of state or defense to Minsk are not signs of support for the regime, and they matter profoundly for maintaining normal dialogue with an emerging military and foreign policy leadership and for accurately gauging conditions in the country. Small programs that focus on the after-effects of denuclearization, or on securing and disarming neglected stockpiles of Soviet conventional munitions, will have a real impact on both the military and the population at large.

2. Encourage regional initiatives with Belarus. A common thread runs through the writing of the Polish, Lithuanian, and Ukrainian authors in this volume: Belarus is too important to isolate; engagement must begin in the neighborhood. The conclusion of a Belarusian-Ukrainian border treaty in 1997 was a positive start. Lithuania, too, took a positive step in inviting Belarusian representatives to the Vilnius meeting of East European states in 1997. Polish president Aleksander Kwasniewski included a visit to Belarus on his itinerary in early 1996.

These efforts must be sustained. Poland's eastern policy in particular needs a boost. Polish foreign minister Bronislaw Geremek is an enthusiastic supporter of an expanded *Ostpolitik*. He is reported to have encouraged joint U.S.-Polish initiatives toward the Baltic states and Ukraine. There is no greater challenge to the stability of Poland's eastern border than Belarus. The whole question of Polish-Belarusian relations is a historically sensitive one, but nothing like that which Poland has already overcome with Ukraine.

Efforts designed to strengthen regional cooperation—such as the Baltic Sea Council or ongoing programs between Poland and Ukraine—ought to invite positive contributions from Belarus. Working-level delegations and observers ought to be invited to meetings. Belarusian cooperation ought to be actively sought on issues such as regional crime, migration, and drug trafficking. There must be NATO and European support for this kind of engagement. In the past several years, Polish officials were often left to wonder whether dynamic Eastern policy initiatives helped or hurt their country's chances for membership in Western institutions. These institutions should send a strong signal that such initiatives are encouraged.

3. Enlist Russia as an ally in promoting Belarusian reform. Helping to get Belarus back on track should be a broad-based effort bringing together the United States, Western Europe, Russia, and Belarus's neighbors. Precedents for such a cooperative effort already exist in the negotiating structures that produced the soft landings negotiated on Baltic troop withdrawal and Ukrainian denuclearization. Although the structures themselves did not eliminate deep disagreements, often over basic issues, they did bring together at a single table the key players from the states of the region, Russia, and the outside world.

Russia is just such a key player. It is the driving force in creating a bilateral military and security relationship with Minsk, although NATO countries seem to be largely ignoring this issue in their bilateral and multilateral discussions with Russia on security matters.

There are no forums where discussions could take place with Belarus on this issue. Russia is also vitally concerned about Belarusian stability, as evidenced by its intervention—to little avail—in Belarus's November 1996 constitutional crisis. At various times Russian representatives have pushed Lukashenko to hold early parliamentary and presidential elections, a goal also sought by the Western community. And the Russian foreign minister supposedly played a key role in persuading the Belarusians to accept the establishment in Minsk of the OSCE monitoring group in early 1998. Although many in Russia who define Russian interests in purely geopolitical terms want nothing to do with encouraging reforms in Belarus, others see the importance of change there. A reforming Belarus automatically makes Russian-Belarusian integration more open to Europe.

Any effort involving Russia requires Western countries to acknowledge the strategic link between Minsk and Moscow. It requires including a Russia that is unlikely to see eye to eye with the West on many key issues. However, it will also require both Russia and Belarus to face certain facts. In particular, it would force both parties to admit that integration is unlikely to resolve the problems they face. The two nations are not—nor can they be—building an eastern version of the EU. Russia and Belarus can both get the maximum benefits they seek from each other by relying on close ties that fall well short of integration. These ties would be nothing for Belarus's neighbors or Europe as a whole to fear, provided they do not lead to the redeployment of Russian nuclear or combat forces into Belarus. Both sides have to work hard to see that the restraint on military deployments in the region continues. Here, too, however, the West is not without the means to shape their choices. If well constructed, this round of conventional arms control in Europe can provide an incentive to avoid further impetuous or destabilizing military initiatives in and around Belarus.

The West needs to understand that, along with continued fragmentation and the failure of the CIS as a whole, a variety of forms of cooperation are likely to emerge in the former USSR. Western policy must understand the trends and distinguish good from bad. The West also has to think about policies that increase the transparency and interaction between both halves of Europe. The last thing needed is the construction of a new wall in Europe.

4. Create incentives in favor of Europe. The free flow of people and goods between Belarus and the outside world needs encouragement. The current obstacle is, of course, Lukashenko himself. In the long run the problem will also be complicated by EU enlargement. Poland is already under pressure from its future partners to put in place greater restrictions on its eastern borders.

The long-term enlargement of Europe's great institutions will create dilemmas for Belarus and its neighbors. NATO has succeeded in defusing the most obvious security tensions arising from enlargement. Its voluntary military restraint on the deployment of nuclear weapons and large-scale conventional forces in Poland and the creation of a special forum with Russia appear to have called forth a restraint in turn from Belarus and Russia. Time is needed for both sides to live with the new arrangement.

The European Union must devise the economic and political equivalent of this NATO policy, keeping the EU–non-EU border in the region as open and transparent as possible. This is a tall order, since Belarus and other states such as Ukraine must exercise sufficient control over their sides of the borders to create EU confidence in a relaxed regime.

Without efforts to think through the parameters for future borders in this region emanating from the EU itself, there is a real likelihood that the region will be redivided into haves and have-nots. Such a division would have deep and enduring security consequences, helping to underscore the notion that a stable, secure, and prosperous Europe is coterminous with membership in NATO and the EU.

5. Lend support to progressive elements within Belarus. Even with the best of intentions on the part of the outside world, all these suggestions to stimulate a more productive relationship with Minsk stand or fall on whether Belarus begins to change internally in ways that permit it to escape the isolation that the current regime has imposed upon the country. Belarus cannot remain a state bent on building "socialism in one country" and still be a full participant in Europe under present conditions. The fate of such a political strategy is not to occupy center stage in Europe, to instead be the ominous "other," and to be marginalized, with harmful consequences for Belarus and for Europe as a whole.

Other countries may be able to lend support on the margins to the forces for change within Belarus. In part, the conditions for such an internal trigger are present. Economic stagnation, generational change, the limits of what Russia can provide, the example of markets working in Poland and Russia, and fissures within the leadership itself already constrain Lukashenko's political options. Western policies designed to deny Lukashenko legitimacy and recognition have had a significant impact. EU- and OSCE-sponsored efforts to mediate between Lukashenko and the opposition have been less effective but need to be sustained. Much more thought needs to be given to ways in which Russia could be included as an additional lever for change within Belarus.

No one can or should expect Lukashenko's conversion to Western-style political and economic reform. He currently has genuine support among the broad populace. While he personally shares few of the West's core values, other elements in society do understand and respect the advantages of democratic practice. Still others, less preoccupied with political principles, recognize the importance of integrating Belarus into the larger European economic setting. With these elements the outside world can and should have a serious conversation. Meanwhile, Belarus's neighbors, the United States, and West Europeans should continue to press for a state that operates within the law and heeds the voice of a democratic opposition; they should continue to back the efforts of those who want to promote economic and political reform. But the outside world should also invest more in long-term changes that no dictator can control. These investments should aim at supporting core elements of a still-weak civil society. Support for the everyday activities of labor, religious, and social organizations is important, even without a direct link to today's demonstration or tomorrow's election. Improving the basic health and education infrastructure of Belarus ought to be another goal.

Outside help can provide only a small fraction of what Belarus needs, but scholarships, exchanges, training, and material assistance to selected institutions would demonstrate the outside world's continued concern about the country and its people. Lukashenko will obviously oppose many of these programs. He will try to use others to end the isolation imposed on him. His resistance need not be the last word, unless the prevailing indifference of the major Western powers makes it so. Lukashenko would find it more difficult to oppose a concerted and coordinated external effort to help Belarus and its people, particularly as the shortcomings of the Belarusian economy become more apparent.

Outside observers need to remember not only Belarus's importance to the long-term health and stability of the region and Europe as a whole, but also the fact that there are allies within the country that seek change. This change would not be simply a favor to Europe or a rejection of Russia. It would, as Anatoly Rozanov makes plain in chapter 2, accord with Belarus's deepest interests. Activating what he calls the "European vector" creates more leverage for constructing a Russian-Belarusian relationship open to Europe, and one more in keeping with the needs of Belarus itself. It would address the rising generation, whose members are looking for something beyond the conservatism of the collective farm.

AN INTERDEPENDENT FUTURE

None of these recommendations can ignore the very real obstacles that keep Belarus a reluctant participant in Europe. Lukashenko is a comparatively young man, seemingly in firm control of his country and believing that his and his country's future lies to the East. The slow progress made by Belarus has justified its isolation in the minds of many Western policy makers. Some of these same policy makers assume that Belarus is part of Russia's geopolitical space and thus is Russia's problem. Such conclusions ignore the structure of international relations in the region.

This structure is multipolar, although not in the ideological sense used by Primakov. The collapse of the old order in this part of Europe—as evidenced by Russia's weakening and transformation, the creation of new states, and the increased activity of the outside world—creates a new pattern of diplomacy. Small and medium-sized states have the "breathing space" to make their weight felt. Long-term stability in the region no longer depends solely on Moscow or Brussels, but on the interaction of these capitals with Warsaw, Kiev, Stockholm, Vilnius, Minsk, and others.

If there is a single lesson to be drawn from this volume, it is that the defection of Belarus from the region, either by direct challenge to the emerging order or its isolation from it, will affect the stability of its neighbors and of Europe at large. What happens in Belarus is not just a curious side show or socialist holdover. Contrary to the expectations of many Western observers and policy makers, the stakes are high in Belarus. Now is the time for those who understand these stakes to make political efforts commensurate with this insight.

NOTES

1 Sherman W. Garnett, "Europe's Crossroads: Russia and the West in the New Borderlands," in Michael Mandelbaum, ed., *The New Russian Foreign Policy* (New York: Council on Foreign Relations, 1998), pp. 64–99.

2 *RFE/RL Newsline*, February 4, 1999.

3 Lukashenko has said: "Not a single Belarusian citizen will ever be engaged in warfare outside our territory." See "Lukashenko Speech on Union with Russia," transcription from Minsk Radio, March 27, 1996, in *FBIS Daily Reports: Central Eurasia*, March 27, 1996.

4 See Sam Glebov, "Where Has All the Food Gone?" *Minsk News*, no. 18 (May 12–18, 1998), and Alexander Vasilevich, "IMF, Concerning Belarus's Economy," *Minsk News*, no. 7 (February 23–March 2, 1998).

5 See the account by Viktar Kuklow in *Minsk respublika*, March 14, 1998, p. 4.

Chronology of Key Events, 1990–1999

1990

July 27 — The Supreme Soviet of Belarus formally adopts the Declaration of State Sovereignty, which proclaims Belarus a nuclear-free zone and neutral in international affairs. Minsk reserves the right to raise its own army and security forces and to establish its own national bank and currency.

1991

August 25 — The Belarus Supreme Soviet temporarily suspends the Communist Party and gives the July 1990 Declaration of Sovereignty the force of law.

December 10 — The Belarus Supreme Soviet ratifies the Minsk Agreement creating the Commonwealth of Independent States. A new Communist Party of Belarus is formed.

1992

July 20 — Russia's deputy prime minister Yegor Gaidar and Belarusian prime minister Viacheslau Kebich sign twenty-one agreements on economic, political, military, and cultural cooperation.

1993

February 4 — The Belarus Supreme Soviet ratifies the START-I treaty, the Lisbon Protocol, and Belarus's adherence to the Nuclear Non-Proliferation Treaty.

April 9 — The Belarus Supreme Soviet agrees to adhere to the May 1992 CIS Tashkent Treaty on Collective Security, but Stanislau Shushkevich, chairman of the Supreme Soviet, refuses to sign the treaty.

July 22 — Shushkevich signs the Nuclear Non-Proliferation Treaty.

September 8 — Russian prime minister Viktor Chernomyrdin and Belarusian prime minister Viacheslau Kebich sign preliminary agreement on Russian-Belarusian monetary union.

1994

January 3 — Shushkevich signs Tashkent Treaty on Collective Security.

January 15 — President Clinton visits Minsk and meets with Supreme Soviet chairman Shushkevich to discuss nuclear disarmament.

January 18 — The Belarusian parliament ratifies the CIS charter.

January 26 — Shushkevich, opposed by pro-Russian forces in Belarus, is ousted as head of state amid charges of corruption.

March 11 — Russia and Belarus sign a set of agreements for defense cooperation, including provisions for joint border protection.

March 15 — The Belarusian parliament ratifies a new constitution establishing the presidency and setting a date in June for presidential elections. The constitution also says that Belarus intends to become a nuclear-free and neutral country.

April 12 — Kebich and Chernomyrdin sign a new agreement on monetary union to establish free-trade and ruble zones.

June 23 — Belarus holds presidential elections, and Aleksandr Lukashenko receives 45 percent of the vote, placing him ahead of Prime Minister Kebich (17 percent). Runoff elections are scheduled for July.

July 10 — In second-round elections, Lukashenko is victorious. He receives 80 percent of the vote, with 70 percent of voters turning out.

September 15 — Chernomyrdin states that Russia's monetary union with Belarus cannot take place without economic reform.

1995

January 6 — Russia and Belarus sign agreements governing a customs union and Russia's continued use of military facilities in Belarus over the next twenty-five years.

February 21 — Russian president Boris Yeltsin visits Minsk and signs three treaties with Lukashenko: the first, an accord on friendship and cooperation; the second, an agreement on customs regulations; and the third, an agreement on the joint protection of borders.

March 27   The National Security Council of the Republic of Belarus
            adopts the National Security Concept that contains an
            official description of Belarus's policy of neutrality.

April 12   The Belarusian parliament ratifies the treaty on
            friendship and cooperation with Russia, which was
            signed by Yeltsin and Lukashenko on February 21, 1995.

May 15   Belarus holds a referendum in which all four questions
            proposed by President Lukashenko are approved: 83.1
            percent agree that Russian have equal status with
            Belarusian as a state language; 82.4 percent vote in favor
            of Lukashenko's efforts at economic integration with
            Russia; 75 percent support the return of Belarus's Soviet-
            era state emblem and flag, and 77.6 percent favor giving
            the president the authority to dissolve the parliament if
            it violates the constitution.

May 24   The Russian State Duma ratifies the treaty on friendship
            and cooperation with Belarus, which was signed by
            Yeltsin and Lukashenko on February 21, 1995.

May 26   Yeltsin and Lukashenko sign a joint statement in
            Moscow reaffirming the customs union created on
            January 6, 1995. At the signing ceremony, Yeltsin says,
            "The border between Russia and Belarus no longer
            exists."

July 17   Ukraine and Belarus sign the Treaty of Friendship, Good
            Neighborliness, and Cooperation in Minsk. Presidents
            Lukashenko and Kuchma also sign accords on citizens
            working and residing in the other country, the terms for
            changing to the residency of the other country, air links,
            and cooperation in health care and medical services. The
            bilateral talks between the two presidents also focus on
            broadening cooperation in the trade and economic
            sphere and at dealing with the aftermath of the
            Chernobyl nuclear accident.

September 12 Two American balloonists in an international race are
            killed when their hot air balloon is shot down by the
            Belarusian Air Force.

December 8–9 Russia and Belarus sign eighteen military agreements
            regarding the withdrawal of the last two strategic missile
            regiments from Belarus, joint Russian-Belarusian regional
            security planning, joint use of Belarusian infrastructure,
            common use of air defense structure, and military-
            industrial cooperation.

1996

January 18   Lukashenko warns that Belarus will seek redeployment of Russian nuclear weapons that were withdrawn if NATO expands eastward.

April 2   In Moscow, Yeltsin and Lukashenko sign an agreement creating the Community of the Sovereign States of Belarus and Russia. The agreement calls for the formation of an integrated political and economic community that coordinates its foreign policies and cooperates in policing its common outside border. The two countries also pledge to form a common economic space with harmonized labor, pension, customs, taxation, and investment policies by the end of 1997.

April 4   Over 20,000 people demonstrate in Minsk against the Belarus-Russian Union Treaty signed on April 2. Lukashenko threatens to expel diplomats who attend such rallies and withdraw accreditations from journalists who cover demonstrations.

April 26   On the tenth anniversary of Chernobyl, fifty thousand people demonstrate in an unsanctioned rally in Minsk, demanding that Lukashenko resign. The demonstrators clash with police; about two hundred are arrested and several are admitted to the hospital with injuries.

August 31   Lukashenko presents a draft constitution for approval in a November referendum, which extends his term of office and gives him the right to reject decisions by local councils, set election dates, call parliamentary sessions, and dissolve parliament.

November 6   Lukashenko issues a decree that says that the results of the November 24 referendum will be legally binding and do not need to be confirmed by the Constitutional Court.

November 24   In a national referendum with a voter turnout of 84.1 percent, 70.5 percent of voters support Lukashenko's draft constitution. The United States and Europe condemn the vote and amendments as contrary to the democratic process.

November 26   The last Russian nuclear weapons are removed from Belarusian soil.

November 26   Lukashenko sets up a new parliament, in which the lower house includes 110 members from the disbanded parliament and the upper house comprises the president's appointees.

November 29 — Lukashenko signs a bill terminating the authority of the old parliament.

December 2 — Lukashenko signs his new constitution.

December 7 — Lukashenko signs several decrees that authorize a reorganization of the Constitutional Court of Belarus, biasing it in favor of his regime.

1997

February 28 — The U.S. government formally downgrades its relationship with Belarus, issuing a strong rebuke of the Lukashenko leadership and beginning a policy of "selective engagement."

March 7 — Yeltsin and Lukashenko sign a joint statement "covering the whole range of bilateral relations." The agreement echoes the April 1996 Russian-Belarusian Community Agreement and calls for establishing a common legal system and currency, and unifying budgetary and other economic policies. The presidents create a commission to prepare an action program for deeper integration in advance of the April 2, 1997 Yeltsin-Lukashenko summit.

March 21 — The United States suspends $40 million in aid to Belarus because of the country's poor human rights record.

April 2 — Yeltsin and Lukashenko sign the Treaty on the Union of Belarus and Russia in Moscow, the text of which was abbreviated from the longer draft version that had been approved by the Parliamentary Assembly of Belarus and Russia. The two presidents sign the "declaration" version of the treaty and initial a charter, both of which are published widely in the press for nationwide discussion. The treaty establishes three governing bodies of the union—the Parliamentary Assembly, the Supreme Council, and the Executive Committee. It is speculated that opponents of the treaty—such as Anatoly Chubais and Boris Nemtsov—persuaded Yeltsin at the last minute to reject the longer Union Treaty in favor of an abbreviated version.

May 12–13 — President Kuchma of Ukraine and President Lukashenko meet in Kiev to discuss a full range of bilateral relations, signing an agreement on the mutual border and its delimitation, and recognizing the existing—and never disputed—border as final.

May 23	Yeltsin and Lukashenko sign the Charter of the Union of Belarus and Russia in the Kremlin. The charter was significantly emasculated from its initial draft—which called for a single Slavic state with a supranational parliament—that Yeltsin and Lukashenko initialed on April 2, 1997. The charter does stipulate that the two countries coordinate their foreign policies and offers citizens of each country a series of social and political guarantees, such as the right to obtain free education and medicine in either country.
May 27	Russia-NATO Founding Act signed in Paris.
June 6	The Russian State Duma ratifies the Charter of the Union of Belarus and Russia.
June 14	First session of the Parliamentary Assembly of the Union of Belarus and Russia.
July 8–9	NATO Summit in Madrid; Hungary, Poland, and the Czech Republic are invited to begin accession talks for NATO membership.
July 22	Belarusian authorities arrest and jail Russian television journalist Pavel Sheremet and his cameraman Dmitry Zavadsky on charges of crossing the Belarus-Lithuania border unlawfully. Sheremet spends ten weeks in jail, Zavadsky, six. Sheremet eventually receives a two-year suspended sentence and is barred from traveling outside the CIS or working as a journalist until January 1999.

1998

June 22	Ambassadors of European Union countries and U.S. ambassador Daniel Speckhard are recalled from Minsk after Lukashenko forces foreign envoys to abandon their embassies and residences in the Drozdy district of Minsk (near the presidential compound).
August 17	Russian finances collapse as Russia devalues the ruble and defaults on some of its debt.
September 10	Yeltsin nominates Yevgeny Primakov as prime minister. Primakov's first visit outside Russia is to Belarus on September 30.
December 25	Yeltsin and Lukashenko in the Kremlin sign a declaration of further unification of Russia and Belarus, a treaty between the Russian Federation and the Republic of Belarus of equal rights for citizens, and an agreement between the Russian Federation and the Republic of

Belarus on the creation of equal conditions for economic entities. The declaration commits the two countries to take further steps in 1999 to create a full-fledged unification treaty, supranational governing bodies, a unified budget, a single legal environment for economic activity, and a single currency.

1999

January 17   Ambassadors of European Union nations return to their embassies in Belarus. The U.S. ambassador does not return.

March 12   Hungary, Poland, and the Czech Republic become full NATO members.

April 23–25   NATO's fiftieth anniversary summit occurs in Washington, D.C.

July 2   The Twelfth Session of the Parliamentary Assembly of the Union of Belarus and Russia takes place in Minsk. At the assembly, Lukashenko gives a speech in which he lashes out at Moscow, blaming Russia's political elite for sabotaging the integration process.

July 20   The United States and European Union say that Lukashenko's legitimacy as president has expired, calling the 1996 referendum that extended Lukashenko's term to 2001 flawed and unconstitutional. Both call for free, democratic, and fair elections to restore the legitimacy of Belarus's political authority.

THE EDITORS AND CONTRIBUTORS

SHERMAN W. GARNETT is professor and dean of the James Madison College at Michigan State University. From 1994 to July 1999, he was a senior associate at the Carnegie Endowment for International Peace, where he directed the project on Security and National Identity in the Endowment's Russian and Eurasian Program. Specializing in the foreign and security policies of Russia, Ukraine, and other states of the former USSR, Dr. Garnett has published widely. His book *Keystone in the Arch: Ukraine in the Emerging Security Environment of Central and Eastern Europe* was published by the Carnegie Endowment in 1997. Before joining the Endowment, Dr. Garnett served at the U.S. Department of Defense as the acting deputy assistant secretary of defense for Russia, Ukraine, and Eurasia. He also was director for European security negotiations and representative to the CSCE for the Defense Department. Dr. Garnett received his Ph.D. in Russian literature from the University of Michigan

ROBERT LEGVOLD is professor of political science at Columbia University, where he specializes in the international relations of the post-Soviet states. His most recent work includes a book with Alexei Arbatov and Karl Kaiser, *Russian Security and the Euro-Atlantic Region* (Institute of East-West Studies, 1999), and *After the Soviet Union: From Empire to Nations* (Norton, 1992), co-edited with Timothy Colton. Dr. Legvold was director of the Harriman Institute, Columbia University, from 1986 to 1992. Prior to going to Columbia in 1984, he served for six years as senior fellow and director of the Soviet Studies Project at the Council on Foreign Relations in New York. For most of the preceding decade, he was an assistant, then associate, professor of political science at Tufts University. He received his Ph.D. from the Fletcher School of Law and Diplomacy

ALGHIRDAS GRICIUS is a professor at the Institute of International Relations and Political Science at Vilnius University, president of the Lithuanian Association of Political Science, and distinguished specialist of international relations and foreign policy of Lithuania.

In 1996, Dr. Gricius was a member of the Delegation of the Parliamentary Assembly of the Council of Europe and worked as a monitor of the presidential elections in Russia.

ANTONI KAMINSKI has been a professor and leader of the Department of International Security at the Institute of Political Research of the Polish Academy of Sciences since 1994. He was formerly director of the Department of Strategic Research at the Ministry of National Defense of Poland (1993–1994), director of the Polish Institute of International Affairs (1991–1992), and director of the Institute of Sociology at Warsaw University (1984–1990). He is the author of many publications on the problems of international security and the building of political and economic institutes.

VYACHESLAV NIKONOV is president of Russia's Fund "Politika" and a doctor of historical science. From 1993–1995, Dr. Nikonov chaired the subcommittee on international security and arms control under the State Duma International Affairs Committee. Prior to this work, he served as a counselor to the Reform Fund of the Presidential Apparatus of the Soviet Union, and as head of a department of the Central Committee of the Communist Party of the Soviet Union. From 1978–1988, Dr. Nikonov taught in the Department of Modern History at Moscow State University.

HRIHORIY PEREPELITSA is head of the Department of Military Policy at the Ukrainian National Institute of Strategic Studies. Since 1991, he has worked in the Analytical Department of the General Staff of the Ukrainian Army. For more than twenty years he served in the navy of the Soviet Union.

ANATOLY ROZANOV is a professor of the Faculty of International Relations at the Belarusian State University. He is a doctor of historical science and a specialist on the problems of international and European security, Belarusian foreign policy, and military-political doctrine, as well as coauthor of the book *Security: A Western Approach*.

The Carnegie Endowment for International Peace is a private, nonprofit organization dedicated to advancing cooperation between nations and promoting active international engagement by the United States. Founded in 1910, its work is nonpartisan and dedicated to achieving practical results. Through research, publishing, convening and, on occasion, creating new institutions and international networks, Endowment associates shape fresh policy approaches. Their interests span geographic regions and the relations among governments, business, international organizations, and civil society, focusing on the economic, political, and technological forces driving global change. Through its Carnegie Moscow Center, the Endowment helps develop a tradition of public policy analysis in the states of the former Soviet Union and improve relations between Russia and the United States. The Endowment publishes *Foreign Policy*, one of the world's leading journals of international politics and economics, which reaches readers in more than 120 countries and several languages.